# Willie Horton: 23

### Detroit's Own Willie the Wonder,
### the Tigers' First Black Great

## Willie Horton and Kevin Allen

TRIUMPH
BOOKS

First Triumph Books paperback edition 2023

This book is available in quantity at special discounts for your group or organization. For further information, contact:
Triumph Books LLC
814 North Franklin Street
Chicago, Illinois 60610
(312) 337-0747
www.triumphbooks.com

Printed in U.S.A.
ISBN: 978-1-63727-290-9
Design by Nord Compo

# Contents

# Foreword

My first Willie Horton contact was with his bat. It was the fall of 1961, after my first season with the Detroit Tigers. They had asked me to come to winter ball in Dunedin, Florida, to work on a few aspects of my game.

As I walked onto the field, there were bats lying on the ground. I grabbed one, and I couldn't believe how heavy it was. It was like I was holding a tree trunk.

"Whose bat is this?" I said to no one in particular.

Someone pointed to a young man in the outfield. It was Wille. From then on, Willie had no problem with me. That bat was so heavy that I remember thinking, *"How in the world could anyone swing this?"*

I don't know how heavy it was, but it felt like a 50-ounce bat.

But once you realize his stature you understand. He was about to turn 19 when I met him and he was 5'11", and more than 200 pounds. Willie was built like a fireplug, and he was a strong, strong individual.

When you are playing baseball, there is a certain sound you hear that automatically draws your attention. Every bat has a sweet spot. And when you hit the baseball on that sweet spot it makes a sound that tells you that you have hit it well.

Willie's sweet spot was three-quarters of his bat, and mine was maybe three or four inches. That was a big difference.

Willie told me that his father had gone down to Briggs Stadium to watch the Tigers and saw me play and that had influenced the family decision to have Willie sign with the Tigers. Before then, Willie thought he was going to sign with the New York Yankees.

I always joke with Willie that the reason why he ended up on the Tigers was because his father saw me and thought, *"Wow, if the Tigers signed this guy, Willie can make the Hall of Fame."*

Willie wanted to be a catcher. He loved to catch. But when he signed with the Tigers, they put him in the outfield. He never complained. That tells you something about Willie's attitude. They never said, if we sign you, we are going to do this, that, or another. They signed him first and put him in the outfield. I don't know why they did it. But I watched Willie and he just handled it.

When you are a good ballplayer, you grow up with your parents loving you and your fans loving you. You are all of this and all of that. Hey, I was All-State in New Jersey when I signed with the Tigers. But when you go to spring training, there is an All-State guy from New York, an All-State guy from Texas, an All-State guy from Mississippi, an All-State guy from California and we were all competing against each other.

It's about how you handle that mentally. Some guys could, some couldn't.

Some guys can't handle it because they have been patted on the back so much and people have raised them up. Now their head is swollen. So now that you are competing against players who are at your level, how do you respond?

Now we come to Willie and how he responded to having to compete in the outfield. An unfamiliar position. How did he respond? With flexibility and a goal in mind. And to this day, that's what he teaches to others.

Baseball is a life experience. In baseball, you fail more than you succeed. If you succeed three out of 10 times as a hitter, you are considered a good hitter. I always tell little kids, "Have you ever seen anyone bat 1.000? I haven't."

But throughout my life I've seen the contributions that my teammates have made that don't show up in the newspaper. That's what Willie has always tried to instill in others. Still does today.

Here we are in 2022 talking about an experience I had with Willie in 1961. That's the kind of impact he has on people.

I was with the Tigers when Willie came up in 1963 and 1964, but he solidified himself in the lineup in 1965. But even in that process, it did not change his character or who he was. It didn't change his demeanor.

When some guys get to that level, there is not a hat big enough to fit their head.

Even to this day, he has achieved so much, and yet he retains his humility. When I've been fortunate to go down to spring training as a guest of the Tigers, I still see him working with younger players, trying to instill confidence in them. It's a mental thing. He is always trying to encourage these young men, He can tell them about the ups and downs. Willie can speak from experience.

The game was hard for everyone, not just the African American players. When I came up there were only 10 teams in the American League and eight teams in the National League. The Dodgers had the same guys in their lineup, the same team, every year, same as the Cardinals. When you got on a team, it seemed like you were there for life.

When I was at Denver in AAA ball, I came across African American players who had been in the minor leagues for eight or 10 years. They could play. Believe me. But they were going nowhere. Opportunities didn't present themselves.

I thank God for an opportunity that was presented to me. In 1960, the Tigers traded second baseman Frank Bolling to the Milwaukee Braves for center fielder Billy Bruton. That opened up the second base position. And I'd just had a fairly decent season (24 doubles, 18 triples, 12 home runs, 34 stolen bases, and .305 average) at Denver.

You have to take advantage of that opportunity. That's the attitude that Willie still instills in people today. You have to be prepared when your opportunity comes. You can't live off what happened last season. You have to produce every season to stay in the major leagues, because there are a thousand guys waiting to take your place.

Willie has accomplished so much in the game. But he's given back to the game. Some do not do that. I've seen some players accomplish things and say, "I got mine; now you go get yours." They don't want to help you. That's not Willie Horton.

When you enter a clubhouse with Willie, you see the respect that even young players have for him. It's amazing. It's because he is always reaching out to others.

I don't have any regrets about my baseball career. I thank God for players like Jackie Robinson, who in 1947 integrated the great game of baseball. I'm grateful for all those who played the game and had an impact, especially players like Willie. Still today, he paves the way for people after him.

His humility is even more impressive than his hitting was.

—*Jake Wood*
*Detroit Tigers infielder, 1961–67*

# Foreword

WHEN I FIRST met Willie Horton at the Detroit Tigers winter ball instructional camp in 1961, I couldn't believe what a powerful build he had. His arms were huge. He was stronger than heck. Every time he swung the bat it felt as if the ball was heading out of the park. I had heard about him, but it was different seeing him in person.

We are only three months apart in age, and after seeing him, my first thought was: *This is my competition?*

Willie had power like no one I had seen. He also worked at his game. He was the hardest worker of any of us. I remember he wore this red rubber suit under his uniform. Even during exhibition games he wore it. He wanted to sweat off pounds. No question about his drive to be a major league player.

Even though Willie and I were competing against each other for a place on the Tigers roster, we became friends quickly. He's such a good guy. In this book, Willie will tell you how difficult it was for Black players in certain cities where segregation was still present in the early 1960s.

It was embarrassing to me, and probably to other White players, that this was still going on. I certainly can't pretend to know what it was like to be a Black player in that era. All I know is Willie and I were close friends in the minors and at the major league level. We are still friends today.

Willie was a good all-around athlete. Jim Northrup was faster than Willie and me from first to third, but we all had about the same speed from home to first. Willie wasn't just a power hitter. Willie has credited me for helping him become a better outfielder. The truth is he was never a bad outfielder. He had good hands. He went from being a good outfielder to a damn good outfielder.

If I helped Willie at all, it was getting him to throw over the top. That paid off. If you watch the video of Willie throwing out Lou Brock at home in the 1968 World Series, then you see those perfect over-the-top throwing mechanics.

Willie and I had some memorable times together, and I still have a crooked finger to prove it.

When we were playing for Duluth-Superior in the Northern League in 1962, Willie and I were horsing around. My hand became caught in his sleeve and he swung his arm and broke my finger. There were only three weeks left in the season.

It's hard to describe how strong Willie was. When we played for Knoxville in 1963, we became involved in a skirmish against the Lynchburg team in Virginia, and tempers flared. The locker room there was really a pole barn. And when we got back there, Willie was still angry. He yanked the padlock and hinge right off the door with his bare hands. It was like shrapnel flying through the air.

Another time we were playing winter ball in Puerto Rico and our team had a spat with our opponents. Everything was straightened out, and Willie and I trotted to our outfield positions. Then somebody from the other team said something and Willie started moving toward the infield. I cut him off and grabbed him by his jersey.

Willie simply picked me up off the ground and walked me into the infield. When this book was being written, I was reminded that there is a photo that shows me with a bear hug around Willie during a bench-clearing brawl.

I can tell you that I never worried about Willie hurting me on those occasions. He would not harm me. I'm confident of that. Willie wasn't mean. Everyone snaps at some point. But Willie would be careful around me.

But what I remember most about Willie was how he swung the bat. I marveled at his ability to swing for the fences on every pitch. He swung so hard that he once broke a bat just swinging. No contract with the ball. The bat broke from the force of his swing.

Willie had some strikeouts, but nothing like we see today from power hitters.

He made contact. And when he did, there was a good chance the ball was leaving the yard. I saw him fooled by pitches and still clear the fence. He would end up with a one-handed swing and the ball still rocketed off his bat. It was always fun to watch him bat.

*—Mickey Stanley*
*Four-time Gold Glove winner*
*Detroit Tigers, 1964–1978*

# Introduction

WHEN FANS EXCAVATE MEMORIES of Willie Horton, they remember the fire in his eyes and the thunder of his bat. When "Willie the Wonder" stepped to the plate in the 1960s, it was a Motown happening. You didn't mow the lawn or wipe the kitchen countertop during a Willie Horton at-bat. You put your life on hold just long enough to turn up the volume on Ernie Harwell on the radio, or to adjust your rabbit-ear antenna to get a clearer view of what Willie would do. When Willie swung the bat, it was not to be missed. In the 1960s, he was baseball's most marvelous physics exhibit.

When the force of Willie's swing connected with a baseball traveling at a high velocity there was a reaction the likes of which most of us had never witnessed. The impact was explosive enough that it could be heard from Detroit to Traverse City to Port Huron to Ishpeming. Every home run seemed nuclear-powered, like they would be more accurately analyzed with a seismograph than a tape measure. When Willie launched a baseball into orbit you could hear people gushing on every street, in every city, in Michigan.

The 1960s were perilous times in America, as society struggled through a civil rights battle that was long overdue. Not everyone had made their peace with racial issues. The racial divide seemed perilous. Protests. Riots. Tension. Even Willie found himself, in his full Tigers uniform, in the middle of the 1967 riot. He stood on 12th Street, not far from where he developed his mighty swing, and tried to persuade Detroiters to stand down.

Some listened to Willie because he was a leader in his own way. Others did not. He was the Detroit Tigers' first Black star, developed on Detroit's inner-city playgrounds. But his stardom was not divided along

xiii

racial lines. Like all Black athletes of his generation, Willie received his share of hate mail. But in Detroit, Willie was as revered by White fans as he was by Black fans. White or Black, young or old, rich or poor, fans loved Willie Horton because he played baseball with boyish passion. He symbolized the American dream that a child can rise up from a poor neighborhood to become a sports hero. Fans loved Willie because he entered the batter's box with a menacing stare that could melt the confidence of All-Star hurlers, and yet he wore a smile everywhere else on the diamond. The curious aspect of fans' allegiance to Willie Horton was that they fell in love with him without ever really knowing that he was a better man than he was a ballplayer. The truth is Willie is as much about his God, his people, and his family as he is about baseball. He loved the game because he loved its people. He loved his teammates like they were his brothers, and he always had time for the fans.

Some athletes see a fan seeking an autograph as an imposition, but Horton sees it as an honor. When Willie makes reference to his family you can't be sure if he's talking about his wife and children, his former teammates, or members of the Tigers' ground crew. They're all family to Willie.

This is a man who awakens at dawn every morning to read the Bible, and who spends hours on the phone talking to friends and family. During the course of a day, he has a kind word for everyone he meets and a hug for many of them. He is a 79-year-old sports icon and yet he refers to the late Tigers owner Mike Ilitch as "Mr. Ilitch." And he pays similar respect to many others in his life.

But if people call him "Mr. Horton," he begs them to call him "Willie" instead and he punctuates every goodbye with a reminder to give his best to your family. The worst criticism his friends can lay on Willie is that he has trouble saying "no" to anyone for any reason. Imagine what a pleasant world this would be if that were the worst of all our faults. The reflection of a man's character is often revealed in the company he keeps, and it's noteworthy that many of Horton's closest chums are the same friends he possessed 60-plus years ago when he was living in the Jeffries Projects. They were all there at Tiger Stadium in 1959 when Horton, then a sophomore at Northwestern High School, hit the light tower in right-center field with a monumental home run. They were there the night in 1963 when Willie hit a home run in his first Tiger Stadium appearance wearing a Tigers uniform. They were at Comerica Park in 2000 when his No. 23 was officially retired and his impact was immortalized with a statue. And they were all there at his home in October 2004, when his family hosted a gathering to celebrate the state of Michigan's passage of a resolution annually recognizing Horton's birthday, October 18, as Willie Horton Day throughout the state. As friends and family told stories about Willie's life of giving, his former Northwestern teammate and close friend Walt Terrell (who shares his name with a former Tigers pitcher) allowed his love of Willie to bubble up in an emotional testimony.

"I can't hold this in any longer," Walt said. "I have to say this—Willie Horton loves Detroit. Willie Horton is Detroit."

"Amen," the crowd murmured, nodding their heads in agreement.

At that moment, spirituality circulated in the room to the point that it felt like a Baptist revival.

That was 17 years ago. But the love for Willie remains as vibrant as it was on that special day. He still works for the Tigers and he's the man the media wants to talk to when there is a discussion about the organization's history or former players.

Without question, Willie is the most important living athlete to grow up in Detroit and play for a Detroit team. Willie's story needs to be told. Long before baseball was talking about launch angle he was rocketing fastballs into orbit. No upper deck was out of reach. No pitcher seemed too dominant for Willie to conquer. How many Michigan children of the 1960s have beautiful memories of Willie the Wonder striding to the plate?

The 1960s were confusing times, particularly if you were poor and unsure of where you fit in a world that was changing dramatically. You tried to develop your self-esteem by idolizing those who had an abundance of it. In that era, you longed to be as proud and defiant as Muhammad Ali and as strong and confident as Gordie Howe. But it was allegiance to our hometown baseball teams that got us through the difficult summers when we had too much time to think about what might lie ahead. Back then, adults weren't trained how to allay children's fears about the

Cold War. Race relation discussions were never had at the dinner table. We didn't have counseling; we just had baseball. And Willie Horton was great therapy. There was something about his aura that we wanted to rub off on us. It was his attitude. He put his soul into every swing he took. Willie was never cheated on his cuts. When he rolled his wrists at the pitch, he swung with gale force. Sometimes when he missed, his helmet would spin off his head. Most of us were sure he was going to corkscrew himself to the center of the earth. Even when Willie failed, he walked from the plate in his gait, comfortable knowing that he had given the game his best effort at that particular moment. This was a kid who escaped poverty to live his dream, and that mentality never left him.

Maybe some of us who watched him started to believe we could do that in our own lives, in our own way. It didn't matter what I did with my life. Thanks to Willie, I began to believe that I was not going to allow myself to be cheated on my swings. Willie taught us to swing for the fences with all of our being. It was his gift to us all.

*—Kevin Allen*

# Chapter 1

# Pride and Prejudice

THE TRUTH IS, I didn't experience true racism until I signed my first professional contract with the Tigers in 1962.

My initiation to being a Black man in America came on my first trip to spring training in Lakeland, Florida. Excited and brimming with confidence, I flew to Tampa and took a Greyhound Bus to downtown Lakeland. From there, I tried to hail a taxi for the final leg of my trip to Tiger Town.

The first cab driver rolled down his window and said he couldn't take me.

"Why not?" I asked.

"Because you're Black," he said. "You have to call Wigs Taxi. They can take you."

I started to laugh because I believed someone was playing a joke on me. That didn't sound like a legitimate cab company. In Detroit, we had the Checker Cab Company or Black and White Cabs or Yellow Cabs.

"Wigs," I repeated. "That sounds like a barbecue place."

Remember, I had been at winter ball in Tampa the previous fall after signing with the Tigers. Teammates were always playing tricks on you. I had been warned that in spring training veterans liked to have fun at the rookies' expense.

He finally convinced me that he wasn't pulling my leg. But I didn't call Wigs Cab Company, the designated cab company for Black people. Instead, I flung my duffel bag over my shoulder and walked the seven miles from the bus depot to Tiger Town. Can't say for sure why I didn't dial Wigs. Maybe I wasn't sure I believed the cab driver. Probably I was too proud.

Keep in mind that 15 years had passed since Jackie Robinson had become the first Black player in the major leagues. He debuted for the Brooklyn Dodgers on April 15, 1947.

The Boston Red Sox became the last major league team to insert a Black player in their lineup when they started Pumpsie Green in 1959.

But in 1962, I showed up for my first major league spring training and discovered the experience was different for me because I am Black.

Clearly my life in the Jeffries Projects didn't prepare me for what I would discover in Lakeland. Black and White folks lived in the Jeffries Projects when I was young. We drank out of the same hose. When someone bought a Coke, we all took a swig. We all got along fine.

We knew about segregation only because the Detroit Federation League didn't have any integrated teams. When coach Ron Thompson organized the Black and White kids from the projects into one ball team, he wanted to put our integrated team in that league.

League officials suggested to Thompson that our Black players should join the all-Black Mohawks team and White players should join one of the all-White teams. Thompson decided players would vote on whether we should split up.

We voted to stay together, even though it meant we had to play in a lower level recreation league. It was a secret vote, but my hunch is that the vote was unanimous. My parents had done a good job teaching me not to see color when it comes to getting along with people.

It was hard for me to accept that a group of us kids wouldn't tolerate segregation in the 1950s and I had to accept it as a professional baseball player.

I was shocked by what I experienced in Lakeland. Down in Florida, it didn't matter whether you were a professional player or not. If you were Black, you were going to be treated differently than a White person.

At Lakeland, in 1962, Black fans still had to sit in special sections of the baseball park. Drinking fountains and restrooms were designated for either Black or White fans.

Even at the Tiger Town dormitories, Black players were assigned to sleep in different buildings. They were barracks left over from the days when the place was an Air Force base.

Black, White, and Hispanic players could be on the field, but we couldn't sleep in the same room or eat together. We sat in different sections of the cafeteria for meals.

I was not the only player who found the situation intolerable. The Tigers' 1961 starting second baseman, Jake Wood, called it a "culture shock" for him, coming from New Jersey where there was no segregation.

"We were together on the field but out in society we were separated," Jake said, describing our life in Lakeland.

Many White players thought the dormitory setup was just as ridiculous as the Black players did. Mike Christino was a White 18-year-old first baseman from California in 1962 and he would jokingly say he was going "to burn those dormitories down."

That's what happened a couple of years later, but Mike had nothing to do with the blaze. Those buildings were built out of pinewood and they burned to the ground fast as hell. Not sure whether they ever figured out the cause.

Christino played nine seasons in the minors, advancing as high as AAA baseball, but never made it to the majors.

The blatant racism of the times was probably harder on the Black major leaguers than it was on us. We were just getting started and we expected to be treated poorly. But the guys who had made it to the major leagues had hoped their treatment would be better. But the hotel and dining issue was just as bad for them when they were down South.

The late Detroit Tigers pitcher Earl Wilson told me that he "went through hell" as a Black man playing for the Red Sox during spring training in Winter Haven, Florida. A hotel wouldn't let him swim in the pool with his teammates.

One day when he wasn't pitching he decided to anger the hotel management by jumping in the pool. There was one problem: the pool was deep and he couldn't swim.

He made some headlines when teammates had to jump in to rescue him.

That form of protest caught people's attention. Pools were another Whites-only destination in the early 1960s in the South.

When I first joined the team, there were no hotels in Lakeland that would accept Black players. Veteran Black players relied on local families to open up their homes to them for the duration of spring training. That's how I met George and Madeline Brooks. The Brooks family made sure Black players had places to live in Lakeland.

Knowing some restaurants in Florida didn't allow Black diners in those times, the Tigers would have box lunches for players to eat on the bus rides home after road exhibition games.

At night, after games and practice in Lakeland, the Tigers would pick-up the young players—Black and White—at Tiger Town and bus them to town. Black players were dropped off along the road and we walked another quarter-mile to the Black area of Lakeland to find a place to eat.

None of us really had much money so we would find the best food with the cheapest prices. The bus would transport White players into the downtown area. If it was a nice night, many of us would walk, rather than take that bus. Maybe that was our form of protest. The bus would come back and pick us up at night.

At my first spring training, I wasn't old enough to enter the place Gates "Gator" Brown and the other Black players wanted to go. They liked a bar called "Half a Pint." Wigs Taxi was next door and I would sit out front of that building on a bench waiting for the boys to come out of the bar. The woman that ran the taxi—we called her "Momma"—sat out there with me.

Sometimes we all went down to Ellis barbecue and ate together. Sometimes if Gator knew they were going to be there a while, he would come outside and tell me to head back to Tiger Town. If he was heading over to Epps to play cards, I knew it would be best to go home. Gator loved his cards and he was going to be there a while.

I did plenty of waiting for Gates, but I would not have traded those nights for anything. I always learned plenty from Gates on the bus ride there or the walks home.

Jake told me that he recalls a woman asking him how the players got back to Tiger Town. When he told her that Black players sometimes walked, she was mortified.

"She went into a rage about what could have happened to us," Jake recalled. "That's when the fear came into our heart."

Lakeland wasn't built up the way it is today. Orange groves were everywhere. It was dark along the road home. These roads weren't paved. They were sand and gravel. We could have been in trouble if the wrong people saw a couple of us walking by ourselves.

When spring training was over, everyone was assigned to different teams. If you didn't earn a spot on the major league roster, you received a minor league assignment. After my first spring training, I was assigned to Duluth, Minnesota, to play for the Duluth-Superior Dukes. We traveled from Lakeland to Duluth by bus. That's a 1,636-mile trip. We had difficulty finding a hotel that would accept our Black players.

Our manager, Al Lakeman, a former major league catcher, was clearly bothered by that.

"If we can't stay together, you just keep driving straight through," he told our bus driver.

Back then, that trip took roughly 30 hours. To make sure our driver could rest, some veteran players drove for a while. Lakeman even took a turn.

The Northern League was a rough ride. It wasn't just in the South where our integrated team had trouble finding hotels. During my first pro season, sometimes our White players would stay at one hotel and our Black players would be at another.

That season I remember traveling to play the Aberdeen Pheasants in South Dakota and our six Black players were forced to stay in one room while White players were two to a room.

In Duluth, I lived at the YMCA. Once I went up to the front desk to complain about a problem with my room and the man said: "Look [n-word], just be glad you have a room."

That's not a word I heard in my neighborhood, but I had started to hear it from fans as well. That's a word I won't use today, even in the telling of a story.

I remember a phone call with my dad about the confusion I felt because my grandmother—my father's mother—was White. I loved her dearly.

"Poppa, I don't want to stop loving my grandma," I said.

Because it was difficult to find hotels that would take us all, we would drive all night sometimes. We would clear the luggage out of the overhead space and take turns sleeping up there. It doesn't sound comfortable, but at least you could stretch your legs out.

Playing in the minor league was not always comfortable for Black men in the 1960s. When I played for Knoxville in the 1960s, a pitcher knocked me down with an inside pitch in a road game in Lynchburg, Virginia. That caused a major team brawl.

Police came on the field to break it up. They locked me up in a storage room they had at the ballpark. As soon as the police left me, I just knocked the door down and headed back to my dugout.

At the time, some of my brothers were still living in West Virginia and they climbed in a truck and drove to Lynchburg the next day after they heard what happened.

My oldest brother, James, did the talking. He called me by my family nickname, "Boozie."

"Did they hurt you, Boozie?" he asked pointedly. "Did they lay a hand on you?"

"No, they didn't hurt me," I said.

"That's good," James said.

My answer to that question probably prevented a whole lot of trouble. My kin was there to look after me.

The New York Yankees had a farm team in Augusta, Georgia, and the Reds' affiliate was in Macon, Georgia. Both cities invoked a midnight curfew for Black people, and if we played twilight doubleheaders in those cities I would remind my manager that I may need to be pulled in the second game.

It wasn't as if I was going to be walking with the team back to the hotel. The Black guys had to walk to the Black hotel, which was always farther away.

"I came to this town to play baseball, not get involved with a curfew issue," I told manager Frank Skaff.

One night we were playing in Asheville, North Carolina, where the Pittsburgh Pirates had a farm team. The game ran late and the city had a curfew. We had a bus and it was going to leave the highway and drop me off and I would walk the rest of the way.

My fellow outfielder Mickey Stanley thought that was unacceptable. He said he was getting off with me and would stay at the Black hotel.

The only problem with that plan was the Black hotel wouldn't allow a White man to stay there. Mickey and I just sat in the lobby and talked all night.

Mickey and I were already friends, but that night strengthened our bond. What I remember most about Mickey was that he was the best center fielder I ever saw. And he went out of his way to help me be a better ballplayer.

He helped me get to the Tigers by working with me to improve my outfield skills. He taught me how to play the ball off the wall and where to put my glove to make sure I could handle a shot into a corner.

Mickey was the first one to get me thinking about preparing myself before the hitter stepped into the batter's box.

"Know how your pitchers pitch," he would say.

Mickey showed me that if you understand your pitcher's approach "you should always be within 10 or 15 feet of where the ball is going to be hit."

If you think about that plan, it makes perfect sense. If you know your pitcher is going to jam right-handed batters, you know you should cheat toward the left-field line. If he is going to keep the ball away from a hitter, you need to move toward the gap.

I laugh when I see outfielders pull a cheat sheet out of their pocket to know where to play hitters. We would never have done that because we would want our manager to know that we had studied the opposing team and knew where to play each batter.

My advice to young players is to learn your pitchers and learn the hitters in the league. That will help you as much as pure skill.

And remember we were competitors trying to earn a spot on the Tigers' roster. I played left and Mickey played center, but when you first get called up you are just a spare outfielder. That can be a center fielder, left fielder, or right fielder. Mickey didn't care. He did what he could to help me.

I played with many different ballplayers throughout my career, many of them from the South, but I never felt I had a teammate who acted in a racist manner.

But I had one manager who troubled me.

Bob Swift replaced Charlie Dressen when Charlie suffered a heart attack during spring training in 1965. I knew Swift's appointment as interim manager was not in my best interest.

After spring training, we played an exhibition game in Atlanta. While we were there, I met my brother Robert and had dinner with him. It was a few minutes after curfew when I ran into Swift. I introduced him to my brother. He seemed fine about it all.

But the next day, Swift called me into his office and said: "If you don't start taking your career seriously I am going to send you back down and you aren't going to be called back up."

I was stunned. Anybody who knew me knew I was very serious about playing baseball.

It wasn't the first time I made him mad. When my parents were killed in an automobile crash, I was playing for him in Puerto Rico. When the funeral was over, I decided not to return to Puerto Rico. I was leading the league in homers when I left. But I was still mourning. My heart wasn't into playing ball. I heard Swift wasn't happy with my decision.

When I made the Tigers roster in 1965, I thought my problems with Swift were behind me. I was among a few Black guys who had made the team. Several games into the season, none of us had started a game. We had one pinch-hit among us.

Sometimes you can experience subtle racism. Nobody may be calling you a name or making you ride in the back of the bus, but you aren't treated the same as a White person. Even if you couldn't prove it, you could feel it.

As a Black player in the 1960s, I always had the impression that some managers subconsciously had a quota system in their head when it came to Black players. It felt as if a Black player was going to earn a starting spot, it was going to be at the expense of another Black player.

For example, when Ike Brown was called up by the Tigers in 1969, he was an infielder. But he was told to come out and work out in left field.

"Why don't you go and work out in right field with Al Kaline because he will be leaving before I will," I said.

I also felt that Black players couldn't report injuries the way a White player could. You didn't dare tell anyone if you had a toothache or a headache or sore arms and legs. You were fearful that if you left the lineup, you would never get back into the lineup.

During my time in Detroit, I received my share of hate mail and death threats, much of it with racial overtones.

One other form of racism I noticed during my time with the Tigers. Tigers managers always talked to the White star Al Kaline about what was happening with the team. But Tigers managers and coaches never talked to me about anything.

Don't take that wrong. I loved Al. This wasn't about him. He deserved everything he got from the Tigers. My point was that some members of the Tigers didn't treat me the same.

# Chapter 2

# Jake the Snake

WHEN I BROUGHT Jake Wood to meet Mike Ilitch for the first time, the Detroit Tigers owner knew who Jake was and his importance to the club's history.

"Jake the Snake," Ilitch said, extending his hand to greet him. "In 1961, as a rookie, you stole 30 bases, hit 11 home runs, and led the American League with 14 triples."

Wood signed with the Tigers in 1957, only two years after an injury forced Mike to give up baseball because of an injury suffered while playing in the minors for the Tigers organization.

Most baseball fans, even in Detroit, don't know about Wood and that is shameful. He was the first Black player born in America to rise up through the Detroit Tigers farm system to play regularly for the Tigers.

Ozzie Virgil is listed as the Tigers' first Black player, but he was born in the Dominican Republic and moved to Brooklyn when he was 13.

Virgil came to the Tigers on a trade. I do not want to diminish the value of Ozzie's accomplishment. He was the first player born in the Dominican Republic to play in the major leagues. A Dominican Republic airport is named after him.

The celebration of Virgil being the first player of color to play for the Tigers happened only 35 months before I signed with the team.

The fact that the *Detroit Free Press* headline read: "Tigers call up first Negro" speaks to where America was at in race relations in 1958.

In the story announcing Virgil's call-up, it was noted that the Tigers had 19 Black players under contract. According to the article, the Tigers also denied that the call-up had occurred "as a result of pressure from Negro groups."

The Tigers became the second-to-last major league team to use a non-White player. Virgil had been acquired from the San Francisco Giants the previous winter. On June 6, 1958, Virgil went 1-for-5 to help the Tigers pound the Washington Senators 11–2 at Griffith Stadium.

On June 17, Virgil was 5-for-5 when he made his Tigers' debut at Briggs Stadium. He received a standing ovation from the 29,000 fans.

It is appropriate to note that Virgil made his debut in Briggs Stadium, because it is widely accepted that it was owner Walter Briggs who had dictated that the Tigers were to have an all-White roster.

That is the only explanation why the Tigers lineup had no players of color for 11 years after Jackie Robinson made his major league debut—scoring the game-winning run—for the Brooklyn Dodgers in a 5–3 win against the Boston Braves on April 15, 1947, at Ebbets Field. Eleven weeks after Robinson joined the Dodgers, Larry Doby was inserted into the Cleveland Indians' lineup to give the American League its first Black player.

Twelve seasons later, Doby was traded to the Detroit Tigers for Tito Francona and he became the second Black player on the Tigers. His first game was April 10, 1959. He played only 18 games for the Tigers before being sold to the Chicago White Sox for $30,000. Late during the 1959 season, Black pitcher Jim Proctor was brought up and pitched in two games. Those were the only two games he played in the major leagues.

As I said earlier, the Boston Red Sox became the last major league team to integrate when Pumpsie Green played for them on July 21, 1959. The Philadelphia Phillies had become the last National League team to integrate when John Kennedy played for them on April 22, 1957.

Briggs died in 1952, but his estate owned the team until July 16, 1956, when a group headed by John Fetzer bought the team. According to a *Detroit News* article, the Tigers did invite some Black ballplayers to training camp after Briggs' death in 1953, including outfielder Grover Moses, 18, from Northwestern High School. Others included an 18-year-old outfielder named Claude Agee and a shortstop named Henry Gaskins. The Tigers also purchased the contract of Arthur Williams, a pitcher who had been very impressive in the California State League. None of them made it to the major leagues. Briggs' influence on the racial makeup of the Tigers' roster seemed to last until Fetzer officially took over the team.

Virgil's debut occurred when I had just started at Northwestern. It was an important step, but I couldn't help wondering if Virgil's accomplishment would have been more meaningful if he had been a Black kid whose heritage wasn't jointly shared by two countries.

He was a man of color, and certainly had American roots. He moved from Monte Cristi, Dominican Republic, to America when he was 13. He graduated from a Bronx high school and served in the U.S. Marines. When he made his debut for the New York Giants in 1956, he became the first player from the Dominican Republic to play in the majors. Felipe Alou and Juan Marichal would soon follow.

What I can tell you is that my father was more excited about the arrival of Jake Woods as a Detroit Tigers player than he was about Ozzie's debut. He let me and my friends Johnny Mack and the late Jimmy Slate skip school to go see Jake play his first game on April 11, 1961, at Tiger Stadium.

Jake homered off Jim Perry and you could tell the Black folks at the game were excited to see him in the lineup.

Because of Jake's speed, he created a buzz at Tiger Stadium in 1961. You could feel the crowd's excitement when he was on base. "Go, Jake, Go," they would yell every time the pitcher was in a stretch.

I call Jake Wood the "Abraham Lincoln of Baseball" because he is so well respected. He was low-key, always cool and composed. Jake always says he learned so much from me, but the truth is I learned much from him. He was a mentor.

Jake experienced racism in the minor leagues just like every other Black ballplayer did. He told me he grew up in an accepting multiracial New Jersey community.

"You grew up not realizing that society is not like that," Woods said. "I grew up in a neighborhood where there were Italian kids, Jewish kids, all kinds of kids. We were out there all day, not on grass fields, but gravel fields and playing what? Baseball. And we played stickball in the street. And whoever's house you are in front of you went in and had a sandwich at noon and then came out and played again. We didn't care whether you were Catholic or Jewish, we just knew you as Harry or Buddy."

Jake told me it was hard on him when he came down to spring training and realized, "I could not even go downtown and see a movie."

When he was in the minors, he remembers taking a trip to his team in Erie, Pennsylvania, and en route, when the bus was still in the South, the White players went to the hotel and he and another Black player "went to a lady's house to stay."

"We were not allowed to be with our teammates," Jake recalled.

He remembers on a bus trip when the team stopped for dinner and the Black players waited on the bus. Teammates brought them sandwiches.

When Jake was playing for Idaho Falls in the Pioneer League, he turned 21. The team was on the road in Montana. Naturally, the guys wanted to take him out for beers.

"They wouldn't serve me because of the color of my skin," Jake remembered.

In the one season he played in Idaho Falls, he remembers seeing only one other Black person in the city.

When he played in Erie in 1957, he had one Black teammate, Jim Branch from Detroit, but he was released 14 games into the season. At the time, he was batting .263.

Wood became lifelong friends with a White player named Ted Brzenk from Milwaukee, who had signed with the Tigers after playing one season of college baseball at Northwestern.

In 1958, Wood started out the season in Durham, North Carolina, where he caught up briefly with Brzenk and his new bride, Barbara. Wood has retold the story many times about Barbara greeting him with a hug in Durham.

"She came running out to see me and was hugging me," Jake recalled. "I said, 'What are you trying to do, get me killed down here?'"

Wood laughs about it now, but a Black man and a White woman didn't hug in public in the South in those days. That speaks to the difficulty Black players experienced trying to climb to the major leagues in the 1950s and early 1960s.

Fighting your way to the top is hard enough for White players, but they didn't have as many hurdles to clear as Black players.

Fans were rough on Jake in some of his minor league stops, maybe because he was a dynamic player. He could spray the ball around the diamond and fly around the bases.

"I've heard words that were not in the dictionary when it comes to the fans describing me," Jake said.

One night in Charleston, South Carolina, Wood remembers that a fan called him a "horrific" name and one of Wood's White teammates had to be restrained from going after the fan.

"It was hard to believe that people who didn't even know me would say such horrible things," Wood said. "It was not just the Black players who heard this. My heart went out to the Spanish-speaking players. Sometimes we would have one Spanish-speaking guy on the team who didn't speak the language. How did he get by? You are in a strange land and you don't have a clue about this kind of environment you are coming into. And you are absolutely alone. It was difficult when you were a Black person, but you might have two or three of us on a team. When you were Hispanic, you were probably the only guy. How did they survive?

Wood was a smart player and a good hitter. After he turned pro in 1957, he hit .300 or better in each of his first four seasons in the Tigers' system. He hit .318 for Erie in his first season, then .306 in a combined 1958 season with Durham and Idaho Falls, and then .309 in a combined season with Knoxville and Fox Cities.

In 1960, Jake had a monstrous season, batting .305 with 54 extra-base hits and 76 RBI for Denver. That earned him his trip to the big leagues.

Based on his start, Jake looked like he would enjoy a long career in the majors. That appeared even more likely when he finished sixth in the American League Rookie of the Year race in 1961. He had 171 hits, scored 96 runs, and drove in 69 runs as a leadoff hitter.

Only Al Kaline and Norm Cash had more hits for the Tigers than Wood did in 1961.

This was a few years before Maury Wills and Lou Brock reminded the baseball world that speed can be a major factor in helping you win a game. If the Tigers had given Jake the freedom on the basepaths that

Brock and Wills enjoyed, he might have swiped 60 bases. Wood was as fast as any ballplayer I knew in those years. Ron LeFlore came along a number of years later and I believed Jake in his prime was comparable to LeFlore. Wood was so fast that he would make errors on defense because he would run past the ball.

Back then, the Tigers organization didn't believe much in running. They were worried about the players' legs. Mickey Stanley and I stole 18 bases in my first pro season in Duluth and they really didn't want me to run that much.

Who can say whether racism cost Jake any votes for American League Rookie of the Year in 1961? But there were six players who received votes for Rookie of the Year that season, and the two Black players finished third and sixth in the balloting.

Boston Red Sox pitcher Don Schwall won the award on the strength of a 15–7 record and Kansas City Athletics shortstop Dick Howser finished second. He had the same number of hits as Jake (171), and Howser stole 37 bases, seven more than Jake. Howser also batted .280, compared to Jake's .258. But Wood had more RBI, triples, home runs, and extra-base hits. Howser received six first-place votes and Jake had one.

Chicago White Sox outfielder Floyd Robinson, from Prescott, Arizona, was the other Black player in the race and his .310 batting average was best among the competitors. But he only received two first place votes.

At the least, we can say that the National League was quicker to embrace the use of Black players than the A.L. was. The American League didn't name an African American Rookie of the Year until 1966, when Chicago White Sox player Tommie Agee won the honor. In 1964, Cuban player Tony Oliva won the award.

In contrast, the National League by 1966 had already named 10 Black players Rookie of the Year, including Jackie Robinson, Willie Mays, and former Negro League stars Sam Jethroe (1950) and Joe Black (1952).

After Wood's strong rookie season, you would have thought he was set up for a long run of major league success. But that isn't what happened. He went from playing 162 games in 1961 to playing 111 games in 1962. His batting average dropped to .226. In 1963, Jake played only

85 games. He managed to hit 11 home runs in those 85 games. That is a pace for 21 home runs over a 162-game season. Wood also batted .271.

You would have thought he would have played more after that showing. But he played even less in 1964 because the Tigers made a major trade.

After the 1963 season, the Tigers acquired second baseman Jerry Lumpe in a five-player deal that sent Rocky Colavito to the Kansas City Athletics. Now Wood was Lumpe's backup. It's difficult to have consistency in your swing and performance when you are not playing every day.

As Wood told me when he wasn't playing regularly, "a 90 mile-per-hour fastball started to seem like it was 150 miles per hour.

"Some guys can play a couple of times per week and play well," Wood said. "I didn't play well."

He ended up playing a utility role until his contract was sold to the Cincinnati Reds on June 23, 1967. That meant he missed being part of the Tigers' 1968 championship team by one season.

"To this day, I wonder why [they moved me,]" Wood said. "You think about some of the personnel they kept and you wonder what made them different from me. But all I know is they got rid of me. Then you go to any organization and you are tolerated but not wanted."

Jake said it never occurred to him until he retired that in the 1960s that Black players were competing against each other for the limited roster spots available to Black athletes. At that time, major league teams still weren't necessarily taking the best players for their roster. Teams still weren't comfortable with the idea of having multiple Black players on the roster. It wasn't yet a fair competition for starting positions or roster spots. Quality players were left off rosters because they were Black.

"You talk about players with five tools, but I saw some Black players with six tools and they never made it," he said.

Jake and I have talked many times about how it is hard to explain why New Jersey–born Jesse Queen never got his chance with the Tigers. He batted .284 throughout his 12-year minor league career. But he never got a sniff at making the major leagues.

In 1961, he batted .321 with 22 doubles, 11 triples, and 18 home runs between Double-A Knoxville and Triple-A Denver.

The following season he played the whole season at Denver and batted .316 with 34 doubles and 20 home runs.

He was 25 then. Seemed like the right time to call him up to the major leagues. He was one of the finest ballplayers I saw in the minors. But it didn't seem to matter what he accomplished in the minors.

Would it have been different if he were White? We just don't know.

I always thought Rufus Anderson, a Black player from Valdosta, Georgia, was talented enough to play in the majors. When I played my first pro season in Duluth, he was my teammate. That was a tough league and he helped the other Black players get through the season. He was tough. He played with a chip on his shoulder. He didn't turn the other cheek. He was the type of guy if you hit him, he hit you back. He always carried a switchblade in his pocket. I always felt safer around Rufus.

We called him "Snake." He was the first small player I ever saw who used a long, heavier bat. He could hit the ball a long way. He batted .264 the season we played together in Duluth. That was an interesting place to play. That city is on the shore of Lake Superior and when the fog rolled in you couldn't tell whether a hit down the right-field line was fair or foul. We had a good group; Mickey Stanley, Pat Dobson, and Jim Northrup were on that team.

We used to call Northrup "Sweet Lips" because he always had something to say.

In 1962, he started in Class A Knoxville and then was sent down to Duluth.

"I'm here to help you guys start winning," Northrup would say, laughing.

"You're here because you weren't hitting," I would remind him.

Jake said it was always challenging to know where you stood with your manager or general manager because no one talked about racism back then.

"People say things in life in general in front of your face," Jake said. "But behind the scenes, when they make decisions, you don't know what they are saying."

Wood was a quiet man, similar to Al Kaline in his soft-spoken nature. He just took care of his business and didn't say much. Very classy man.

Everyone likes Jake. When he started working for Abraham & Straus department store in Brooklyn, New York, as a receiving manager, he ended up staying there through many management changes. It became the Federated Department Stores, which included Macy's. He worked 32 years there before retiring.

He said he had no regrets about his baseball career. The only regret I have is that the Tigers haven't recognized Wood more for being the first American-born Black player to move through the system and play full time.

Mr. Ilitch helped me get Jake invited back often these last 15 years to be recognized for his accomplishment. But that wasn't enough. I wanted more for Jake. The Tigers honored him again in 2021, and the plan is to have his accomplishment commemorated at Comerica Park in some way, probably a plaque.

I am happy about that. Baseball is in Jake's soul. He's 84 and still playing competitive ball. In July 2021, when we called him about this book, he had just walked in the door after playing a weekend tournament in Roanoke, Virginia.

In the winter of 1960, the Tigers acquired Billy Bruton from the Milwaukee Braves to play center field. Chico Fernández, born in Havana, Cuba, was the team's starting shortstop. So in 1961—the year I signed—the Tigers had three minorities among their eight starting position players.

When I got to Tiger Town in 1962, former Negro League pitcher Sam "Red" Jones was on the team. He'd played for the Cleveland Buckeyes in the Negro Leagues and then signed with the Cleveland Indians in 1951. But he didn't find true success until he joined the National League with the Chicago Cubs in 1955. In his first full season with the Cubs, he pitched a no-hitter. A two-time All-Star, Sam won 21 games for the San Francisco Giants in 1959. He won 18 the following season.

Sam was 36 years old when he was dealt to the Tigers before the 1962 season, and he still parked a toothpick in his mouth, which had become his trademark over the years. He was also known as "Toothpick Sam."

In my first spring training, Sam had a habit of picking up the Black players and driving them over to a local family's house for a cookout. He turned me into a barbecue specialist, and I carried that tradition through the years at Tiger Town.

More importantly, Jones, Bruton, and Jake Wood would tell stories about the Negro League and their experiences as Black men in a sport that struggled with integration for years. Jones was a lighter-skinned Black man, and that spring when he was injured he was hospitalized in the White ward. He told us he didn't want his wife to visit him because he knew when the nurses saw her that he was going to be transferred to the Black unit.

But she did go to visit him, and that's exactly what happened. Jones said the quality of care was so inferior in the Black ward that he checked himself out. It was a sad commentary on what was happening at that time in American history, but Sam made it a funny story. "It was like driving a Rolls Royce and then suddenly I was behind the wheel of a Chevrolet," he said.

The Black players who paved the way for me to the major leagues had a much more challenging road to travel than I did, and I had great respect for them. It seemed as if the Black players looked out for each other. Jake wouldn't come knocking on our door, but if you approached him, he was always there for you, always willing to put his arm on your shoulder and tell you what you needed to hear.

Once I made it to the majors, I also became friendly with Larry Doby, who was coaching by that time. His stories really made me appreciate the struggle that Black athletes endured—like the day Doby was promoted to the Indians in 1947, when some of his new teammates wouldn't even shake his hand. He heard racial taunts from the fans in the stands, and some of them tried to provoke him into lashing out. But Doby wouldn't stoop to their level.

Early in his career, he also had to stay at different hotels than his teammates did. And even though Doby was the first Black player in the American League—in the same season Jackie Robinson broke into the National League—I can't help but wonder why Doby never got the same recognition as Robinson. In 1998, Doby was voted into the National Baseball Hall of Fame by the Veterans Committee.

Based on my conversations with Doby, my understanding is that he believed he was ready for retirement in 1959. But he decided to ask for a trade to the Tigers instead. He wanted the last laugh on the late Walter Briggs. Doby believed, as others did, that the former Tigers owner had vowed the Tigers would never have a Black player on their roster. Even though Virgil had been the first player of color to play in Detroit in 1958, Doby wanted to wear a Tigers uniform as his way of protesting Briggs' position.

He also made his voice heard when he joined with Jake and Jim Proctor to demand that Black players be given rental cars for road games during spring training.

When I joined the Tigers in 1962, the civil rights fight was far from over, particularly in the American League. Gates Brown was already on the team when I showed up. He was three years older and took me under his wing. Young Black players looked for an older Black player to help them find their way. My guide was the Gator, who was street-smart and wise beyond his years.

When Gates and I had played winter ball together in 1961, he already had two years of professional baseball under his belt. In 1961, he hit .324 with 33 doubles and 15 home runs playing for the Durham Bulls in the Carolina League.

He was just 22 and his chest seemed enormous to me. One day, he invited me to his home. The way he said it made me laugh.

"You need to come up and meet the Gator," he said like I was going to meet someone new.

He gave me directions to a place he was renting in Tampa. I'll never forget that when I walked up, it was like I was meeting someone new. He was sitting on the porch wearing a silver smoking jacket, a long flowing robe that made him look like a king. He was a king in my eyes.

"Have a seat," he said.

When I plopped down on the steps, he began his line of questioning. "Was that for real, when I read in *Jet* magazine about you signing for big money—more than $50,000?" I told him I thought it was, but I didn't know for sure because my father and Judge Damon Keith had handled everything. The Gator just whistled.

From that point on, Gates Brown and I became the best of friends. We played together for 13 seasons, and I learned much from him during my career. Going through that period of integration in the American League seemed to make us stronger. Maybe it made us closer. I called Gates all the time. There wasn't a day that passed that I didn't talk to him. In fact, I even introduced him to his wife.

Billy Bruton was a first-class man, and probably the closest thing we had to a civil rights activist on the Tigers in those days. He was supposedly 36 years old when I came to the Tigers in 1962. However, the rumor was that Billy was actually in his forties. He was the son-in-law of Judy Johnson, the Hall of Fame Negro Leagues star. Billy knew about the Negro Leagues, and he'd lived through the integration of the National League. He spent eight years in Milwaukee, leading the N.L. in stolen bases three times (1953–55) and triples twice (1956 and 1960).

As a young Black player, I looked up to Billy because he was willing to take a stand. He was appalled that the American league was years behind the National League in terms of racial equality. And he wasn't afraid to say so. "I went through this early in my career with the Braves," he said, "and I'm not going to do it again."

Billy was angry at the lack of hotels willing to accept Black players, and he told the Tigers he wouldn't report to spring training in 1963 if the situation didn't change. Sam Jones stood beside him on that issue.

That's when Tigers general manager Jim Campbell went to the city and persuaded officials to get moving on the construction of a new hotel.

But even after the Holiday Inn was finished, the Black players couldn't eat with the White players. We had to eat in the press room. That wasn't good enough.

At one point, Billy told the Tigers, "If you can't treat me properly, I'll just meet the team back in Detroit."

Billy educated me on how to pick up the torch and do my part. Billy and I remained friends through the years. In 1995, he was on his way to meet me at a family reunion when he suffered a heart attack driving in Delaware. With Billy incapacitated, his car veered off the road and struck a tree. He died at the hospital.

When Charlie Dressen was hired as manager of the Tigers on June 17, 1963, the organization brought in an honest man who believed in racial equality. When it came time to choose his players, Charlie was color-blind. He'd managed Jackie Robinson in Brooklyn as well as the great Roy Campanella. He later managed Bruton with the Milwaukee Braves. Dressen clearly wanted to give me and Gates Brown the opportunity to play in Detroit. Most Tigers fans have forgotten that Dressen toyed with the idea of moving Al Kaline to center and using Gates in left and me in right.

Dressen was an old-school manager who mastered his craft in the Dodgers organization, guiding the team to back-to-back pennants in 1952 and 1953. Charlie brought a sense of family to the Tigers' organization. He was the one who wanted to bring Tiger Town and the major league team closer together. He wanted the Tigers' minor leaguers to be closer to the team's major leaguers. And he tried to bridge the gap between the A.L. and N.L.

When Charlie died in 1966, I mourned his loss. I learned so much from him in such a short period of time. He was tough on me, but he did so like a parent trying to get the best out of his child. Charlie tried to work with me, and inspire me, in my battle to keep my weight down. He told me how Campanella had the same problem in Brooklyn, but was able to overcome it. I figured if Campy could do it, so could I.

To motivate his Detroit players—particularly me—Charlie would also tell the story of George Crowe, the former Negro League player who made it to the majors when he was 31 years old. Crowe began his baseball career with the New York Black Yankees and the New York Cubans in the Negro Leagues in the late 1940s. He had also played in the National Basketball League with the Dayton Rens in 1948–49. Before then, he had played alongside Jackie Robinson on the Los Angeles Red Devils basketball team in 1946–47.

Crowe was clearly a superior athlete, but he didn't get a chance to play in the majors until the Boston Braves promoted him in 1952. And he didn't get an opportunity to play full time until Cincinnati gave him the first baseman's job in 1957. At age 36, he belted 31 home runs and drove in 92 runs. Despite the late start, he played nine seasons in the majors.

"Sometimes you get stuck in one organization or you don't get an opportunity," Charlie would say. "So when you're given that chance, you have to take advantage of it, because you don't know when you'll get another one."

One day when the Tigers had a day off in New York, Charlie took me to meet Campanella, who owned a liquor store in the area. We spent all afternoon there with Campy. Clearly, Charlie was trying to motivate me, and it worked. Charlie was a fiery 150-pound manager who loved the game more than life itself.

Given the young team we had coming up, I wonder how far Dressen could have taken the Tigers if he had lived longer. Could we have won two or three pennants? We will never know. But I do know he was one of the best managers I've ever had. And it seemed to me that the American League could have been a better league if it had brought over more managers like Dressen from the National League.

The A.L. didn't just lag behind the N.L. in race relations. The A.L. trailed the N.L. in many aspects of the game. Most of it had to do with attitude. In the older National League, which many in baseball called "the senior circuit," managers and players seemed to understand that everyone played more aggressively when they enjoyed coming to the ballpark every day.

In 1965, I was named the American League's starting left fielder for the All-Star Game in Minneapolis. Shortly after taking my defensive position in the field, Willie Mays homered, Willie Stargell singled, and Joe Torre homered. Bang. Bang. Bang. We were down 3–0 before we had our stirrups on straight. Cleveland Indians outfielders Vic Davalillo and Rocky Colavito were in center and right and I yelled over to them, "Do we have any business playing these guys?"

We did come back to make a game of it before the National League won, 6–5. But it was clear to me that there was a major difference in the two leagues that went beyond talent. It's no coincidence that the National League went 23–2–1 in All-Star games from 1960 to 1982. Back in the early '60s, they played two All-Star games a year, giving the N.L. two chances to wallop us.

At the 1973 All-Star Game in Kansas City, I can remember quietly sitting on the bench with my fellow American League teammates watching the N.L. players running around out on the field in the midst of talking to themselves and fans. There was plenty of horseplay when the National Leaguers were on the field.

Cincinnati Reds outfielder Pete Rose spotted us all on the bench and yelled over to us, "Look at all you guys getting ready to get your behinds whipped again. You guys are so tight, you can't even talk."

Rose was right. The N.L. players always seemed to be having a good time, and we always seemed subdued by comparison. That attitude seemed to flow from the top down. In the A.L., we had rules against talking to fans. We really did. In the N.L., there were no such rules. The National League was people friendly.

One time in the late '60s, we were in Chicago to play the White Sox. Gates Brown and I found time to go across town to see our former Tigers teammate Willie Smith, who was then playing for the Cubs. We were sitting in the stands at Wrigley Field, and Cubs players Smith, Ernie Banks, and Ron Santo came into the stands to sit with us before the game. They were shocked when I told them we wouldn't be allowed to do anything like that in the American League.

With that kind of mindset, it's really not surprising that it wasn't until halfway through my career before we had some form of racial equality in the American League.

As I've often said, I only caught the tail end of the ugly discrimination that Black players faced in the major leagues. But it was clear to me early in my career that some people within the Tigers organization still weren't ready for the team to have a Black star in its lineup.

Word spread around the team that our opponents had been given a scouting report on how to pitch to me. It detailed my strengths and weaknesses, and it had been sent to them from someone within the Tigers' front office. Mr. Campbell and Charlie Dressen found out about this and were furious. So were some of my teammates. Campbell fired the person who was responsible, but clearly, not everyone was ready for racial equality in baseball in Detroit, even in the 1960s.

I witnessed enough incidents, and heard enough stories from Billy Bruton, Larry Doby, Sam Jones, Roy Campanella, and others to believe that I owed it to those who came before me, and to those who would come after me, to stand up for civil rights. In 1969, it would be my turn to stand up for racial justice and I did that. You will read about that later.

When I was playing for Syracuse in the minor leagues, I stood in a line one day just to shake Jackie Robinson's hand. He didn't say a word. And he didn't need to. Just shaking his hand was enough for me. I understood that he had opened the door for so many of us. And when it came time for me to meet him, I just thanked him for all he had done.

# Chapter 3

# The Coward's Call

WHEN I DRIVE around Detroit, I avoid the intersection of Michigan and Trumbull Avenues because I don't want to see where Tiger Stadium used to be. Even though we have another baseball field there now, it's not Tiger Stadium.

I want to remember the old ballpark the way it was when I was stationed in left field, Mickey Stanley was in center, and Jim Northrup in right. Tears filled my eyes on September 27, 1999, when the last Detroit game was played at Tiger Stadium. That ballpark was home to me, and I don't want to think about my home being torn down. In my mind, I still see Michigan and Trumbull like it was on September 17, 1968, when the Tigers won the pennant on Don Wert's RBI single. I remember the roar erupting in the Tiger Stadium stands after I threw out Lou Brock at home in Game 5 of the 1968 World Series.

It doesn't seem possible that it was 53 years ago when umpire Doug Harvey signaled Brock was out. It seems like only yesterday I was in the clubhouse with Gates Brown, Dick McAuliffe, Earl Wilson, Norm Cash, Mickey Lolich, and the others.

When I close my eyes, I can still see myself as a kid walking over to Tiger Stadium from my home in the Jeffries Housing Projects. We would play the game "strikeout" against the outside walls of the stadium and then sneak into the stadium to watch the games for free. I've been blessed in my life to have such special memories. I'm especially blessed when you consider that in 1963 I almost quit baseball.

Every baseball player has endured a hitting slump where it feels as though he doesn't even know which end of the bat to grip. It feels like you've never held a bat in your hands before. Your stance feels unnatural. You can't get comfortable in the batter's box. And every pitch

27

seems impossible to hit. It's either just out of your reach on the outside corner of the plate or it's burrowing in on your hands like a guided missile. When you're in a slump, borderline pitches are always called strikes. When you're in a slump, you swing at bad pitches and foul off good pitches.

When I was playing Triple-A baseball in Syracuse in 1963, I went through one of those slumps. I was 20 years old and maybe I doubted myself. I was probably homesick. I don't remember exactly what I told my mother when I called home to Detroit, but I remember that she was pouring her love through that phone line.

Lillian Horton, called "Sis" by almost everyone who knew her, might have been the best listener God ever put on earth. If you had troubles, she had buckets and buckets of sympathy. And she believed that if she could get you to her supper table, she could solve all your problems. She had given birth to 21 children, and yet she always acted as if she didn't have nearly enough people at her table for meals. She was always bringing someone home to eat. She would whip up some biscuits and homemade syrup and whatever troubles you had seemed far less bothersome.

When I told Mom that I was wondering if I was good enough to play in the big leagues, she was sympathetic and caring. She didn't even flinch when I told her I was thinking of quitting.

"Baby," she said, "if you decide baseball's not for you, don't you feel bad. You just c'mon home. This will always be your home, and I'll be here to take care of you."

Poppa must have figured out what the conversation was about. I could hear him stomping across the room saying, "Sis, give me that phone.… Give me the damn phone!"

James Thomas Clinton Horton was not a man to mince words, and he certainly didn't on that night.

"You aren't going to jump up and leave the job you've been given," he said sternly. "You aren't going to give up this opportunity the Tigers have given you. You're not going to let down Judge [Damon] Keith. And you're not going to let down your family. You have responsibilities, Willie, and you're going to live up to those responsibilities. What are you going to do if you come home—work in an auto plant?"

As I tried to explain the self-doubt that was dancing through my mind, Poppa didn't want to hear it.

"What do you have to complain about? You're nothing but a damn coward," he said, and slammed down the receiver. His words were like a knockdown pitch, and it was a struggle for me to dust myself off. Poppa shocked me. And it was the worst feeling I'd ever had.

Immediately, I called my oldest brother in West Virginia.

"James, did Poppa ever call you a coward?" I asked.

"Nope," he said. "You must have done something bad. What did you do?"

That didn't help me, so I called Ray. Same question. Same answer. Poppa had never called him a coward. Next up was Frank, and that was a mistake because he was the brother most like my father.

"Frank, did Poppa ever call you a coward?" I asked.

"No," he said. "You must've really messed up if Poppa called you a coward."

As one of 21 children of Lillian and Clinton Horton, I had plenty of folks to call. And I called them all. When I ran out of brothers, I called my sisters, and none of them had ever been called a coward. I even called my brother-in-law George, who had helped raise me in Kentucky. We looked up to him almost as a parent.

"Poppa said what?" George said, incredulous.

When I wouldn't tell him what I had said to warrant Poppa's wrath, George would only say, "You must've done something very wrong for him to say that." That night might've been the turning point of my career. Maybe it turned my life around because it was the first time I really thought about accepting my responsibility as a man.

By that time, I was already married, and I had my first son, Darryl William. That night, it occurred to me that my dad was telling me that baseball wasn't just my hobby anymore. It was also my job. And if my job wasn't going well, I had to figure out a way to perform better. He really shouldn't have said that to me because I saw my parents live that philosophy every day of their lives.

My father was working in a coal mine in Virginia when I was born, and when the mine closed, he came to Detroit because that's where he thought he had the best opportunity to find work. He accepted his responsibility and he did whatever he could to help us survive. He did what he had to do to feed his family. He always had two or three odd jobs. And even though we didn't have much, my mother always wanted to share what we had.

Today, we have reunions to bring families together, but back then, we had reunions every weekend. My parents believed in family and community. That night, my dad made me realize that I'd been blessed with a gift to play baseball, and that it would have been a sin not to use that gift to the best of my ability. I never called home to complain again—and I didn't need to.

Everything started to fall into place that night. I stopped worrying about what had gone wrong and started to concentrate on how to improve my game every day. Although I was demoted to AA Knoxville that season, I ended up batting .333 with 20 doubles, nine triples, 14 home runs, and 70 RBIs down there.

In September, the Tigers called me up to the majors. In 15 games with Detroit in 1963, I batted .326. And by the end of that season, my confidence was soaring. If I would have listened to my mom, I might've come home that night. And who knows what would've happened after that? To be honest, I'm not a quitter. I loved baseball, and it's hard for me to believe that I would've quit the game. But I can't be sure. All I know is that I've carried Poppa's powerful words with me for 58 years.

The lesson he taught me wasn't just about baseball. It was about life.

# Chapter 4

# Poppa's Rules

CONSIDERING HOW MUCH RESPECT my dad had for Negro League baseball, it's funny to recall that the first time he met Negro League legend Buck O'Neil, he chased poor Buck out of our house. O'Neil played in the Negro Leagues from 1937 to 1955, as a player and a manager, and he was credited with helping prepare George Altman, Ernie Banks, Elston Howard, and several others for the major leagues. By 1957, O'Neil was working as a scout for the Chicago Cubs, and one day, he showed up at our door with a plan to sign me as a 15-year-old.

At the time, the Cubs were aggressively trying to sign underage Latin American players because, apparently, there were no age restrictions on foreign players. O'Neil told my dad that we just needed to say that I was Puerto Rican or Latino and the Cubs could sign me. That's when my dad told O'Neil to leave our house.

I had great admiration for Buck because I knew he was a great baseball man. But up until he died in 2006, I would often tease him about how my dad had him on the run at our house in 1957.

To this day, I'm still not sure why Poppa was so upset with Buck. Maybe he was insulted because Buck wanted him to lie about our ethnicity. Or maybe he believed that Buck shouldn't be trying to sign a 15-year-old boy. Or maybe the money he offered was too low for Poppa. I can't be sure because Poppa never discussed those things with me. What I do know is that O'Neil's arrival at our house was my first indication that I might be able to play in the majors.

Poppa was working at a coal mine in Arno, Virginia, when I was born in 1942. I was their 21st and youngest child. By then my dad was 43, and my mother was almost 40. My brother would tease me about being the "accident baby" long before I knew what that meant. In fact, some of my brothers and sisters were so much older than me, they seemed kind of like surrogate parents. And their children seemed more like my brothers and sisters. We were a close-knit family, and it was commonplace that I would spend weeks, or even months, living with one of my siblings.

During my major league career, I had several nicknames: "Willie the Wonder," "Boomer," "the Ancient Mariner," and "Mull Digger," which is a Southern term passed down from my grandfather to my father to me. But the one nickname some of my relatives still call me is "Boozie."

Even some of my nieces and nephews call me "Uncle Boozie." When I was just a boy, I was big for my age and a little uncoordinated, too. My relatives said I looked "kind of boozy" when I walked. And even before that, I had several adventures as a toddler. One day, I was exploring our cupboards and discovered some canisters of lard and flour. By the time adults found me, I'd been eating it by the handful. Apparently I was enjoying it so much that I looked tipsy, and they stuck me with the nickname "Boozie."

Although I feel as if I'm a Detroiter, the roots of my baseball career are actually in the South. In fact, my family roots are in the South. My brother Billy and I were the only two sons of Clinton Horton who didn't work in the mine at some point. And in 1954, when I was just 11, we were living in Stonega, Virginia, a small town in the midst of a mining area. I had heard that there were tryouts for a baseball team in Appalachia, which was about four or five miles down the road.

My dad said I could try out for the team, but I couldn't convince any of my friends to walk to Appalachia. I was upset, and I started walking down the tracks with tears rolling down my cheeks. After a while, I stumbled across a boy named Larry Munsey, who was fishing. Sure enough, he said he'd go with me to the tryout.

When we got there, there must've been 60 or 70 kids at the tryout. Former pro ballplayer Junior Strong was one of the coaches. Junior took charge and essentially loaded his team with the best players. I was the only Black player on the team, and we were sponsored by Wolfe Hardware store. It was the first uniform I ever wore, and I don't think any of us took off those uniforms for a few days.

The year before, I'd actually played a half-season of youth baseball in Tennessee when I was living with my brother Ray and his wife, Pinkie. I actually used my brother Billy's name to play, and even today folks still think I'm Billy, who was also a talented athlete. But that Wolfe team seems more memorable, maybe because of Larry Munsey or maybe because I really started to develop as a player.

Years later, Coach Strong told me he saw my potential, and that's why he wouldn't let me bat against other kids in batting practice. He insisted on pitching to me himself. He wanted me to face a higher caliber pitch to help me improve. Coach Strong had a decent knuckleball, and today, Munsey likes to remind me that Coach couldn't sneak it past me even when I was 11.

After I moved to Detroit, I didn't see Munsey for more than 35 years. But one year my niece organized a charity outing in Kingsport, Virginia, where, unbeknownst to me, Munsey was serving as vice mayor. Just as I was about to go on the air at a local radio station, Munsey showed up and surprised me. We hugged and cried and talked as if we'd just played a game together that morning.

Looking back on my youth down South, I can honestly say that my family situation wasn't crystal clear to me. Having more than 20 years between the oldest and youngest child was rather confusing. We always had relatives and friends over at our house, and it didn't seem all that important to me to sort out who was who.

That summer that I played baseball in Appalachia, Munsey and I would often stop at the store and buy a Moon Pie or some other treat. One day, a man that I recognized—we called him James—drove alongside us and offered us a ride.

"Noooooo," I said, because Poppa had warned me never to hitchhike. He'd always told me to walk the tracks home, and that's what I was going to do.

"Suit yourself," the man said. "I have to stop by to get some fish for Mom."

As we were walking, it occurred to me that his mom was *my* mom. When I got home, everyone laughed because I didn't know my oldest brother.

Even though I was the only Black player on a team in the South in the 1950s, I really didn't grasp the concept of racism. Even today, Munsey and I both recall that I was treated like every other kid on the team. If kids were passing around a Coke, I got my swig. My parents always taught us to be color-blind, and they always had both Black and White friends around the house. My father's mother was actually White, but again, our family was so large and continually coming and going, I didn't even know she was my grandmother until I was older. I just thought she was some White lady that hung around the house.

My sister Helen and her husband, George, were almost like parents to me, because I would frequently stay with them in Kentucky. When the mines closed for good, I stayed with them in Kentucky while my parents relocated to Detroit. My parents lived on Canfield and Avery with my two nephews, Mike and Joe. A year later, I rejoined them. We moved to Sixth and Forest in a duplex with a shared bathroom. My sister Faye lived on the 11th floor in the Jeffries Projects, and I would spend as much time over there as I did at my parents' house. My buddy Walt Terrell lived on the sixth floor in the projects, and he used to joke that by living on the 11th floor I was "in the penthouse."

Once I finally moved to Detroit, my baseball career began to blossom. The late Ron Thompson, the legendary football coach at St. Martin de Porres, was attending Wayne State University back then, and he organized a neighborhood youth team of Black and White players out of Poe School on Canfield. He managed the team out of the back of his station wagon, and we began to think in terms of leagues and finding the highest level of competition. We called ourselves the Ravens. Mr. Thompson taught us about teamwork and about the fundamentals of baseball.

As kids, many of us would frequently be down at Tiger Stadium playing "strikeout" against the stadium's outside walls. To play "strikeout," you draw a box on the wall, and if the pitcher hits the box and you miss, you're out. If you hit it a certain distance, it's a home run. Before Tiger Stadium was razed, I wish we could have peeled off the paint and found the spot on the wall where the strike zone had been drawn for our "strikeout" games.

But it was also strategic for us to play "strikeout" at Tiger Stadium, because we often tried to sneak into ball games without playing. When the delivery trucks would show up, we'd follow behind them and then climb into the dumpster. Near game time, we'd simply climb out and watch the game for free.

It seemed like a foolproof plan. But one day, we miscalculated and came out of the dumpster too early and were apprehended by the security guards. Just as we were being hauled away, the Cleveland Indians walked by. Rocky Colavito and Don Mossi—I remember him specifically because he had those gigantic ears—came over to see what the trouble was all about.

Once the Cleveland players were told of our crimes, Colavito asked if we could be released into his custody. The security guard obliged, and Colavito took us down to the visiting clubhouse and asked the visiting clubhouse attendant, Rip Collins, to give us jobs. I've never forgotten the kindness that Rocky showed us that day. Years later, when Rocky and I were teammates, I discovered his big heart wasn't just a one-day event. That's just Rocky's way.

Money was always an issue for those of us growing up in the Jeffries Projects. That's why my buddy James Slate was revered, because he figured out we could earn money by carrying people's groceries home from the store. That's how we bought our bats and baseballs.

Slate was the only one in our group who didn't actually play sports, but I don't think he ever missed one of my games or my boxing matches when we were growing up.

Believe it or not, I made "big" money as an actor when I was a kid. In those years in Detroit, there was a locally produced television series called *Juvenile Court*. Local kids were paid $25 to portray the troubled youths who were supposed to be showing up in court. Now that I think about it, it was a great way to keep us all out of trouble. First, it kept us busy all day and gave us some much-needed cash. And by acting as a kid going to juvenile court, we all understood we didn't want to go there in real life.

But mostly every waking hour was reserved for playing baseball. Mr. Thompson's Ravens were a very good team. We had a shortstop named

Al Melvin who we used to call "Little Al Kaline." This was probably about the time that Poppa began to realize I had some natural baseball ability. Although my dad never talked about it, I found out later that he had played some baseball in the Negro leagues in the South, particularly around Birmingham, Alabama, and in Tennessee. He was an infielder. Poppa understood the game, but didn't pressure me the way some kids are pressured.

He was a tough, principled man—not the kind of dad who played catch with his son. He believed that I should learn to do things on my own. He taught me to find a wall and to bounce a few hundred balls off it to improve my catching skills.

Poppa never praised me, and he was always quick to point out if I messed up in a game. "Willie, you need to practice more," he'd say. "You just aren't concentrating enough."

My father always stressed respecting the coaches and the opposition. If I wasn't listening to my coaches, I was in trouble with Poppa. My father didn't drive, but I remember he made it to all my games anyhow. We'd play all over the city, but somehow, he always managed to be there by game time.

My mom, meanwhile, heaped out praise as if she was doling out mashed potatoes. Everybody received a second helping of praise from here. There was just something about Momma that made everyone feel better. And she could make a meal out of anything. She would make her own syrup on the stove better than anything you could find at any store in town. She'd cook up some bacon and a pan of biscuits, and you would have yourself one fine meal. Some of the food that people think of as dinner food—pork chops, gravy, etc.—was breakfast food in my mother's kitchen. And I used to love to watch her eat because she enjoyed her food so much.

Although my dad was tough, he was also a thinker when it came to my baseball career. The best move he made was to let me play for more than one team at once. I would play with the Ravens at my age level, and then I'd play with older players on different nights.

That's how I ended up playing against Bill Freehan and Dennis Ribant, both of whom would later become my teammates with the Detroit Tigers.

Freehan was from Florida, but he lived with his grandparents in the Detroit area in the summer so he could play baseball for Lundquist Insurance. One season, the Lundquist team qualified for the inter-city sandlot World Series in Altoona, Pennsylvania. The team was permitted to add local players, and I was one of the players they chose, along with Ribant and Alex Johnson. I think I made only three or four outs that entire tournament.

Detroit's sandlot team ended up beating Cincinnati's that year, and Cincinnati boasted Eddie Brinkman, who would one day play with Freehan and me on the Tigers. John Havlicek, who would eventually star in the NBA for the Boston Celtics, also played on that team. I was told that the year before, Pete Rose played with Brinkman, and believe it or not, Brinkman, who was a light-hitting major leaguer, was the better player back then.

One memory of my childhood illustrates the differences between how my mom and dad approached parenting.

In the mid-1950s, they were still building the Lodge Freeway near the Jeffries project, and for some reason I started trying to hit bottle tops over the highway with a broom handle. Soon, I was able to hit a bottle top all the way over the freeway. I was pretty excited about it, and I went home to brag to my parents.

My dad didn't believe me. "Quit lying," he said, "or I'm going to spank your behind."

But Momma didn't doubt me. "You keep doing that, baby. You keep hitting 'em over the highway."

If I got myself in trouble, the consequences were severe, such as the time I swiped a $1.98 baseball cap from Cunningham's drug store on Trumbull Avenue. It was an Ivy League cap with pinstripes, and I didn't have money for it. So I just walked out of the store with it.

That night Poppa saw me wearing it. "That's a nice cap," he said.

"Thank you, sir," I said, knowing this probably wasn't going to end well for me.

Once he determined the cap had come from Cunningham's, he had a few more questions for me.

"Did you work for Cunningham's to pay for that cap?"

"No, sir."

"How did you pay for it?"

"I didn't. I just walked out of the store with it."

Lying about it only would've made it worse, although I don't know how it could have been. Poppa whipped me from our house on Sixth and Forest all the way to Cunningham's. Once we got there, my dad told the manager that I would be working there all summer to pay for that $1.98 cap. That meant I was going to miss baseball games, but Poppa didn't care. He wouldn't even budge when Mr. Thompson appealed on my behalf, and on behalf of the team.

It was a harsh penalty but it taught me a valuable lesson. My dad wasn't shy about passing out the whippings, but he was a wise man. He was sure he could teach me the lessons of life, but he also felt that I needed more help than even he could provide me.

Before I headed off to Northwestern High School, my dad told me that he'd decided to make Judge Damon Keith my legal guardian.

That kind of news is shocking to a teenager who doesn't quite comprehend the legal system.

"You aren't giving me away, are you, Poppa?" I asked.

"Nah," he said. "But I think Judge Keith can help you."

Poppa didn't elaborate then, but now I know that he just wanted me to understand both sides of the tracks. We were living in the Jeffries Projects with my sister Faye, and Judge Keith was a successful African American man and a good role model. Legally, Judge Keith may have been my guardian, but in reality, he was becoming my mentor and adviser, too.

When I started spending time with Judge Keith, I began to dream of a better future. The judge didn't counsel me about being a better baseball player; he led me down a path to be a better person. Back then, I was very far removed from knowing what real life was all about.

Judge Keith always tells the story about the time he confronted me after my parents told him I was driving without passing the state's driving test.

"Your mom and dad told me you were driving without a license," he said.

"Well, Mr. Keith," I replied. "I have a driver's license." I handed him a driver's license with another man's name and address on it. I didn't understand the licensing process. I was just told you needed a driver's license, and I had acquired one from someone else.

Essentially, I was recruited to go to Northwestern to play for their coach and athletic director, Sam Bishop. Coach Thompson was an alumnus of Northwestern, and he clearly had an influence. Judge Keith supported the idea. Based on my address in the Jeffries Projects, Northwestern would not have been my school. So in order to enroll there, I moved in with my sister, Virginia, during the week, so I had the right address.

Coach Bishop knew who I was before I arrived at Northwestern but I didn't know who he was. On the first day of classes, my buddies Sam Blue and James Slate and I were leaning against the cannon that stood guard in front of the school. Out of the school came a man dressed in a white suit, and he was heading directly at us. With the way he was dressed, I thought he was with the janitorial service. He told us to get off the cannon, but we refused. The next thing I knew, he was chasing us down Grand River Avenue.

A few weeks later, we all lined up in the hallway to sign up for sports. Soon I noticed that the man taking down information at the front of the line was the man who wore the white suit. I was looking for somewhere, anywhere to hide, but Coach Bishop just shook his head at me. Coach Bishop to me was like General George Patton; he could be hard on you to keep you disciplined. But he might hug you, too.

At Northwestern, I started out as an outfielder/third baseman, but after two games, I was moved to catcher, where I played for the rest of my prep career.

As it turned out, the distance between Northwestern and Tiger Stadium wasn't very far, both literally and figuratively.

Word seemed to spread quickly that I could be a major league talent. Northwestern Field, located along Grand River near the junction of West Grand Boulevard near Northwestern High School, had six diamonds back then, and scouts were always around. Detroit scout Louis D'Annunzio told me years later that he had a scouting report on me that dated back to my days playing in Virginia. Apparently, he had seen me play there as an 11-year-old when he was visiting with a Detroit team.

With good grass and a spiffy infield, the Northwestern Field was the best in the city. Sandlot and high school baseball was a bigger event in those days, and the games always drew a crowd. There were no home run fences, so outfielders played deep. But they weren't allowed to leave the outfield grass. They were forbidden from positioning themselves on Grand River Avenue, and that was important because I began to hit the ball onto Grand River and beyond. According to the ground rules, anything hit on Grand River or beyond was a home run.

The other field where I began to draw some notice was Manz Field, near the corner of Conner and Mack Avenue. One day, I hit a ball that cleared the fence, crossed the street, and broke a window in an employment office on the other side of the road. After that, word spread quickly.

Northwestern had a strong athletic tradition, and I was just one of several athletes getting media attention for their exploits. Henry Carr was a three-sport star at Northwestern when I was there, and he went on to win two gold medals in the 200 meter and the 1,600-meter relay at the 1964 Olympics. He also played in the NFL for the New York Giants. We called him "The Ghost," because when he ran, he was there and then he was gone. He just disappeared right in front of you.

Future American League batting champion Alex Johnson was on my baseball team. Alex's brother is former Michigan and NFL running back Ron Johnson. The crazy thing is Ron might've been a better baseball player, and Alex might've been a better football player. Matt Snorton also played on my baseball team, and he later played football at Michigan State and signed with the Denver Broncos. And much of the Motown explosion came out of Northwestern High. Elbridge Bryant and Melvin Franklin of the Temptations, along with singer Mary Wells, were also from our school. And big John Mayberry, who played in the major leagues with Houston, Kansas City, and Toronto, went to Northwestern, too.

Plenty of Northwestern students enjoyed their moment in the spotlight back then. Mine came on June 9, 1959, when I was a 16-year-old sophomore playing in the Public School League championship game at Briggs Stadium, which later became Tiger Stadium. It was Cass Tech vs.

Northwestern, and in the first inning, I hit a home run that people still talk about more than 60 years later.

My opposite-field shot, hit off right-handed pitcher George Cojocari, landed on the stadium's right-center-field roof, struck a light tower, and fell into the stands. It's the same light tower that Reggie Jackson—a left-handed hitter—hit in the 1971 major league All-Star Game. It's been estimated that my drive traveled more than 450 feet.

Alex Johnson played with me on that Northwestern team, and he tells me what he remembers most about my home run was that my dad was standing behind the dugout, yelling, "Dammit, that's my son! That's my son!"

The *Detroit Free Press* has called my home run "one of the greatest individual baseball accomplishments in state high school history." The ball exploded off my bat, and it kind of shocked me. I had never hit a ball quite that hard before. I just stood there. In fact, the home plate umpire had to remind me to run the bases.

To be honest, not many people in the stands cheered when I hit my blast, because in the early innings the fans were mostly Cass Tech supporters. Northwestern's principal wouldn't let students out of school early to see the game, so our fans didn't show up until the middle innings.

We were actually down 6–1 to Cass Tech after two innings, but we came back with three runs in the third, six in the fifth, one in the sixth, and two in the seventh to win 13–10 for Coach Bishop's third PSL crown. I think that once our fans got to the park, we suddenly found some energy.

In the third inning, I just missed another home run when I hit a long drive to the upper deck in left field, just a few feet foul. I ended up 2-for-4 with a double, a home run, three runs scored, and three RBIs. Snorton also homered in the game and Alex Johnson was 1-for-3.

Talk about a game overflowing with talent. Carmen Fanzone hit a home run for Cass Tech and went on to play five seasons with the Boston Red Sox and Chicago Cubs.

Curiously, after our three home runs in that 1959 game, no high school player hit another homer in a championship game at Tiger Stadium until 1980. Detroit St. Andrew's first baseman Mark Gniewek hit a two-run homer into the lower deck in right field on May 28, 1980, against Detroit St. Hedwig. The next time a high school player reached the upper deck was in 1998, when Casey Rogowski of Redford Detroit Catholic Central launched one into the upper deck in right field in the Catholic League title game.

Not long after that game, there was talk of me turning pro. But Judge Keith and my father decided to wait until just before I turned 18—then it was time for me to sign a contract as a hardship case. Many teams were interested, and I couldn't have guessed where I was going to sign because I had tryouts with several teams, including the Boston Red Sox and the Cincinnati Reds. The New York Yankees' chief scout, Mr. Patterson, gave me a catcher's glove, and I assumed I would sign with them.

I met Yogi Berra with the Yankees when I visited them. I was 14. He gave me advice I never forgot.

"Don't let no fastball or nothing straight get to the catcher," Yogi said. "Why worry about all this other stuff?"

My tryout with the Reds also went well. I met Vada Pinson and Frank Robinson. They had a little bitty park named Crosley Field. I was hitting balls up onto the freeway.

But my dad came in and told me I was going to sign with the Detroit Tigers.

D'Annunzio had pushed aggressively for the Tigers to sign me. What was interesting was that he had only recently joined the Tigers. Before then, he had worked for the Orioles and had signed Milt Pappas out of the Detroit area. Had D'Annunzio still worked for the Orioles, I could have wound up in Baltimore.

In the 1960s, clubs would negotiate with your parents. I was still a minor, and no one told me precisely what kind of deal I got. But from what I was able to piece together later, I believe I received a signing bonus of $50,000–$70,000 and a car. With the bonus money, I bought a new house and furnishings for my parents, and the rest went into a 10-year pension for my parents.

On August 7, 1961, right before I signed my contract, my dad offered me some words of wisdom.

"Don't sign that contract unless you're willing to make a commitment to the people," he said firmly. "You have to promise that you'll serve the community as a player for the Detroit Tigers."

The purchase of the house was primarily for my mother. She had always liked a certain house, once owned by the Henry Ford family, at 112 Edison. At first, we didn't tell her about the Tigers buying it. Instead, we told her we were going to look at some houses. We went out for a drive, and when we turned down Edison, her eyes lit up. There was her favorite house—all wrapped up with a big bow. Mama couldn't have been happier.

The house had five or six bedrooms, and people wondered why my mom wanted such a big house. But we knew she had visions of grand-children running all over that house and yard. She wanted a big house, like she'd owned down South.

Along with the furnishings came a new modern stove. But Momma wanted no part of it. She wanted her old gas stove. Poppa and I were worried to death because once we moved all of their belongings to the new house, we left the old stove out on the street. Usually the junkman or someone from the neighborhood would swoop in and pick up something like that in a matter of hours. But when we got back to our old place, her stove was still sitting out by the road. So the new stove went into the garage, and Momma's old stove went into her new home—just the way she wanted it. When reporters asked me about the home I bought for my mom, I told them: "It's in the suburbs."

To me, that section of the city of Detroit *was* a suburb compared to where I came from.

Also, I always tell my kids that out of my original signing bonus, I probably didn't spend $200. I didn't even receive the car. Poppa sold it, saying, "You don't need a car until you're 21 years old."

Shortly after I turned pro, the Tigers were paying me to play winter ball, and my dad was still giving me about $50 every two weeks to live on. The first time I met Gates Brown and told him that he started laughing. He insisted that I tell my dad that I needed a raise.

"I can't be telling my dad I need a hundred dollars," I said. "No, no, no."

When I finally made it to the big leagues, I had to live by Poppa's rules when I was home. Back then, Ford Motor Company was supplying players with cars, and Al Kaline gave me his Galaxie XL one season. When pitcher Dick Egan was demoted to Triple-A, I got his car. After the season was over, I bought it. I was so afraid to tell Poppa about it, I parked it at my buddy James Slate's house.

But in retrospect, I wouldn't change anything about how we handled my first contract because what I really wanted most was to help my parents. The best bonus I received from the Tigers was to see the smile on my mother's face when we drove her to her new house.

The Tigers sent me to winter ball with the sole purpose of converting me from a catcher to an outfielder. To be honest, the Tigers never told me why they wanted me to make the switch. However, logic suggests that they had spent a bundle of money—reportedly over $100,000—to sign Bill Freehan out of the University of Michigan. They probably figured that by the time I was ready for the big leagues, Bill would already be the team's starting catcher.

The Tigers' winter league team played at Al Lang Field in Tampa, Florida, and I played for manager Phil Cavarretta, who had played in the major leagues, mostly with the Cubs, from 1934 to 1955. Actually, it's hard to say that I played for him, because I only got one at-bat. Primarily, Phil's son, Corky, and I were assigned to chase balls during the games. Then they'd work us out after the game. We played the role of waterboy and batboy, and did whatever chore they wanted done. But the funny thing is the lessons I learned there I carried with me for the rest of my career.

My dad told me to go down to Florida and learn to be a professional, and that's what I did. I learned to respect my coaches at winter ball. As a catcher, I had developed a quick release, so they had to retrain me to throw from the outfield. I did what I was told, paid attention to details, and I ate a lot of hot dogs during the games.

From the time I signed with the Tigers, it took me exactly 25 months to arrive in the major leagues. In my first professional season, I hit .295 at Duluth in the Northern League. In 1963, I started at Syracuse, then was sent down to Knoxville, where I began to hit with authority. But I certainly didn't think I'd be called up to the major leagues that year.

On September 10, 1963, Knoxville manager Frank Carswell told me to pack my bags and catch a flight to Washington, D.C., because the Tigers had called me up to the big leagues. But Carswell liked to horse around to keep his players loose, and I had been one of his favorite joke targets. So I was convinced that this was just another one of his pranks.

In baseball, it's commonplace to pull pranks on your teammates. And in my mind, I was too smart to fall for this one, because it just seemed impossible that I would jump from Double-A to the major leagues. In my mind, I needed to go back to Triple-A Syracuse first before I was ready for the Tigers. So even though Carswell told me to get on that plane, I went to the ballpark to get ready for the Knoxville game.

When Carswell saw me, his jaw dropped. "You're supposed to go to Washington!" he said. "What are you doing here?"

It took him a minute to convince me that this was no joke—and another short while to explain how to make reservations to board the plane headed for our nation's capital. I was a 20-year-old kid from the streets of Detroit, and I didn't know much about "catching a plane."

By the time I finally made it to Washington for my first major league game, it had started without me. I quickly changed into my uniform and hurried into the dugout. The Tigers were trailing the Senators, 4–1. I hadn't even finished shaking everyone's hands when manager Charlie Dressen said to me, "Horton, you bat for Aguirre."

It was only the top of the fourth inning, and starting pitcher Hank Aguirre was none too pleased about this turn of events. Mind you, this was long before the designated hitter rule, so pitchers still batted for themselves in the American League. Aguirre came out of his seat in the dugout and had a few words with Dressen.

"I'm out there trying to win a ball game, and you're going to pull me for some rookie in the fourth inning?" he said. "I can still win this game."

The whole scene scared me. But Dressen just ignored Aguirre's outburst, and I was on my way up to bat. Six-foot-three right-hander Jim Hannan was on the mound. Was I nervous? Excited? Is there a difference? In those situations, you can't explain how you feel. I can't remember anything except that I lined one of Hannan's pitches up the middle for a clean base hit.

I'd finally made it to the big leagues.

A few days later, on Friday, September 13, the Tigers were back home at Tiger Stadium to face the Orioles. It looked like I would get my first major league swings at the corner of Michigan and Trumbull when Dressen decided to insert me as a pinch-hitter for starting pitcher Phil Regan with the game on the line.

It was a 2–2 tie in the bottom of the ninth. We had runners on first and third, one out, and Baltimore left-hander Steve Barber was on the mound. But manager Billy Hitchcock decided to call in right-hander Stu Miller from the bullpen. Dressen countered with left-handed-hitting outfield Billy Bruton to pinch-hit for me. Bruton was walked intentionally anyway, and then center fielder George Thomas hit a sacrifice fly to win the game for us, 3–2.

The next day for some reason, I wasn't thinking that I would get to play. I was in the bullpen talking to my buddies between innings—Mack, Slate, Chapman, and Terrell were all there—when word came down in the bottom of the eighth that they needed me.

We trailed, 2–0, and future Hall of Famer Robin Roberts was pitching a one-hitter for the Orioles. He'd already fanned seven batters and seems to be cruising right along.

Catcher Gus Triandos popped out to start the eighth. Then Gates Brown pinch-hit for our second baseman, George Smith, and drew a walk. Once again, Dressen inserted me as a pinch-hitter—this time for our starting pitcher, Jim Bunning. I stepped up to the plate—my first official big-league at-bat at Tiger Stadium—and hit a Roberts fastball into the left-center-field stands to tie the game. What a thrill!

The game went to extra innings, and in the bottom of the 10th, Triandos hit a home run off Roberts to give us the victory, 3–2.

My home run off Roberts remains one of my fondest baseball memories for a number of reasons. For one, my friends were all there. And of course, my father was sitting in the bleachers. He never liked sitting in the box seats, which I could get for him if he wanted. He liked the bleachers instead. Maybe he felt more comfortable there. Poppa had been such an important part of my rise to the majors, and I was thrilled to know that he was there to see my first major league home run in person. It made it even more special that it came off a pitcher who once won 20 or more games for six consecutive seasons.

Poppa and I planned to meet after the game, and I was eager to hear what he had to say. You never expected praise from Poppa, but I figured he would show some pride in his own way. He was late arriving, and when he finally did show up, he seemed angry, rather than happy. "Let's go," he said simply, and we hurried off.

It wasn't until later that a member of the grounds crew told me that the police had put my father in the stadium holding cell because he got into a scrap with another man in the bleachers.

Apparently when I hit the home run, Poppa yelled, "That's my son! That's my son!" But the bleacher fans didn't believe him.

"If that's your son," someone supposedly said, "why are you way out here?"

And that's how my dad got into a fight on the night his son hit his first major league home run.

# Chapter 5

# Death on I-94

WHEN TIGERS MANAGER Charlie Dressen sent me to the minors early in the 1964 season, he warned me that temporary demotions can become permanent for those who want to whine instead of work.

"You're going down on a 24-hour recall basis," he said. "I've seen guys never come back after going down on a 24-hour recall basis. You have to go down to Syracuse and work hard, Willie, because when we bring you up the next time, we plan to play you every day."

Years later, when I managed the Valencia Magallanes in the Venezuelan League, I tried to incorporate much of Dressen's managerial style into my own. He had a way of making you feel wanted, while still making you realize that if you didn't have "sweat equity" in your investment, you were bound to fail. He made me believe I could be a good major league ballplayer, but he also told me it was possible I wouldn't make it unless I was willing at every aspect of the game.

Although I was only 21 that season, there had still been speculation that I might end up as the everyday left fielder in 1964. Even during my 1963 call-up, Rocky Colavito, who had been the team's left fielder for four seasons, indirectly suggested to me that he assumed I was going to succeed him. I'll never forget the kindness he showed me while he helped me prepare to be an everyday player.

"The fans might boo you at first because they're comfortable with me out there," Colavito told me. "I'm like a pair of old shoes, and everybody loves their old shoes. But if you can just get past the boos, you'll be alright."

He reminded me that fans only boo because they care about the team and about the players. Colavito went out of his way to tell me the aspects of my game that needed improvement. Rocky sure had an arm on him.

In fact, he could throw a baseball from near home plate into the out-field stands. He would talk to me about throwing and about playing the outfield. Whatever wisdom he had about the game, he shared it with me. And he taught me that helping younger players is part of being a professional. I'll never forget what Rocky Colavito taught me.

After the season, Colavito was traded to Kansas City in the deal that brought Dave Wickersham, Ed Rakow, and Jerry Lumpe to Detroit. That's why there had been speculation that I was going to play left field in 1964.

But during spring training in 1964, I got off to a bad start. In February, Gates Brown and I drove to spring training together. We decided to take our time and stop to see family and friends along the way. It seemed like a good idea until we stepped on the scales for the annual weigh-in. With all the good food we had in Virginia and Kentucky, I was 26 pounds overweight.

Dressen was perturbed and told me I had two weeks to lose the weight or he was going to fine me $100 per pound.

By running, drinking nothing but water, and eating nothing but bananas, I lost it all in 10 days. The newspaper ran a photo of Dressen presenting me with a 26-pound ham as a prize for my weight loss.

But that rapid weight loss had a negative effect. I was severely weak-ened from shedding those pounds so fast. It felt as if I couldn't even swing the bat properly. It affected my hitting to the point that I didn't feel right for most of the spring.

To make matters worse, Gates Brown was sharpening his spikes with a scalpel one day, and I inadvertently walked into the blade and severely cut my arm.

That injury also bothered me for weeks, and I really didn't feel com-pletely healed until just before I was demoted. In fact, I remember hitting the ball well the night before I was sent to the minors early in the 1964 season, so I was surprised when Dressen sent me to Syracuse.

"You remind me of a young Roy Campanella," he told me. "But you have to play every day, Willie, and you can't do that up here."

Dressen had known former All-Star catcher Campanella from their days together with the Brooklyn Dodgers. And even though I no longer played the position, I think Dressen thought I had the toughness of a catcher.

At the time, I was hitting only .167, with four extra-base hits and eight RBIs. But the timing of the demotion bothered me the most. I had just started to feel good hitting the ball. My injury was finally healed, and I was just starting to feel strong again. I wondered why they didn't just give me a few more weeks to see if I was ready to be a regular.

In light of the Colavito trade and of Dressen's faith in me, I was surprised that I only got 72 at-bats to prove myself early in the 1964 season.

What I found out later is that my father had something to do with my demotion. He didn't like me sitting on the bench, and he had gone to Mr. Jim Campbell and expressed the opinion that I'd be better off playing regularly in the minors. Mr. Campbell had become a family friend, and he respected my father's opinion. And he had also been thinking along those same lines.

Dressen's word was the law then, so I went down to Syracuse with the idea that I would be the Tigers' starting left fielder by 1965. I hit .288 at Syracuse, with 28 home runs and 99 RBIs in 1964. It seemed as if I was in a good position to win the job.

After the 1964 season, the Tigers asked several of us to play winter ball for Mayagüez in the Puerto Rican League, and we did what we were told. My game was truly coming together, and by the holidays I already had 10 home runs to lead the league. I smacked a couple long home runs in Ponce that had everyone talking. One was estimated at more than 480 feet.

Jim Northrup was also there, and was leading the league with a .350 batting average. Based on what I saw from Jimmy in Puerto Rico, I thought he'd be a major league star. He was a five-sport star at Alma College, playing everything from football to golf. A gifted quarterback, Jim had offers from the New York Titans of the AFL and the Chicago Bears of the NFL, as well as from the Tigers. He accepted the Tigers' offer because their money was guaranteed, and he had to make the team in football. Jim was banging the ball that winter, and given how I was hitting and the confidence I had, it seemed as if I was about to enter a wonderful period in my life.

I could not have been more wrong.

Over the holidays, I tried to call my parents, but across-the-ocean tele-phone communications in those days were spotty, even in ideal weather conditions. It took me about 10 days, but I finally reached them. I dis-tinctly remember that my mother kept asking me to come home because she missed me. Obviously she knew I couldn't do that. But she seemed sad about the distance between us.

Over the New Year's break, I drove to see my friend Alex Johnson, who was also playing in Puerto Rico. On New Year's morning, 1965, I was awakened by a group of players that included Alex, Roberto Clemente, and José Pagan. They soberly informed me that my parents had been in an automobile accident on I–94, just east of Battle Creek, Michigan. My father was dead and my mother and brother Billy were in critical condition. My two nephews, Mike and Joe, were also injured, but not severely.

My parents were in my brother's car, en route to see my sister Frankie and her husband, Ken. In blizzard conditions, the car, which was being driven by one of my brother's friends, ran into the back of a salt truck.

It took me half a day to travel from San Juan to Detroit, and Gates Brown met me at the airport. The plan was to go directly to Albion Hospital to see my mother and brother but the roads were nearly impas-sible. Albion was a two-hour drive in good weather but the conditions were so bad we could only make it as far as the house on Edison Street.

Just as soon as I walked in the door, the phone rang. It was a doctor from the hospital. I identified myself as one of the Horton sons, and almost 60 years later, I still remember what he said to me: "I have some more bad news for you. Your mom just passed."

Poppa had been sitting in the front seat, in the center, and he died instantly. Billy suffered head injuries, and he was in a coma for a lengthy period; we didn't know whether he would live or die. We delayed my parents' funeral for a week as we prayed for Billy's recovery. Doctors didn't think he was going to make it.

My mom had been in the backseat with my nephews Joe and Michael. Joe was my brother Joe's child and Michael was my sister Faye's son. They were like brothers to me, and I honestly think that my parents thought of them as their kids. They were small, and I was told that my mom wrapped herself around the kids to cushion them from the impact. She took the full force. The driver escaped with just a scratch.

It was certainly the worst time of my life. I was 22 and I was still as close to my parents as I was when I was a child. It was still important to me to please my father. His presence always helped me stay on the right path, to do what was right. I wondered how my life would change without my parents.

In the midst of our grief, Tigers president and general manager Jim Campbell paid me a visit. After offering his condolences, he shook my hand and handed me a check to pay for the funerals and the hospital bills. The check was for $20,000. Remember this was 1965, and $20,000 was a tremendous amount of money. I tried to pay him back in the months that followed, but he would never accept my money.

It started to become clear to me that the Tigers had become like a second family to me, and Mr. Campbell was like my surrogate father. Gates Brown used to say about Campbell, "When it came to business, Mr. Campbell ruled with an iron fist. But when it came to his friends, Mr. Campbell had a heart of gold."

Through the years, I would disagree with Mr. Campbell on occasion, but we always remained close. My relationship with him was probably as complicated as my relationship with my father. In some ways, they had the same attitude. On one hand, I think Mr. Campbell was proud of what I had done for the Tigers. On the other hand, I think he believed he had to push me to be the best. Mr. Campbell knew the role Poppa played in my life, and I think he felt he needed to fill that void after Poppa was killed.

Throughout my career, I spent many hours talking baseball with Mr. Campbell, and I had the utmost respect for him. But as close as he felt to me, he always put his role as general manager first. Just like a father and son, we had our disagreements, particularly about money.

Almost as soon as I became the regular left fielder, I developed a kinship with the fans in the stands out there. I didn't know all their names, but I knew them. Some had known me since I was 12 or 13 years old.

It became my habit to take a few balls out of the bag before every game and throw them into the stands. One day, Mr. Campbell saw me do that and said he was going to charge me five dollars for every ball I threw up there. The next day, I took the entire bag of balls out in the outfield, and threw every one of them into the stands.

"Charge me whatever you want," I told Mr. Campbell. My next paycheck was short due to a miscellaneous deduction for those baseballs. It was worth it to me, though, because the relationship I developed with the fans in left field was as important to me as my relationship with my friends. Eventually, I started buying tickets and bringing kids to sit in left field. It wasn't hard to fulfill my promise to my dad because I truly enjoyed the fans.

When it came to contracts, Mr. Campbell always wrestled with players over every last dollar. There were some basic rules: Nobody was going to make more money than Al Kaline. If you didn't play as well as you did in the previous season, you were going to get a cut in pay. Not even Kaline was safe from the threat of a salary reduction. In 1955, at age 20, Kaline won the American League batting title with a .340 batting average. Over the next four seasons, he averaged an impressive .312. But in 1960, his average slipped to .278. In the following off-season, the *Detroit Free Press* ran a story about how Kaline's salary would be cut by a couple thousand dollars.

Judge Keith had one of the attorneys in his office, Nate Conyers, serve as my agent, and after we won the 1968 World Series, Conyers asked Mr. Campbell to raise my salary from $28,000 to $60,000.

Mr. Campbell didn't like that too much. "Willie isn't going to own the damn team!" he said.

Officially, I became a spring training holdout, and I was probably the most antsy holdout in the history of baseball. I didn't help my negotiating leverage because everyone knew I was anxious to get back in uniform. When my Tigers teammates were on the diamond, I didn't want to be in street clothes. Before long, I called my agent. "I'm going on the field, Nate, so you have to get this done."

Needless to say, although I received a healthy raise to more than $50,000, Mr. Campbell didn't give me exactly what I wanted.

Mr. Campbell did fight you for every nickel at contract time, but when he came back from his winter vacation, he would always have a box of candy from the Grand Canyon for his players.

Sometimes, Mr. Campbell would shock you. For instance, in 1975, I made $94,000, and after the season I was hoping that Mr. Campbell wouldn't knock my salary below $90,000 for 1976. I'd hit 25 home runs, but my strikeouts were up and I was nearly 33 years old. I knew that Mr. Campbell could often find reasons to drop you a few thousand dollars.

But when I got my contract in the mail it was for $125,000! Honestly, I thought that Mr. Campbell's secretary, Alice, may have typed in the numbers incorrectly. I went down to Mr. Campbell's office to get it corrected.

"Alice," I said, "there has to be a mistake with those figures."

"No, Willie," she said, "that's the correct amount."

When I asked Mr. Campbell about it, he explained that when Tigers acquired Rusty Staub from the Mets, he brought along a contract for $150,000; Mr. Campbell didn't think it was right that Staub, who'd batted .282 with 105 RBIs in 1975, should be making that much more than I was. Although we viewed Campbell as a skinflint, he did have a code of fairness that he followed—one that probably only he understood. That raise was the biggest of my Tigers career.

Many times, I would go up to Mr. Campbell's office and talk for a couple of hours, and sometimes we didn't discuss baseball at all. We were like family members talking—maybe even friends.

But Mr. Campbell was tough on me, just like my father was. In 1973, I was hitting over .340 in mid-June, and Mr. Campbell summoned me to his office for a chat. As I walked toward the meeting, I truly thought that Mr. Campbell might reward me with a new contract and nice raise.

But instead of praising me, he chewed me out.

"What are you doing, slapping those dinky singles out there?" he said. "You're doing what every team wants you to do."

"What are you talking about?" I asked. "Are you looking at my average?"

He then asked whether or not I was sick, or feeling ill, because he said my strength was no longer evident. It was true that my home run numbers were down at the time. He then began to tell me that my game was about home runs and run production. That's what the Tigers wanted from me, and he didn't need me—or want me—to be out there trying to prove I was a .300 hitter.

"What I want you to do for this team is hit .270 with lots of home runs," Campbell said.

I'll never forget that conversation, because it made me realize that your role on a successful team is determined by how you can best serve the team—not by what you want it to be. Statistics matter only if they are the right statistics. No matter how well you think you're performing, if you aren't fulfilling your role on the team, you're letting the team down.

Conversations about baseball with Mr. Campbell always included some of his philosophy that he wanted you to think about. You could talk to him for only 15 minutes, and then spend the next couple of days chewing on the message he wanted to give you.

We didn't always agree. Much like my dad, Mr. Campbell wouldn't hesitate to tell me if he thought I was making a mistake. He and Judge Keith were both against my idea to open Club 23—my sports bar on Livernois.

They just didn't want my name associated with a bar. They thought it could be trouble, even though I explained that my concept was more of a restaurant/bar. In some respects, I was ahead of my time, because I put together the kind of sports-themed bar that's commonplace today, with the memorabilia on the walls and games playing nonstop on the television. I think we had one of the first big-screen televisions in the city, maybe even the state.

But even though Mr. Campbell was against my decision, he would still bring his secretary, Alice, down to the club for lunch. He always supported me, even if we disagreed. To me, Mr. Campbell was family.

He and I also had different opinions on other matters, too. For instance—the Hall of Fame Veterans Committee. I wouldn't allow my name to be submitted to the committee because I don't believe I belong in the Hall of Fame. To me, the Hall of Fame is for players like Willie

Mays, Hank Aaron, Frank Robinson, Al Kaline, and others. You say their names and you think "Hall of Fame." I put those players on a pedestal.

Mr. Campbell would argue vehemently, comparing me to other players. "Richie Ashburn is in, and he was a good player," Campbell said. "But I would take you over him."

I would laugh, and he would continue to disagree, only conceding that it was fine if someone wanted to submit my name to the Veterans Committee after I'm gone. We debated that point 10 days before he died in October of 1995. He was 71. What I've always told people about Mr. Campbell is that he was as devoted to his team as anyone I've ever met. Near the end of his life, he was a bit hurt that the Tigers organization had discarded him in 1992.

He was a smart baseball man who cared about his team and his players, even though many of his players were often ticked off at him over salary issues.

A few weeks after he died in Lakeland, Florida, I got a call from an attorney who wanted to talk to me about some financial matters. Much to my surprise, he told me that Mr. Campbell had named me as one of his beneficiaries in his will. He left me enough money that I was able to set up a college fund for the 11 grandchildren I had at the time.

Through the years, I've always believed that my relationship with Mr. Campbell was special. He wasn't the kind of man who laid out his feelings, but his will proved to me that he valued my friendship. And that meant more to me than the money he left in my name.

# Chapter 6

# Professor Gator

THE BEST HITTING ADVICE I ever received sounded like gibberish the first time I heard it.

Early in my Tigers career, I would often walk back to the dugout, cursing at myself for striking out. Gates Brown would say something to me like, "Hey big man, it's the bottom of the ninth, you're two runs down, with two runners on base against the Yankees. Who are the Yankees going to bring in from the 'pen to pitch to you?"

Honestly, I thought my good friend "the Gator" was losing his mind. "What are you talking about?" I'd say, waving him off.

He never stopped jabbering at me. When I wasn't playing, the Gator would often quiz me as we sat on the bench. He'd give me various scenarios to consider—just to see how I would answer.

"Let's say [Baltimore's Dave] McNally's on the mound," Gator would say to me. "How would he pitch any differently than this guy?"

Or we'd be one game into a three-game series against the Yankees, and Gator would want me to name all the pitchers we'd be facing in our next series against Cleveland.

He drove me crazy for weeks with his badgering. But one day, it all started to make sense to me. Gator was trying to teach me that hitting isn't just about mechanics. It's basically a mental exercise, about knowing the opposing pitchers and about studying their tendencies.

Gates understood the science of hitting better than anyone I'd ever met. And he changed my approach to hitting. Basically he forced me to think about hitting long before I stepped into the batter's box. He inspired me to develop my own hitting philosophy. I started to utilize some of the advice that Tigers coach Wayne Blackburn had also given me about hitting, most of which fit nicely with what Gator was preaching. It all began to come together for me.

When Mayo Smith was Detroit's manager from 1967 to 1970, Wally Moses was our batting coach, and he always had some funny expressions about his craft. "I can help you," he'd say, "but you have to walk to the plate yourself."

Moses would continually tell his players that if they didn't master the mental aspects of hitting, it was "a long walk from the on-deck circle to the plate."

"I'm tired of everyone always blaming the hitting coach," he told me one day. "I'm not swinging the damn bat."

Although we would laugh at Moses' approach, I understood that his message was similar to the Gator's: If you want to have a successful at-bat, your mind has to be right.

I also learned to hit by watching how the league's most skilled pitchers approached their work. Baltimore Orioles southpaw Mike Cuellar was a nightmare for me, but he made me a better hitter because he forced me to figure out why he was so successful against me.

Cuellar threw a screwball that seemed to dance away from right-handers' bats. And he changed speeds masterfully. Sometimes it seemed as if he was just lobbing the ball up there, but you still couldn't make contact.

In one game, I remember striking out two or three times against Cuellar. When I came back to the dugout, I announced loudly, "He's not going to strike me out again."

Gates Brown responded quickly. "Good, big man. That's the right attitude. You'll get him next time."

"No, you don't get it," I told the Gator. "The next time, I'm going to catch one of his pitches."

Everyone laughed, but I was serious.

In my next at-bat, Cuellar threw me a change-up, and I just reached up and caught the ball. Umpire Nestor Chylak was so surprised, he didn't initially seem to know what to do with me. When he finally signaled for me to trot down to first base, Baltimore manager Earl Weaver went berserk. I'm not sure that Weaver could cite a specific rule that I'd violated, but he was fairly confident that I wasn't allowed to catch a pitch that wasn't going to otherwise hit me. It might've been a strike if I hadn't caught it. He protested the game but it really didn't matter because we ended up losing anyway.

If I had a chance to replay that moment, I wouldn't change a thing. I'd catch that pitch all over again. Once I'd done that, I felt as if I'd pushed Cuellar out of my head. I'd found a way to get on base against him, and I'd accomplished my mission. One of my philosophies as a hitter was not to let any pitcher ruin my tomorrow.

Through the years, I learned that doing your job wasn't just about getting base hits. When you had a runner on first base and less than two outs, you had to be more mindful of staying out of the double play. You had to hit behind the runner. You had to work the count and take a walk if that's what the pitcher gave you.

My dad had always taught me to respect every pitcher whether he won 20 games or lost 20. Gates helped teach me to respect the player on deck. Think about setting the table better for him. He might be swinging the bat better than you are. My hitting plan became all about winning. And as I gained more experience, the scoreboard dictated my batting stance and how I'd approach each pitcher.

I faced Hall of Fame right-hander Ferguson Jenkins many, many times in my career, and I don't think he ever threw me a strike. His best pitch was a sinker, which looked like a strike—until it suddenly seemed like it fell through a trap door. You'd swing at it, but it'd be in the dirt every time. If you really wanted to hit Jenkins' best pitch you needed a shovel—not a bat. After a few at-bats against him, I learned to move up in the batter's box and meet his pitches before they fell through the trap door. My objective against Jenkins was just not to get cheated out of my at-bat. Unless I had two strikes on me, I wasn't about to swing at his best pitches.

It always amuses me when a player says he hit a pitcher's best fastball. "No, you didn't," I wanted to say. "You hit a fastball, but it wasn't his best. The pitcher clearly didn't locate that pitch where he wanted it, or you wouldn't have hit it."

Part of learning to be a good hitter is understanding that every pitcher has a knockout pitch, just like every boxer has a knockout punch. At some point the knockout pitch is coming, and you'd better understand that.

For instance, to best Yankees reliever Sparky Lyle, you had to hit his slider. You had to figure out a way to make it look like a fastball. Either you had to move your body in the batter's box or you had to foul off his best sliders. I always felt that a pitcher would almost rather walk you than have to throw you his third best pitch.

That's why it was always tough to face Luis Tiant, Catfish Hunter, or Dave McNally in my era—because they could really paint the corners. Those guys could feed a fastball through a mail slot if you asked them too—and it would move, too.

One of the toughest pitchers I ever faced was Hoyt Wilhelm. He was the only knuckleballer I ever faced who seemed like he could put the knuckler wherever he wanted to. Wilbur Wood had a decent knuckleball, but he would throw you a fastball every now and then. Not Wilhelm. He threw a knuckle curve, a rising knuckler, and a sinking knuckler. By the time you decided you would swing, his pitch would fall right off the table. He would move that ball all around, depending on the count. With every other pitcher in the league I had a plan when I stepped into the batter's box. With Wilhelm, I was always just guessing.

Throughout my career, I never minded facing the hardest throwers, because they seemed to make more mistakes. Most of the overpowering pitchers were accustomed to getting by on their fastballs, and they made mistakes on their breaking pitches. Eventually they would hang a breaking pitch. Wayne Blackburn taught me how to push pitchers deep into the count until they made a mistake. Guys like Tiant, Hunter, McNally, and others had better breaking pitches than they had fastballs. I learned to foul off good breaking pitches and wait on a mistake. Thanks to the Gator, I began to study pitchers and learn how they pitched. Did they pitch outside or inside? I understood how they moved the ball around in different zones, and I adjusted to the way they threw. I always looked for pitches in specific highways near the plate.

I wouldn't teach my batting stance to anyone, though, because it was pretty unorthodox. I held my hands high and I had a wiggle in my bat. The funny thing is that I didn't use that stance when I took batting practice. My regular stance didn't seem natural to me in batting practice, when there was no pressure. But when I was facing live pitching, I would allow the pitcher to set me up to hit. The stance I used evolved from watching the pitcher and allowing my eyes and my head to tell my hands and my feet where I needed to be. The idea was to relax until the instant the pitcher began his sequence.

Essentially as he went into his motion, or into his set position, I would get in sync with him. I might move closer to the plate, or up in the batter's box as the pitcher started his process. I would be set in my hitting stance at the moment he delivered. If the pitcher spotted me moving up in the box, it was too late for him to adjust. It worked for me. You have to understand the plate, and you have to make that batter's box seem as comfortable as your living room. Another good way to approach hitting is to just think of it as playing catch with the pitcher. He's throwing the ball to you, and you have to send it back to him.

At Tiger Town in Lakeland, players now use the "Willie Horton Training Station." When I came to the Tigers, Blackburn helped me improve my swing by swinging at a rubber tire. When I was a minor league hitting instructor, I took that concept, and developed a method of training hitters using different tire setups. I taught players such as Jose Canseco, Terry Steinbach, and Mickey Tettleton, using this method. Every hitter is different, so every tire setup has to be different. Using a tire allows you to develop a good foundation.

Being comfortable with your equipment is also important to the process. Early in my career, I'd check my swing and the bat would snap in two pieces. My teammates seemed shocked and people began talking about my strength. Shortly thereafter, Tigers manager Charlie Dressen convinced me to start using a heavier bat.

Before that, I was using bats that weighed 32 to 34 ounces, and were 34-and-a-half inches long. On Dressen's advice, I started using bats that weighed 38 to 40 ounces, and were 35-and-a-half inches long. I saw the difference in my hitting immediately. I started using more of the field, and I wasn't pulling every pitch.

During my career, I didn't see too many players using bats as heavy as mine. I always noticed that players who came over from the National League seemed to favor heavier bats because the N.L. was a fastball league. Orlando McFarlane isn't considered a power hitter, but when he came to the Tigers from the Pittsburgh Pirates in 1966, I noticed that he swung a heavy bat. Tony Taylor also came from the N.L. and he used a heavy bat, too. In the American League, only Frank Howard seemed to use a bat like mine.

Bat manufacturers customize bats for each major leaguer, but when I first came into the league, I used the K75 Rocky Colavito model because I liked the barrel of that bat. But when I finally got the opportunity to customize my own bats, I combined three different styles. I took my handle from the Al Kaline S2, the barrel from the K75, and the meat of the bat from Gates Brown's M110 model. It was probably no coincidence that I chose the bat styles of three players who I admired immensely.

To be comfortable at the plate, everything had to be perfect for me, including my helmet. That's why the two helmets I got from the Tigers early in my career were *the same two helmets* I was using when I retired after the 1980 season. Everywhere I went, I just repainted them to match the colors of my new team. When I was beaned in 1971, I was urged to switch to a helmet with an ear flap. But I simply couldn't get comfortable at the plate in a helmet like that. Believe it or not, there were plenty of players who weren't picky about their helmets. In fact, Norm Cash couldn't even get comfortable wearing one. He stuck with the protective liner that went inside his cap.

To me, one other piece of clothing was important on the field. To this day, when I see people selling Willie Horton "game-used jerseys," I can tell you if it's really mine by looking at the bottom. I had a 54-inch chest, but I'm only 5'11", so my shirts came long. I would cut all my shirts the same way because I didn't like that extra material hanging down.

As a rule, ballplayers don't like new equipment. On the Tigers, Mickey Stanley was the best at relacing a glove, so we went to him to fix our old gloves rather than get a new one.

People marveled at my strength in the 1960s, but I never did a lick of weight training. My strength developed naturally, although my training as a boxer with the medicine ball and the heavy bag probably helped.

I boxed out of the local recreation center, and I usually fought older competitors. When I was 17, I won a Golden Gloves championship. It was held in Windsor, Ontario, Canada, across the river from Detroit, and it was televised.

Unfortunately, my dad saw me on TV and he told me I was to never box again.

In those days, you were expected to work in the off-season. When I came home from winter ball in 1961, my dad got me a construction job laying bricks and building walls. A summer of that kind of work will probably help you more than weightlifting. It seemed to me that you wanted to stay away from weightlifting because you didn't want to become muscle-bound to the extent that it would slow down your bat speed. Flexibility was always my objective. And for a great, inexpensive training session, I'd slice a tire inner tube and just stretch it between my arms.

It's hard to say exactly when I started to understand how to be a major league hitter. But there was a hot stretch near the start of the 1965 season where I began to realize the vulnerability of most pitchers. That May, I batted .389 with 17 extra-base hits and 25 RBIs in 26 games. In one three-game series at Washington from May 11 to 13, I went 8-for-13 with 10 RBIs. At one point, I reached base 10 consecutive times. And I set a new record of five RBIs in one game at D.C. Stadium.

"It took them two years and $22 million to build D.C. Stadium," wrote the late *Detroit Free Press* sportswriter Joe Falls. "Willie Horton all but demolished it in three days."

Falls kept track of my first seven home runs that 1965 season, and according to one of his stories they traveled 440, 420, 400, 390, 420, 400, and 425 feet.

Right after the trip to Washington, we went to Boston, where I had another two–home run game. One of my home runs cleared Fenway Park's Green Monster in left field, along with the screen, and landed in downtown Boston.

"If I had his power," Gates Brown told Falls, "I'd be hitting 50 home runs and making 70 grand."

At that time, Bob Swift was the Tigers' acting manager because Charlie Dressen was recovering from a heart attack. "[Willie] is my left fielder now, no matter who pitches," Swift told Falls. "I hope he stays out there until 1985."

Today, baseball managers rely heavily on statistics to make in-game decisions. I always told former Tigers hitting coach Bruce Fields—a man I admire greatly—that there's both good and bad that comes with that. When you look at a player's statistics against a certain pitcher, you don't know whether all of his hits came at a time when he was in the best streak of his career, or whether they came when the pitcher was in the worst slump of his career. Maybe the hitter had 10 bad days all season, and three of them came against one particular pitcher.

All I know is that when I was hitting well, I didn't much care *who* was on the mound. I just wanted to know how he'd been throwing the ball lately—how's his control? The history is important, but it shouldn't be an overriding factor.

As a hitter, I always respected my scouting reports. They were more useful to me than raw numbers alone. You see, all good pitchers pitch different ways to different hitters. They're either going to pitch you inside or outside—whatever's successful for them. I kept a book on every pitcher I faced. They're not going to change what they do. They're just going to keep pitching you in the same area, so it's up to you to make the right adjustments. You have to learn to foul off good pitches, while still staying aggressive and looking for your pitch.

When I first came to the majors, I played full time. And I'm thankful for that because I'm not sure I would have had such a long career if I was platooned. If I would've been used strictly against left-handers, I might've washed out. Even though conventional wisdom says I should've been able to hit lefties better because I batted right-handed, it simply wasn't true in my case. Initially, I couldn't get comfortable with them. The motion and the look of a southpaw would often confuse me at the plate.

Some left-handed pitchers would add to my confusion by wearing their baseball cap tilted to one side or their uniform bunched to one side. It always seemed to me that their motion purposely included some little tick, stutter, or pause designed to break a hitter's concentration at the plate. To me, they always looked like they were going to throw to first base.

One reason that young hitters struggle against left-handed pitchers is that they're more of a mystery to them. You just don't see too many premium left-handers in the minor leagues. And organizations tend to rush left-handed prospects to the majors quicker because they're often in short supply.

I had brief stints in the majors in 1963 and 1964, and I finally started playing full time in 1965. But I really didn't hit left-handers as well as I should have until 1968. In 1966, for example, I batted .246 against lefties and .271 against right-handers. In 1967, I batted just .236 against lefties and .300 against right-handers. But in 1968, I hit .301 against left-handers. After that, I consistently hit for a higher average against left-handers than against right-handers. I just needed experience to find my comfort level.

My dad always insisted that the route to success involved "keeping your eyes and ears open—and your mouth shut." Early in my career, I embraced that wisdom. I would talk to Rocky Colavito, Al Kaline, and Gates Brown.

One thing I learned specifically from Kaline was how to compose myself after a knockdown pitch. When Al got knocked down, he'd pick himself up, flick the dirt off his uniform, and get himself as if he was just striding up from the on-deck circle. Usually, the next pitch was an off-speed pitch, and Al would hit it right up the middle. His approach began to be my approach.

But clearly, Gates had a big influence on my career because he helped keep my mind on my hitting. He made me think about the game in ways that no one else had. If a coach had tried to teach me that, maybe it wouldn't have sunk in. But Gator was one of my closest friends on the team. We even roomed together early in my career. And one time, I brought him to my old neighborhood and introduced him to my neighbor in the projects, Norma Jean Sterling. They ended up getting married.

In my mind, when the Gator instructed me about hitting, it was like getting singing lessons from Aretha Franklin or acting lessons from Sidney

Poitier. Gates might have been the purest hitter on the Tigers in those days. Kaline and I used to talk about that all the time.

What impressed me is that Gates adjusted to whatever role he was given. He batted close to .300 in his four minor league seasons, and in 1964, he played regularly for the only time in his career. He hit .272 with 15 homers and 11 steals. Gates was a stocky man, but he could run.

During spring training in 1965, some members of the media wrote that I was going to take Gates Brown's job because he had played left field the year before. That bothered me immensely because as a player, you aren't trying to take anyone's job—you're just trying to get in the lineup. It's not accurate to suggest that anyone takes anyone's job in spring training because it's always an open tryout. If it were up to me, Gates and I both would've played. I believed he was good enough to play regularly. In fact, at one point, Charlie Dressen considered moving Kaline to center field and using Gates in left and me in right.

We lost Gator to a heart attack in 2013. I still miss him. When I see players pulling sheets of paper out of their pocket to know where to play certain hitters, I think the Gator would have been upset to witness that. Same thing with pitchers looking at papers in their hat on how to approach batters.

Gator taught me to study the game and know every pitcher in the league. We would have been embarrassed to have to look at a piece of paper to know what to do. Back when we played, the manager expected you to know what to do in all situations. We took pride in our preparation. Gator always told me, "Know your job."

At Gator's funeral, I found out that Gator played football in Crestline, Ohio, with former football coach Jack Harbaugh, father of Jim and John.

Jack Harbaugh said one of former running back Gator's favorite stories centered on a game where Jack had called 16 consecutive Gator running plays to move the ball down the field.

"He took the ball all the way down to the 1-yard line," Jack remembered. "I said, 'Gator you look tired, I think I'll take it in. Quarterback sneak on one.' Gates never allowed that to affect our friendship. We got a great laugh out of it."

Sometimes general manager Jim Campbell would say that he didn't have any trade offers for Gates, but others in the organization would tell Gates that he had five or six offers. Presumably, Campbell wanted to keep Gates because he understood how vital he was to our team, whether he was playing 50 games or 100 games.

Gates was also a great clubhouse guy, making jokes but also always offering words of encouragement. It was no surprise that he became the Tigers' hitting coach after he retired as a player. I wasn't the only one who Gates helped on our team. It was like he had a master's degree in hitting science.

The funny thing is that Gates Brown hated batting practice. In spring training, I always wanted to be in his group because I knew he'd give me his swings in the batting cage.

While we were hitting, Gates would go to the water fountain and spray water all over the front of his shirt so the coaches would think he'd worked up a healthy sweat. When the rest of us were finished hitting, Gates would go to trainer Bill Behm for his rubdown. "Boy, I'm tired," Gates would tell Behm. "I've had a rough day."

# Chapter 7

# Extra Cash, Nightly Poker, Light on the Mayo

MICKEY LOLICH RODE a motorcycle. Denny McLain had a lounge act. Pat Dobson and John Hiller were real pranksters. Norm Cash was the center of attention at every party. Gates Brown was a nightly card player—and he wasn't playing solitaire.

When Mayo Smith gave up his job as a New York Yankees scout to become manager of the Detroit Tigers on October 3, 1966, he must've felt as if he was taking over a fraternity house as well as a baseball team.

Between the lines in that era, no major league team was more devoted to winning than the Tigers were. And outside the lines, no major league team was more devoted to howling at the moon. In 1968, we came from behind after the seventh inning to win 40 different games. We also pushed a plane into the pool at an Anaheim hotel because it seemed like a fun idea at the time. We once produced 97 extra-base hits, including 42 home runs, in a single month. We also were involved in four bench-clearing brawls in a single season. We had rifle arms in our outfield and we had a *real* gun in our clubhouse because McLain had a permit to carry a concealed weapon.

We were a crazy unit of competitiveness and juvenile behavior. On one hand we couldn't wait to start the late night, postgame poker game. On the other hand, we were known to stay in the clubhouse 90 minutes after a game to analyze why we had lost. On more than one occasion a Detroit ballplayer would spend the night at the stadium because he was so angered by his personal performance.

One night in Boston, right fielder Jim Northrup, miffed by a bad day at the plate, called Tigers general manager Jim Campbell at one o'clock in the morning to see if Campbell could get the lights turned on at Fenway Park for some extra batting practice.

Northrup's attitude that night reflected a team-wide commitment toward winning a pennant. It was a team that wanted success very badly. Most of us had grown up together in the Tigers' farm system, and we were like a family. We were a tight-knit, loyal group of guys. When you found one Tigers player in those days, you probably found most of us.

In 1966, we lost our lovable 71-year-old manager, Charlie Dressen—and soon after we lost his replacement, Bob Swift. Dressen suffered his second heart attack on May 16 and died August 10. I wept the night he died. Charlie was my first big-league manager, but he was more like a grandfather to me. He liked to tell me stories about other successful players, particularly Black players, with the hope that I'd be inspired to realize my potential. As a manager, he could be tough, but kind at the same time.

Swift was one of our assistant coaches, and he took over as manager after Charlie's heart attack. But on July 14, *he* was hospitalized with cancer. Bob died right after the season. He was only 51. Our third-base coach, Frank Skaff, became manager midway through 1966, but how can you succeed under those circumstances? The emotion of that season was simply overwhelming. We were 13 games over .500 with Dressen and Swift in charge through the first 83 games, but only one game over .500 the rest of the way. As soon as Swift was hospitalized in July, we lost 12 of the next 15 games. But despite the difficulty of the season, we still managed to win 88 games and finished just 10 games behind the A.L. pennant-winning Baltimore Orioles.

Mayo Smith's personality was probably the right fit for the Tigers going into the 1967 season. Some guys like to manage like they're play-ing a board game, moving guys all around as if they're trying to prove they're worth their pay. Mayo wasn't like that. Although he had managed in the 1950s with the Cincinnati Reds and Philadelphia Phillies, he really wasn't as well-known in the baseball world. He'd been a minor league outfielder for almost two decades and spent half a season with the 1945 Philadelphia Athletics. Mayo was a player's manager. He found a lineup he liked and he stuck with it. He liked veterans. If you were a veteran, he figured you knew what you were doing and he left you alone. Mayo was 52 when he became Detroit's manager, but he always seemed like he was 70 years old.

He didn't like confrontations. Actually, I'm not sure he even liked talking to his players very much. If you asked Mayo a question, he would ask you to elaborate a little bit more. When you were done explaining, Mayo would say, "You answered your own question," and then move along.

Mayo essentially inherited players who were accustomed to policing themselves. The players ran the clubhouse at Tiger Stadium, and we held each other accountable. The manager and coaches laid down some guidelines, and we enforced them. We were comfortable with each other. When a player wasn't performing the way he should, one of us would say something to him. We respected seniority, and we all understood that younger players were supposed to follow the lead of the older players. There was a clear chain of command in the locker room and on the field.

Our catcher, Bill Freehan, was the quarterback. Billy would talk to everyone and we followed him. If Bill told us to move around in the outfield, we moved.

We were all about respect and teamwork. That's what made us so successful. We knew the outfielders needed to listen to the second baseman or shortstop when the throws came in from the outfield. And it didn't matter whether Al Kaline was a better hitter or that I hit more home runs, we knew that center fielder Mickey Stanley was the boss in the outfield. On a base hit up the gap, Stanley would always call us off or let us know if he couldn't get to it.

There wasn't one guy on our roster who wouldn't accept help from his teammates. Some guys were more stubborn than others, but when we walked out the clubhouse door, we were a unified team. That's how you win.

We felt comfortable getting on each other because we were so close. Northrup could kick my butt if he didn't think I was working hard enough, and I would get on him if I didn't like his attitude in a game. Northrup, Stanley, and Freehan had all played together, dating back to their first pro season with Duluth in 1961. I had played with Denny

McLain, Northrup, and Stanley in Knoxville in 1963. I played with Don Wert and Ray Oyler in Syracuse. Norm Cash, Dick McAuliffe, and Al Kaline had played together on the Tigers since 1961. Gates Brown and I had both made our major league debuts in 1963. Bill Behm had been our trainer in the minors and then was promoted to the Tigers with us. Even our team physician, Dr. Clarence Livingood, was also the family physician for most of us. That's the kind of bond that team had.

But sometimes when you entered our clubhouse, it was like a trip to Neverland. The Tigers were a team of colorful characters, and that may have been one of the keys to our success. We were always having fun. You could never be sure what sort of shenanigans would take place behind those doors. Mickey Stanley and I were the best of friends, and when we were in the same room, we were like a couple of puppies—we were always wrestling. Jim Price would come after me all the time looking for a playful wrestling match.

Cash was one of the most fascinating characters. He was also the most superstitious player on our team. If he was in the middle of a batting streak, he wouldn't wash his uniform. He wouldn't even want anyone to touch it. He'd go so far as to call the clubhouse attendants on the road and tell them how to deal with his uniform. It had to go directly from the bag to a hanger. When Cash was going well, his uniform was dirty enough to stand on its own.

The other crazy thing about Cash is that I don't know that I ever saw him use his own bat. That's crazy when you consider he won a batting title with a .361 average in 1961.

He would wander around the clubhouse, pulling bats out of his teammates' lockers. "Hey, this bat feels really good," he'd say. "Are you gonna use this one today? Let me try it out. I think there's a couple hits in this one."

Cash would cork a few of his bats and use them in batting practice to see how far he could drive a ball. Clearly he wasn't going to use those bats in a game because you could see the cork on the end of the bat.

Gates Brown was another player who would occasionally grab another player's bat to pinch-hit. One day, he grabbed one of Cash's practice bats and got busted by umpire Nestor Chylak, who could see the cork sticking out. You could tell they were for practice because he made no effort to hide the cork. Gates had no idea he had an illegal bat in his hands.

Cash could drive Mayo crazy. One day, the Yankees brought in Steve Hamilton from the bullpen with Cash due up next. Hamilton was 6'7" and he'd played in the NBA with the Minneapolis Lakers. More importantly, he had a three-quarter throwing motion and a wicked slider. He was murderous against left-handed hitters. In 1967, left-handers batted only .171 against him. In 1968, they batted just .185.

Standing in the on-deck circle, the left-handed-hitting Cash saw Hamilton coming into the game and walked back to the dugout. He placed his bat on the rack and sat down.

Mayo rushed over and said, "Norm, I didn't put in a pinch-hitter. You're still in the game!"

"Mayo," Cash responded, "I couldn't hit Hamilton when we were in the minors. I've never hit him in the majors, and I probably won't hit him today. Any good manager would put in a pinch-hitter for me right now. If you don't, we're just giving them an out. Why do that when we can still win this game?"

Stormin' Norman liked to win, but he also liked to joke around. In the summer of 1973, Nolan Ryan was throwing his second no-hitter of the season—unfortunately it was against us. In the bottom of the ninth at Tiger Stadium, Norm came to the plate with a piano leg instead of a bat. He'd already fanned twice using a bat against Ryan, and he thought he couldn't do any worse with a piano leg. Umpire Ron Luciano, of course, wouldn't let him use it, and Cash eventually popped out using a regulation wooden bat. But everyone had a good laugh when Cash entered the batter's box with that piano leg on his shoulder.

Mayo would grin and bear most of our antics, but there were some lines he wouldn't let us cross. Once, when we were in the midst of a losing streak, we were headed out west. Mayo never liked those trips because he thought we got into too much mischief in California. He told us we were going to have a bed-check out there, and Tigers coach Wally Moses reminded us when we all gathered to play poker that night.

Gator and I roomed together, and nearly everyone was gathered in our room, either playing cards or watching. Right before midnight, everybody returned to their rooms to await Mayo's call. After each player got the call, he would just come back down to our poker game.

A while later, everyone was back in our room, including right-handed reliever Fred Lasher. He kept asking everyone if Mayo had checked on them. It turned out that everyone had been called but Lasher. That made him furious. He stormed to Mayo's room and busted down the door.

"Aren't I a member of this team, too?" he screamed at Mayo. "I'm as important as anybody else is! You should've checked on me!"

Mayo always worried about us when we played in California—and for good reason. Everyone seemed to have too much fun in the sun, including me. And there was one particular party that got me into trouble. I knew some of the Four Tops from Detroit, and one night in California they threw a party in my honor. The Temptations were also there. I remember telling Gates about it, but he refused to go. He figured that nobody at the party was going to care that the Tigers had a game the next afternoon.

I don't recall too much about the party except that somehow we ended up at a house owned by singer Glen Campbell. The sun came up and we were still there, and I had to have someone drive me straight to the ballpark.

When I arrived, the Gator was there, shaking his head, letting me know that he'd made the right choice not to attend that Hollywood bash.

To be honest, I tried to tell Mayo that I couldn't play that day because I felt lousy. But Mayo, to his credit, said, "You're going to play."

As it turned out, I hit a home run in that game and drove in three runs and probably never felt worse in my life. Mayo took me out of the game before it was over. I was so sick and I went back to the hotel and slept until the next afternoon.

But that's the way we all were back then. No matter what happened the night before, once the game started, we were all about winning. We'd stay up all night talking, but I'd play the next afternoon without thinking twice about it.

The only time I can remember Mayo being truly angry with us came on a road trip to Anaheim to play the Angels. We stayed at a hotel that proudly displayed a vintage fighter plane out in front. Late one night, after too many drinks, some of us "relocated" that plane to the middle of the hotel pool.

At four o'clock that morning, Mayo caught wind of it and promptly hauled us all out of bed. It was the first time any of us had ever seen him mad. I could barely stop laughing, though, because he came downstairs wearing a nightshirt with the slits down the side, and I'd never seen anyone wear one of those except on TV. It looked like an old lady's nightgown from the turn of the century.

"I don't care how you did it!" Mayo said, fuming. "Everyone is going to help get it out of the pool." We tried, but we weren't able to get that plane out of the pool, and a wrecker had to be called to do the job.

We usually didn't get into too much trouble on the road, though, because we were too busy playing cards. On the road, Gates Brown and I held a regular poker game in our room. He was the head organizer, and when we checked into a hotel, Gates would always buy 100 one-dollar bills from the front desk to make sure we'd be ready for the game. Gates, John Hiller, Jon Warden, Pat Dobson, and Tommy Matchick always played. Sometimes Cash, Northrup, McLain, or others would join us.

The regulars always liked McLain to play in those games because he wasn't nearly as good a card player as he was a pitcher. They nicknamed McLain "the Dolphin" because he was a "fish" at the poker table. We would be playing five-card stud and have a two, three, nine, seven, all different suits showing and he'd stay in. Everyone would be looking at each other, like what is he *doing*? But Denny was Denny.

Because we were as close as brothers, we sometimes acted like it—meaning we didn't always play nice. I've never been a successful gambler, so I didn't play much. But I would go to the games anyhow—I saw them as social events. Cash was the same way. He wasn't much of a gambler, but he always wanted to be where the party was. Sometimes, I would simply be the Gator's bank. "Let me hold a twenty," Gator would say to me, and the next thing I knew, we were partners in some poker pot.

McLain always played the role of big shooter in these games. He always wanted to be the big king. When he played cards, he liked to wear a Japanese smoking jacket. He was always talking on the phone during the games. And even though he always had a pocket stuffed with money, Denny was always short when it came time to ante up.

Like I said, we were as close as brothers, and sometimes brothers fight each other. One night, we were in the middle of a game, and Denny was on the phone ordering some food, and his antics started to irritate Northrup.

The game was high-low, split the pot, meaning the best hand and worst hand shared the pot. As usual, Denny was light, so he was pulling chips out of the pot to show how much he owed.

With bets at one or two dollars apiece—and three raises allowed, the pots would sometimes grow to a couple hundred dollars, this one included. The games could get serious because none of us had the contracts that today's athletes do. A couple of hundred dollars was still a nice sum for us.

On this particular hand, McLain ended up winning half the pot, and when that happens the other winner gets your "lights" because you actually owe the pot.

But Denny swept his "lights" into his own pile, and Northrup spotted the move. His temper boiled over. He grabbed McLain's arm, and said "those are mine." McLain claimed he wasn't light on the pot. "You lyin' son of a gun," Northrup said as he reached across the table and ripped McLain's black-and-white smoking jacket right in half.

I really don't remember for us, but I'm guessing Jimmy must've had a bad day on the field because he was angrier than he should've been.

"I'm tired of Jim Campbell protecting you," Jimmy said.

The next thing I know, money was flying everywhere and my teammates were yelling and pushing. Gator and I broke up the fight before it really got out of hand.

Shortstop Ray Oyler probably had had too much to drink because I think he thought he was still in the military. When the scuffle started, he grabbed Gates Brown. I still remember Oyler trying to get in the middle of the scrap and big Gator just holding him by his head.

Meanwhile, some guys—myself included—were picking up the money that was scattered on the floor. It was probably the only time I ever won at poker.

Today, Warden always jokes that when the fight broke out, he got up, stretched, and said, "Where has the time gone? I'd better get to bed" and then scrambled out of the room. His theory was that if management came down to break up a fight they weren't going to punish Northrup, McLain, Cash, or me, but Mayo might have wondered what a rookie was doing up there with a bunch of veterans.

"It would have been, 'Hey rookie, I'll see you in Toledo,'" Warden says, laughing. "So I got my rear end out of there."

I should take a moment to talk about Oyler because he was probably one of the forgotten heroes of 1968. The 165-pound Oyler was probably one of the slickest fielding shortstops I ever saw in the major leagues, but he had trouble hitting his weight when he was with the Tigers.

I never quite understood that because I played with him at Syracuse in Triple-A ball and he hit 19 home runs one season. The season before that, he hit 23 doubles and nine home runs. But at the big-league level, he couldn't find any confidence at the plate. You could've rolled the ball up to him, and I'm not sure he could've hit it.

For a joke, the guys gave Ray a "Popeye bat" with a big barrel on it. He handled the ribbing pretty well.

Supposedly Oyler, who had spent time in the marines, was 22 when the Tigers signed him in 1960. And he was supposedly 29 when Mayo Smith joined the team in 1967, but Oyler looked as if he was in his late thirties. When we acquired pitchers John Wyatt and Earl Wilson, both of them told us that Oyler had been their sergeant in the service. Wyatt and Wilson were listed as four years older than Oyler, and they didn't see how that was possible.

"He must have joined the service when he was 14 years old," Wyatt used to say.

But I respected Oyler because he was willing to bunt, or hit behind the runner, to help the team. He also won games for us with his defense. Often Oyler, batting eighth, would lay down a sacrifice bunt to move a runner into scoring position to allow our pitchers to drive him in. Our pitchers could all swing the bat, and most of them might have been better major league hitters than Ray. Heck, Earl Wilson probably hit more homers in one season than Oyler hit in his whole career.

In addition to their contributions in the field, Warden, Dobson, Hiller, and Price kept us all loose with their antics. And I was frequently the target of their pranks. My concerns about flying were well-known, and the guys liked to mess with me on that. One time, they locked me in the bathroom on the team flight. It was like I was stuck in an elevator, going up and down, up and down. It seemed as if I was in that bathroom forever.

Another time, one of those three guys posted a note on my locker saying I had to call some doctor because tests I had taken for hemorrhoids showed internal bleeding. I was nervous and worried, but then I caught them snickering and I figured out what was going on.

What I liked about our team is that we always seemed to understand when it was appropriate to pull pranks. When we needed to relax, or to get our minds off a losing streak, you could count on funny comments and jokes. And everybody had a nickname, too. Don Wert was "Coyote" because he didn't say much. I became "Roids" because I suffered from hemorrhoids. Freehan and Joe Sparma were dubbed "Big Ten" because Freehan had played tight end at Michigan and Sparma had played quarterback at Ohio State. In 1961, Sparma threw for 200 yards to lead Ohio State to a 50–20 win against Michigan in their annual rivalry game.

Jim Northrup was "the Gray Fox" because he was prematurely gray. And I always called Jim Price "the Big Man" because he always seemed like he was destined to wear a suit some day in the business world.

Price and I actually played against each other in 1964 when I was playing Triple-A ball in Syracuse and he was in the Pirates' organization as a catcher for Columbus.

In one game, Bob Priddy, who eventually made it to the majors, was pitching for Columbus. He hit my Syracuse teammate Oyler "right in the coconut," as Price likes to say. I was up next and I didn't even look at Price as I stepped into the batter's box. But as I was taking my practice swings, I told Price that if Priddy's pitches even got close to my head, I was coming after Price. Price nodded and then went out to the mound for a chat.

Years later, Price told me what he said. "What I told Priddy was that if he threw high and inside to you, you were going to come after him with a baseball bat."

Outfielder Wayne Comer, from Shenandoah, Virginia, was one of my good friends on the team, and we spent a lot of time together. Even today we keep in touch. I recently visited him at home in Virginia to celebrate an anniversary of baseball in that area. When Comer played for the Tigers, we called him "Shank." He was actually a fine outfielder and a dependable role player in 1968. But he also liked to run with the big dogs, and occasionally he'd get himself into sticky situations at various watering holes.

One time, some of us were having a drink and a burger at the Brass Rail in Minnesota, and Wayne spotted a group of soldiers at the bar. Wayne's impishness got the better of him. He went up and one-by-one he asked each soldier where he was from. He would then make an insulting remark about his state. The joke seemed to play pretty well until he got to the last soldier, and he suggested, in his own colorful way, that Oklahoma was the worst state of them all. We ended up fighting our way out of the place. I tell this story simply to show that we had a one-for-all-and-all-for-one attitude. We looked out for each other.

Most successful teams have a player who keeps everyone loose and on their toes at the same time. Gates Brown could help a player out of a batting slump, and he could have the entire team doubled over in laughter because of something he said.

Gates always drew a crowd around him because you never knew what might come out of his mouth. Once we were playing one of those rare 11:00 A.M. games in Minnesota, and Al Kaline had the day off. That shifted me from left field to right field, and Gates started in left.

At that early in the morning, the glare of the sun was directly in your face in left field and I was mighty thankful I was in the right. Bob Allison hit one ball that bounced off Gator's chest, and then Harmon Killebrew drove a ball that bounced off Gator's head.

When Gator came back to the dugout, he was mad about the errors, and he blamed it all on Mayo. Believe it or not, he started cussing out Mayo for giving him the start.

"You know full well that I shouldn't be out playing in left field this early," Gator screamed. "You know that I like to play poker late at night."

Mayo was dumbfounded. He didn't know what to say, so he turned to batting coach Wally Moses and asked, "What is he talking about?"

Moses shrugged, and everyone was laughing because Moses was keenly aware that Gator liked to stay up late and play poker.

Then McLain came into the dugout and decided to needle Gates. That was only fair, because Gator liked to needle everyone else. "It's bad enough that I have to face Minnesota with eight good hitters in their lineup," McLain said. "But now I find out that my biggest enemy is sitting on the bench with me."

We all laughed because with the way McLain was pitching then, he could overcome just about any mistake we made. McLain also knew that the Gator could take a ribbing.

The Gator knew he wouldn't usually be called upon until late in a game, so he liked to hang out down in the bullpen, especially at Tiger Stadium, because the relievers always had plenty of food spread out like a smorgasbord. Hot dogs, pretzels, and peanuts were always on the menu. One night in the fifth inning, Mayo called down to the bullpen for Gates to pinch-hit.

The guys in the bullpen told me that Gates had just dressed up a couple of hot dogs and he had eaten only one of them when he got the call from Mayo.

"You guys will eat this if I leave it here," Gates said as he wrapped up his ketchup-slathered dog and stuck it in his jersey.

This was 1968, and Gates was stroking the ball like he was Ted Williams. Not surprisingly, he ripped a line drive down the right-field line and slid head-first into second with a double. Gator rolled over to get up, and the umpire looked at him with panic in his eyes. "Don't move, Gator!" he yelled. "You're hurt."

There were ketchup stains streaking down Gates' jersey, and it looked as if he was bleeding profusely. Gator told the umpire it was an exploded hot dog and to keep quiet because he didn't want Mayo knowing he was eating every night at the all-you-can-eat bullpen buffet.

As he often did, Mayo inserted a pinch runner for Gator, who came out holding his side because he didn't want Mayo to spot the ketchup stain.

Another time, Gates hit a home run off Boston pitcher Lee Stange and a hot dog fell out of his uniform as he was rounding the bases.

We had many great characters on the Tigers to keep us all loose and enjoying ourselves. But there was no question who the team leader was. Al Kaline was easily the most respected man in the clubhouse. He never played a day in the minor leagues. He was 18 when the Tigers signed him in 1953, and he won an American League batting title when he was just 20. He wore the English "D" continuously from 1953 until 1974. Then he went into the broadcast booth. He was, essentially, a Tiger for more than half a century.

Players called him "The Line" because Mr. Campbell wouldn't pay anyone more than he paid Al. I preferred the nickname "The Lion" because he was the king of our jungle. When he walked in our clubhouse, he was so light on his feet you couldn't even hear his cleats click.

To me, Al was the elder statesman of our team. He was humble, dignified, and quiet, but when he spoke his words they were very powerful.

Some guys wondered why Al never said much. But former trainer Jack Homel explained to me that Al's reserved demeanor probably reflected how he arrived in the major leagues. When Al came to the Tigers in 1953, he was an 18-year-old high school player joining a team that had a lineup heavy with veteran players. Johnny Pesky was 34 and just a year from retirement. Outfielder Pat Mullin was 35. Catcher Matt Batts was 31, and there were a couple of other starters 30 or over.

"He was a kid in a man's world," Homel said. "When you come to a team in that situation, you're just expected to keep your mouth shut and play. That's what Al did and that just became his personality. He just stayed in that world."

Al and I were the best of friends. I learned a lot from hitting behind him, especially the professional manner in which he approached hitting. Early in my career, I kept my distance, mostly out of respect for who he was.

But as I grew into a man myself, I began to realize that if you had a question for Al, he had an answer. He was a private man. He wasn't like Cash or Gates or Rocky Colavito, who all loved to talk. He wasn't going to come up to you and start telling you how to become a better hitter. That wasn't Al's style. But if you went to him, he'd give you everything you needed. He was one of the classiest ballplayers I ever came across in my career. Perhaps my bond with Al was cemented forever on May 30, 1970, when I performed an emergency medical procedure on him that I'm told saved his life.

We were playing a game at County Stadium in Milwaukee when Brewers second baseman Roberto Peña sliced a 380-foot line drive into the right-center field gap. Center fielder Jim Northrup and right fielder Kaline both tried to make the catch, but they collided violently. The ball deflected off Northrup's glove and he immediately started chasing down the ball. The bases had been loaded with Brewers and Jim wanted to keep some of those runners from scoring.

I immediately noticed that Kaline wasn't moving. I was in a full gallop from left field to right. Milwaukee bullpen coach Jackie Moore was the first to get there and he could see Kaline gasping for air, but he couldn't get Kaline's mouth open.

By the time I got there, Al had turned blue. I kneeled over his chest and performed an emergency first-aid procedure that I had learned from my boxing days. Always concerned about a boxer swallowing his mouthpiece, we were taught to push up on the chest to help force open the jaw. I did that and forced my three fingers down Al's mouth and pulled out his tongue. Milwaukee's trainer Curt Rayer was also there helping me. Al had swallowed his tongue after the collision, and the blockage in his throat prevented him from getting air.

Unfortunately, for me, when I got Al's jaw open, he bit my hand—hard! I still have the mark on my hand where Al got me. I often tell people that the bite mark is the best autograph you can get because no one can take that from me.

I'm thankful that my boxing training came back to me when it did. In an emergency, it's easy to forget your training.

Peña ended up with an inside-the-park grand slam and we eventually lost that game 9–7. But I don't think anyone on the Tigers felt bad about the loss after Al survived that scary moment in the outfield. He didn't play the next game, but he was in uniform and didn't have any lasting effects.

Every player on the roster appreciated Al for who he was and what he meant to the organization. He was also one of the classiest players in the game, and on the Tigers, he was the standard by which all others were judged.

Every successful team has players whose competitiveness fuels success. Second baseman Dick McAuliffe and pitcher Earl Wilson were the Tigers who were like that.

Once the game started, we were all business. But McAuliffe was all business two hours before the first pitch. We called him "Mad Dog." Before the game, he didn't want people talking to him. It was almost like he was in a trance, and he'd be perturbed if you disturbed him. He respected players who tried to take him out at second base on a double-play ball. That's the way he played.

And no one competed with more ferocity than Wilson. I remember a game against Baltimore at Tiger Stadium when Wilson was pitching masterfully, going into the ninth inning with a 4–1 lead. He'd given up only three hits and the Orioles weren't making good contact. Wilson had them off balance.

Then, in the ninth inning, Frank Robinson homered on the first pitch, and Boog Powell and Brooks Robinson followed with solo shots in rapid-fire succession to tie the game. Boom. Boom. Boom. To this day, I've never seen a team lose a three-run lead as quickly as we did. Mayo pulled Wilson out of the game, and reliever Tom Timmerman then gave up the winning run on a double by Davey Johnson.

After the game, Earl was furious that Mayo didn't have a reliever throwing in the bullpen to replace him after he gave up the first home run.

Mayo was flabbergasted. "Earl, you were pitching a three-hitter," he said. "You looked like you were coasting, and if I had someone up throwing you would've been mad at me for that." Earl was just steamed that we lost the game, and Mayo was a convenient target. Earl hated losing.

Another time in Baltimore, Earl was saying before the game that Frank Robinson had his number, and he was darn tired of giving up big hits to him. Robinson was perhaps the most competitive player I ever played against. When Robinson slid into second base to break up a double play, he sometimes would knock the pivot man onto the outfield grass. Robinson never received enough credit for his hitting ability. I remember one time early in my career we had a pregame meeting about the Orioles. We started talking about how to pitch to Robinson but Charlie Dressen cut off the discussion because he said Robinson could hit a pitch in any location.

"You just have to go right at him and hope for the best," Dressen said.

On this day in 1966, Earl had a different plan.

"I'm going to drill his ass," he said, "I'm going to bust him between the neck and the collarbone."

In the first inning, Earl gave up a couple of singles to Luis Aparicio and Russ Snyder and then Robinson strode to the plate. Earl threw high—inside smoke up above the neckline. Robinson just raised his hands and blasted the pitch clear out of Memorial Stadium to give the Orioles a 3–0 lead.

Clearly Mayo Smith inherited a team primed to win a pennant. We had the talent, and we were gaining the experience. In 1966—a year before Mayo arrived—everyone in our starting lineup hit 10 or more home runs, except Jerry Lumpe. At 31, Kaline had finished third in the batting race and hit 29 home runs; he still seemed in the prime of his career. I was only 23 and had just completed my second 100-RBI season, Norm Cash hit 32 home runs and Dick McAuliffe hit 23. Jim Northrup had smacked 16 home runs in just 123 games, and looked very much like a consistent 20–25 home run guy.

Freehan was only 24, and he was already a two-time All-Star and one of the top defensive catchers in the game. From 1965 to '66, Bill posted a .996 fielding average and threw out about 36 percent of runners trying to steal on him.

Team president Jim Campbell could see even in 1965 that we had the makings of a championship-caliber team. That's why on June 14, 1966, the Tigers traded Don Demeter and a player to be named later (Julio

Navarro) to the Boston Red Sox for Earl Wilson and Joe Christopher. Earl solidified our pitching staff. He boasted a 2.59 ERA in 1966 and when he pitched it was like having an extra big bat in the lineup. He might've been the best-hitting pitcher in the American League. Also that season, Denny McLain won 20 games for the first time. Mickey Lolich won 14 games, and it was clear that he was going to be a dominant pitcher. We also had high hopes for right-handed pitcher Joe Sparma, the former Ohio State quarterback. Personally, I thought he threw as hard as any pitcher in the American League. When we first started, I thought he was going to be another Sandy Koufax. I would say Sparma threw his fastball in the high 90s.

In 1967, McAuliffe moved full time to second base and Ray Oyler became our starting shortstop. Mayo's theory was that we had plenty of offense, and that Ray would make our defense stronger.

Even dealing with the tragic deaths of Charlie Dressen and Bob Swift in 1966, we had still contended. Now with a fresh start and a new manager, the Tigers wouldn't be content to just contend. We were thinking about winning. When I looked at our lineup and compared it to the rest of the American League, I saw no reason why we couldn't win multiple championships.

# Chapter 8

# 1967

DURING SPRING TRAINING of 1967, I tore my Achilles so badly that a leading orthopedic surgeon recommended I have surgery that would sideline me for the entire season. Amazingly, that wasn't the worst news of the summer.

Playing through that injury wasn't nearly as excruciating as seeing the city of Detroit engulfed in flames, with people dying and tanks rolling through the neighborhoods where I played sandlot baseball as a child. The aching in my ankle wasn't nearly as painful as seeing National Guard troops marching up 12th Street with their eyes panning the houses for snipers.

By July of 1967, I expected to be in the midst of the American League pennant race. Instead, I found myself standing in the midst of an urban riot. There I was, standing in full Detroit Tigers uniform on the hood of my car, pleading with the rioters and looters not to destroy more homes and lives.

This was supposed to be a summer of fun in the Motor City. All winter, fans had been talking about our chances to win Detroit's first pennant since 1945. We were hungry for success. New manager Mayo Smith had been on all of the sports shows, saying we were going to compete for the American League title. We figured our pitching staff was as talented as any in the league. The Red Sox had Jim Lonborg, Gary Bell, and José Santiago. Minnesota had Dean Chance, Jim Merritt, Jim Kaat, and Dave Boswell. We could counter with Mickey Lolich, Denny McLain, Earl Wilson, and Joe Sparma. All four of those Detroit pitchers could easily win 20 games.

After my injury, the Tigers flew me to California to meet with a leading sports medicine expert, and he told me flat-out that my season was over before it began. That answer was unacceptable to me because I had trained aggressively all winter to be ready for our pennant drive. With my German Shepherd, Champ, at my side, I'd run up and down the Lodge Freeway service drive all winter long to reach a high level of conditioning. I was not going to let that go to waste.

Ultimately, it was my decision whether to have surgery. I informed our team physician, Clarence Livingood, that I would try to play through the injury and have my surgery after the season. He consulted with Dr. Russell Wright, who worked with both the Detroit Lions and Tigers, and they came up with the idea of me playing the entire 1967 season in a soft cast. The cast was protected with a high-top boot, similar to the ones that Johnny Unitas wore in the NFL.

The hope was that if I sat out the first three weeks of the season, my Achilles would heal enough to let me play most of our games. We also consulted with Mayo, and we all agreed that if the Tigers had a significant lead, I would come out of the game. The idea was to minimize as much strain on the ankle as possible. It was not an ideal situation, but I was able to play 122 games that season. My injury wasn't the Tigers' only medical woe that season. Al Kaline also missed five weeks midseason with a broken hand.

Injuries or not, the Tigers started the 1967 campaign with a 26–15 record. But we had a rough June, finishing below .500 for the month, and as July rolled around, we were still close enough to make a run for the pennant. We were a confident team, and we mistakenly believed that our pennant would be the big story in Detroit as the summer heated up. But we had no idea that baseball would seem like a trivial pursuit near the end of July.

On July 23, we split a doubleheader against the New York Yankees. But we didn't realize that while we were competing against Mickey Mantle, Elston Howard, and the Yankees, a riot had started in the area around Tiger Stadium. We could see smoke billowing above the stadium roof, but we just assumed there was a major fire nearby.

Even when we were told to exit Tiger Stadium immediately because there was rioting, none of us could really comprehend what was happening on the streets. How do you explain that people—many of whom had never even had a parking ticket in their lives—would suddenly become part of an unruly mob?

People have often asked me why I drove to the epicenter of the riot, and I really can't explain my actions. Thoughts were whirling in my mind and I just wanted to be able to do something to help. This was my community. These were my people. Members of my family were living in the eye of this riot. Honestly, I didn't understand why this was happening. Team officials were pressing us to leave the area quickly and most of the players didn't bother showering. I didn't even change out of my uniform. I jumped into my car and drove over by 12th Street, near the area where I had delivered *Michigan Chronicle* newspapers as a child. I'd walked these streets a thousand times without a fear in the world. But what I saw on those streets that night scared me. Houses had flames dancing across their roofs. Cars were overturned. Small groups of youngsters were roaming the streets, looting and vandalizing the local businesses. It looked like a war zone. To me, it looked like the world was coming to an end.

I got out of my car, climbed on the roof, and started shouting at people until I got their attention.

"Go home, Willie!" somebody said. "Don't stay down here. We don't want you to get hurt."

Supposedly, the 1967 riots began when Detroit vice squad officers raided an after-hours drinking club on 12th Street and Clairmount. There was a large party going on inside in celebration of two returning Vietnam veterans. Apparently, a large group of people gathered outside to protest the arrests. Black people being arrested by White police officers. Racial tension had already been at a boiling point, and this blew the lid off.

There have been studies about why the rioting began, and they pointed to many different factors, including the community's mistrust of the police and economic hardship. It certainly was a changing political climate because of the war in Vietnam and the civil rights movement. But I certainly wasn't thinking about any of that as I stood on my car and asked members of my community to go home and be with their families.

They were burning up and tearing up the neighborhood. "Why are you doing this?" I kept asking. "Why?" But no one had an answer.

"Whatever message you're trying to make will surely be lost in the violence," I said.

People did listen, but not many stopped their assault on the city. More people expressed concern for my safety. Eventually, I climbed down and got back into my car.

The rioting went on for five days. Forty-three people died from the violence, and 1,189 were injured. More than 7,200 were arrested—one of them an 82-year-old man. More than 400 homes were burned and more than 2,500 businesses were either looted or destroyed.

That night, I drove in and out of the riots without incident. People recognized me, and later, some would thank me for at least making an effort to quell the violence, even if it was a failed effort. No one tried to harm me and my car never got a scratch. Maybe that was the night that I embraced my community for the first time as an adult.

I went back down there over the next few days—once because I heard that Mickey Lolich was on one of the tanks. He was in the National Guard, and I was told he had been called to active duty. Other times because I felt I had to do something to help my community. The riot had a profound impact on my life, and it certainly affected our ballclub.

Because of the riots, we didn't play for three days. When we resumed play in Baltimore, we were six games over .500 and starting to make a serious run at winning a very tight A.L. pennant race. We won four of our last six in July, and then posted a 21–14 mark in August to strengthen our position. Going into the final two weeks of the regular season, the Boston Red Sox, Minnesota Twins, Chicago White Sox, and Detroit Tigers all had a chance to win the pennant. The Tigers were trying to win their first since 1945, and we felt confident, although we suspected that the race would come down to the final day. We were right.

In the final two days, Carl Yastrzemski and the Red Sox beat the Twins twice to eliminate them. We controlled our own destiny. All we had to do was sweep a doubleheader on the last day of the season against the California Angels, a team that was in the middle of the pack.

In the first game, I smacked a two-run homer off left-hander Clyde Wright in the first inning, and I doubled later. I ended up scoring three runs, and we won the game 6–4. Joe Sparma pitched seven strong innings, and Bill Freehan went 3-for-3.

But in the nightcap, the Angels played us hard. Jimmy Northrup hit a two-run homer in the second inning to help us build a 3–1 lead, but we couldn't hold it, even with Denny McLain on the mound. Jim Fregosi hit a run-scoring double and Don Mincher hit a two-run homer to give the Angels the lead. By the bottom of the fifth, the Angels were up 8–3. But we wouldn't go down without a fight. With two out in the seventh, Dick McAuliffe hit a two-run single to make it 8–5.

Even trailing by three runs going into the bottom of the ninth, we had some confidence, and it grew when Freehan doubled and Wert walked to start the inning off Minnie Rojas. Then the managing began in earnest. Mayo Smith pinch-hit Lenny Green for Mickey Lolich, who had come out of the bullpen to keep us in the game. Angels manager Bill Rigney then brought in left-hander George Brunet to pitch to the left-handed-hitting Green. Then Mayo brought in Jimmy Price to bat for Green. Even after Price flew out to left, I think we believed we'd rally to tie or win because Dick McAuliffe was up. "Mac" was an All-Star second baseman that year, and in 1966 and 1967, he had a combined total of 45 home runs. He also had some clutch hits, including one earlier in the game.

Mac hit the ball on the nose, but right at Angels second baseman Bobby Knoop, who turned it into a quick double play. McAuliffe only hit into two double plays the entire season. The team was devastated, but nobody blamed Mac.

Even though it looks like we lost on the final day, pennants are never won or lost on the final day. They're lost months, weeks, and days before. We lost it in the final week when we only won three of seven games. We lost it the night before, when we gave up six runs to California in the eighth inning and lost 8–6. We lost it in mid-September when we didn't sweep the seventh-place Washington Senators. We lost it in early July, when we lost seven in a row, including four to the Senators.

Injuries did undermine us in 1967. I like to think that Al and I would've been worth a few wins each had we been healthy. Also, Denny McLain suffered a foot injury late in the season and missed a few starts. No one knew exactly how he hurt his foot. It wasn't the first time he was involved in controversy, and it wouldn't be the last. With the riot as a backdrop to our pennant chase, fans really didn't embrace the battle for first place as they normally would.

But we learned about ourselves in 1967. We came to understand there's a fine line between winning and losing. We realized that those games in July were as important as the games in September. And the riots reminded us that, given the unhappiness in the world, it truly was a privilege that we were getting paid to play a game that we loved.

When we lost to the Angels on October 1, 1967, we couldn't view the loss as having any grand purpose. But early in the 1968 season, it became clear to me that our team had an assignment even more important than winning a pennant. It seemed to me that the Tigers' real accomplishment in 1968 was helping to unify the city of Detroit—to bring Black and White together. To restore harmony to an area that had been a battleground for four days the summer before. To do that, maybe we needed to lose that final game of 1967 to fully appreciate our role. That loss made us even more determined to win it all in 1968.

# Chapter 9

# Sock It to 'Em

THE ECHO OF GUNFIRE that had defined the summer of 1967 on the streets of Detroit was replaced by the sweet tones of Ernie Harwell, whose voice owned the night in the Motor City in the summer of 1968. People still tell me that if you drove down any block in the city that summer it was like hearing Harwell in stereo. His Southern-spun delivery seemed to be coming from all directions. It was a hot summer, doors and windows were open, and Harwell seemed to be a guest on every porch—a visitor in every home. People would be walking down the street with a transistor swinging from a wristband, not wanting to miss a game, an inning, or even a single pitch of the 1968 season. Everyone in the city—Black or White, rich or poor—was listening to Harwell during what can only be described as a magical season.

In 1967, the city was on fire. In 1968, the Tigers were on fire. It was the year of the Tiger in China that year, and fans began to embrace the idea that the Chinese calendar had forecast our success on the ballfield. We really didn't need an omen. No clubhouse speeches were necessary to remind us that we were expected to win the pennant in 1968. We all believed we should have won in 1967, and we were determined to make sure we made no mistake in 1968.

Curiously, we lost on Opening Day, but then we won nine in a row and kept on rolling. Rookie left-hander Jon Warden, who remains a dear friend to this day, won three of those games. He'd made the jump from Class A baseball directly to the majors, and now he was the first three-game winner in the major leagues. When a *Sports Illustrated* reporter asked Jon how many more games he could win as a rookie, Jon said, "I should win 45 or 50."

Jon made the team because we needed an improved bullpen, and with that sense of humor, he fit right into our clubhouse. We were a confident bunch. The Tigers moved into first place on May 10 and we never looked back. Nobody was going to catch us. We won 103 games and finished 12 games ahead of Baltimore.

What I remember about 1968 is that we never believed we were out of any game. In 40 of our victories, we were tied or trailing in the seventh inning. Fans began to expect our comebacks, and because of that, there was always energy and emotion spilling out of the ballpark. If we were trailing going into the seventh inning, people would start to clap and to bang those old, green, wooden seats. As you stepped into the batter's box, you could feed off the rhythm of the cheering. It was intimidating to play against us in Tiger Stadium.

People viewed us as a three-run homer club, but we could beat you in many different ways with many different players.

For example, utility infielder Tom Matchick had just three home runs for the season, but one of those was a two-run shot in the bottom of the ninth on July 19 against Baltimore. We trailed 4–2 going into the ninth, but Tommy's homer gave us the win, 5–4. A week later, reliever Daryl Patterson entered a game against the Orioles at Memorial Stadium with the bases loaded and nobody out in the bottom of the sixth. He struck out Fred Valentine, Brooks Robinson, and Davey Johnson to get us out of a jam. Patterson went the rest of the way and we won that one, 4–1.

During the 1968 season, Jim Northrup smacked four grand slams and broke up three no-hitters. On June 24, Northrup hit grand slams in two consecutive at-bats in a 14–3 win at Cleveland. He was the first major leaguer since Baltimore's Jim Gentile in 1961 to hit grand slams in consecutive at-bats. Then five days later, Northrup hit another grand slam to beat Chicago, 5–2, which set a new record of three grand slams in a week.

My roomie, Gates Brown, also had what is arguably the best pinch-hitting season in the history of baseball. In 1968, he batted .450 as a pinch-hitter, with 18 hits in 40 at-bats. He also drew eight pinch-hit walks.

On August 11, he walloped a home run in the 14th inning to help us beat the Red Sox, 5–4, in the first game of a doubleheader at Tiger Stadium. In the nightcap, we scored four in the ninth—capped by Gator's game-winning single—to beat Boston 6–5.

Gator always liked to remind us how often he had to be the hero. "You guys go out there and screw it up for eight or nine innings," he'd say, "and then I have to come in and bail you out."

Our pitching staff also saved us on more than one occasion. Denny McLain had one of the most remarkable seasons ever by a major league pitcher—and I wasn't at all surprised. The first day I met him, I knew he was destined for major league success.

On April 8, 1963, the Chicago White Sox had to choose between protecting McLain or a right-handed pitcher named Bruce Howard on their roster. When the Sox kept Howard, the Tigers claimed McLain. He started with Duluth that season in the Northern League, but after going 13–2 with 157 strikeouts in 141 innings, the Tigers promoted him to Knoxville, where I was playing.

"I'm not here to stay," McLain told us. "I'm going to the majors."

McLain was an amazing pitcher. With a rising fastball and overflowing confidence, he moved up just as quickly as he had forecasted. By the end of the 1963 season, he was playing with the Tigers. In his first 21 innings in the major leagues, he struck out 22 batters.

It took him two seasons to gain enough experience in the majors to be dominant. And from 1965 through 1969, I don't think there was a better pitcher in baseball. In that time period, I wouldn't have taken Bob Gibson over McLain. For those five seasons, McLain was 108–51 with 1,006 strikeouts. For five years, he put up Hall of Fame numbers.

In 1968, Denny was almost untouchable. He was 14–2 by the end of June, and by July 27, he won his 20th game of the season. He was just blowing hitters away with his fastball. On September 14, with two runs in the bottom of the ninth, we beat the Oakland A's, 5–4. I had the game-winning hit, a single over the left fielder (Port Huron, Michigan, native Jim Gosger) and Denny got his 30th victory.

He would finish the season 31–6 to become the first major league 30-game winner since Dizzy Dean in 1934. Denny was the first American Leaguer to win 30 since Lefty Grove in 1931.

When it came to competition, Denny was a fire-breather at all times. Although I wasn't on the mound when Mayo Smith came to visit, we all heard the stories about what they said to each other. It was never a pleasant experience for Mayo.

"What the heck do you want, Mayo?" Denny would say.

"Well, I just want to see how you're feeling," Mayo would say.

"Do you have anyone in the bullpen better than me?"

"Well, no. But I just want to make sure you're okay?"

"Mayo, get the heck off the mound."

"Okay, Denny, go get 'em."

If Denny had trained more, he could've been one of the greatest players in the game. I don't think he ever ran 100 wind sprints in his life. He also drank a case of Pepsi almost every day. He had cases of it stacked around his dressing stall.

Even if he would've done 20 percent of the training that the rest of us were doing, he might have won 20 games a year for a decade. He had strong legs and a flamethrower arm. He was overflowing with talent, and he wanted greatness. We all loved playing behind Denny because he was a quick worker. He wanted the ball now, and he was usually ready to throw before the batter was set. Two hours and 30 minutes was a long game when Denny was on the hill. He could pitch a complete game in less than two hours. He challenged hitters, and with his stuff, he could be effective with that strategy. With the trust he had in his defense, he didn't fear letting the other team hit the ball.

"The business of pitching up or down or in or out is all bunk," McLain told reporters before the '68 World Series. "You just go out and pitch your game."

True to form, Denny joked about how he'd handle Lou Brock's speed. Denny said he wasn't good at holding runners on base, so he had a unique plan. "I'm either going to get Brock out or let him hit a home run. That'll keep him off the bases."

That was Denny McLain. He pitched the way Frank Sinatra sang: He did it his way.

With McLain in our clubhouse, every day was an adventure. He didn't sing when he played the organ professionally, but he would always be humming around the clubhouse. "Fly Me to the Moon" was one of his favorite tunes, which always seemed appropriate. The first time I ever saw a portable phone was in the visitor's clubhouse in Cleveland, when McLain called his wife, Sharyn, who was in a hospital back in Detroit.

He told her he had a plane waiting for him at the Cleveland airport to fly him back to Detroit.

"The game will take two hours, and with the ride to and from the airports and with the plane ride I will be at your bedside in five hours," McLain told his wife.

He was always confident about his ability to get outs quickly. And that game played out just as he told his wife it would. I bet he was by her side right when he said he would be.

McLain, whose father-in-law was Hall of Famer Lou Boudreau, was involved in plenty of crazy stuff—and most of it we didn't know anything about. But when he started carrying a gun, I moved my locker across the room from him. That just scared me. McLain could be mysterious—and a bit of a loner—but between the lines, he was about winning. There was never any question about his will to win.

His pitching brilliance was a staple of our success in 1968, but our hero changed every day. Almost everybody seemed to have his moment in the spotlight. We really did seem like a team of destiny. In terms of consistency, Dick McAuliffe was unquestionably our spark plug. He scored 95 runs and produced 50 extra-base hits. His batting average was only .249, but he batted 35 points higher with runners in scoring position. He batted .364 with the bases loaded. His aggressiveness at the top of the order gave the team a lift, and maybe we realized that even more after he was suspended for five games for charging the mound and injuring Chicago's Tommy John on August 22 at Tiger Stadium.

On ball four, John's left-handed fastball sailed over Mac's head. Both of them were jawing at each other as Mac trotted to first base. John had good control, and probably that's why McAuliffe believed John was throwing at him. Suddenly, Mac charged the mound and the benches emptied. John went low and turned his shoulder toward McAuliffe, presumably to protect himself. But that backfired when McAuliffe's left knee rammed into his shoulder. John was lost for the season with a separated shoulder. The league suspended Mac for five games. Then we went into New York and promptly lost four out of five to the Yankees. We all realized in that series how important Mac was to the team.

Other than that series in New York, it really did seem as if everything went right for the Tigers in 1968. People talk about our pitching and hitting that season, but they forget that we led the majors in fielding. Bill Freehan and Mickey Stanley were both Gold Glovers that season, and McAuliffe made only nine errors. Ray Oyler had only eight errors at shortstop, and I don't think any other shortstop in the American League fielded his position any better than Ray did in '68.

In terms of hitting, we led the American League in home runs and runs scored. We scored 671 runs that season. The Red Sox had the second best offense, and they finished 57 runs behind us. We clobbered 185 home runs and no team was within 50 of that.

And we didn't even need that much hitting because our pitching was exceptional. Mickey Lolich won 17 games that season, Earl Wilson posted a 2.85 ERA, and Joe Sparma won 10 games. Among our relievers, Don McMahon (2.02), Daryl Patterson (2.12), John Wyatt (2.37), John Hiller (2.39), and Pat Dobson (2.66) all had ERAs under 3.00.

The night we clinched the pennant—when we beat the Yankees on September 17, 1968—was symbolic of how we played all season. We won the game in our last at-bat. We received a terrific pitching performance. We were flawless in the field and Bill Freehan threw out a couple of guys trying to steal second base. It was a team victory, and some of the unsung heroes were in the forefront. Joe Sparma pitched a five-hit complete game, and he walked just one batter.

With two out in the ninth inning of a 1–1 game, Kaline, batting for Norm Cash, drew a walk off Steve Hamilton. We knew Mayo wouldn't let Cash bat against Hamilton, after the grief he took the last time he considered letting Cash face the tall lefty. Next, Freehan singled to left. Then Mayo put in Jim Price to bat for Oyler. The Yankees brought in righty Lindy McDaniel to pitch, and so Mayo countered with the left-handed-hitting Gator. Gates drew a walk to load the bases.

Up stepped Don Wert. "Coyote" had struggled through a tough season—he only batted .200 for the season. But this was his moment in the sun. Two outs. Bases loaded. Bottom of the ninth. The pennant on the line. McDaniel delivered and Coyote singled sharply to right field. Bedlam reigned in Detroit.

The summer of 1968 was special. Everywhere you went in the Detroit area, you saw bumper stickers and billboards that read "Sock it to 'em, Tigers," which was a takeoff on a phrase from *Laugh In*, which debuted that year on NBC. The newspapers were on strike for several weeks that summer, and maybe that relieved some of the tension as well. There were no stories about what had happened the previous season. Everyone was just talking about the Tigers. When we were on television on Saturday afternoons with George Kell doing the play-by-play, everyone in the state seemed to be watching.

Someone even wrote a silly song that was played continually on the radio.

*We're all behind our baseball team,*
*Go get 'em, Tigers!*
*World Series bound and pickin' up steam,*
*Go get 'em, Tigers!*

As we prepared to meet the Cardinals in the Fall Classic, we felt as if we had only one issue to resolve: Where was Kaline going to play?

On May 25 of '68, Al suffered a broken arm when he was hit by a pitch from Oakland A's pitcher Lew Krausse. Al missed a month and during that time it seemed as if our outfield—Mickey Stanley, Jim Northrup, and me—simply took charge.

There was some crazy talk about trading Kaline for a shortstop, but no one in our dugout would have wanted that even though our starting shortstop Oyler was only hitting around .135.

Our team was all about Al Kaline. He made us tick—whether he played or not, and we all knew he had to play in the World Series.

In recent years, ESPN has called the decision to move Stanley from center to shortstop—to open up a spot for Kaline in the World Series—the fourth greatest coaching decision of all time. But it was actually the players who developed the plan. We talked about it frequently, and we even joked about it as we got into September.

I remember Northrup teasing Stanley as the three of us were standing in the outfield before a game late in the season.

"What are you going to do, Mickey?" the Gray Fox asked. "You know Willie's going to play every day and we know the Cardinals have nothing but right-handers in their rotation. So you know I'm going to play every day."

The logical decision was to move Stanley to shortstop. He was the team's best all-around athlete, and we all believed Mickey could play anywhere on the diamond, including pitcher. What's sometimes forgotten is that Stanley would often take ground balls with the infielders before games. He just liked taking ground balls.

Northrup would always joke with Stanley. "You could make more money if you switched to shortstop." Northrup's theory was that there weren't many good-hitting shortstops in the game, and Stanley's .259 batting average with 11 home runs would look great to any general manager looking for a shortstop.

There wasn't anyone else on the Tigers who could've made that move as smoothly as Stanley. Neither Northrup nor I could've played there. And people say that Dick McAuliffe could've moved back there because he'd started out as a shortstop. But then Stanley would've had to move to second base—and then we would have had two players out of position in the World Series. The obvious choice was Stanley. The only question was who would tell Mayo that's what the players wanted.

Eddie Mathews finally said he'd do it, and we knew he was the man for the mission. Eddie had more than 500 career home runs, and given how much reverence Mayo always had for the veteran players, we knew he'd buy into the plan, so long as Mathews presented it to him.

Mayo went along with the plan and issued the order as if it had been all his idea. Maybe he'd been thinking about it. Who really knows? Mayo certainly wanted to find a way for Kaline to play, and this wasn't a charity move by any stretch of the imagination. Even though Kaline got off to a slow start in 1968 and only played 102 games because of injuries, he still batted over .300 after July 1. He batted .327 in September, and for the season he hit .386 with runners in scoring position.

Stanley played the final six games of the regular season at shortstop, and looked very comfortable there, committing only two errors. But the media, especially the national media, thought Mayo's decision was foolish. The World Series was too big a stage, they insisted, to launch such an experiment.

But then again, not many members of the media believed we had much of a chance against the Cardinals. Before the World Series, the Tigers were listed as 8–1 underdogs on the betting line. We were a bit miffed to read, as well, that some of the Cardinals—Bob Gibson, in particular—believed that the opponents they'd faced in the National League had more talent than we did.

Eddie Mathews didn't play much for us in 1968, getting most of his at-bats as a pinch-hitter. He'd already said it would be his last season, but Eddie was an important clubhouse guy, and his leadership was important heading into the World Series. He had played for the Milwaukee Braves in the 1957 and 1958 World Series.

Right before the Series started with Game 1 in St. Louis, I recall that Stanley, Northrup, and I were all sitting in the clubhouse, acting more nervous than we should have been. Eddie came in and shooed us out onto the field. "Go out and have some fun," he said. "Enjoy being in the World Series."

# Chapter 10

# Bob Gibson and the Start
# of the '68 World Series

WHEN THE DETROIT TIGERS played the St. Louis Cardinals for the first time in spring training after I turned pro, my first thought wasn't that I wanted to get a hit off Bob Gibson.

My objective was to ask him for his autograph.

He made his first All-Star team in 1962. By the time I reached the majors for the first time in 1963, he was already established as one of the game's top Black players. He was an intimidating, hard-throwing right-hander.

I wasn't even scheduled to play against the Cardinals that day. I had played the day before. But I told Gates Brown I was going to make the trip because I wanted to ask Gibson to sign something for me. Gator just shook his head in disbelief.

When I got my chance, I walked up to him and asked politely. He said no a little less politely.

Back in the clubhouse, I explained to Gator about my encounter with Gibson.

"Well, you're a damn fool for coming here when you weren't supposed to play," Gator said.

My second significant encounter with Gibson came on October 2, 1968, and it went worse than my first one.

In 1968, we played sharper when we were having fun and we didn't have any fun facing Gibson in Game 1 of the World Series.

Gibson beat us 4–0 as he set a record with 17 strikeouts. We managed just five hits off him. He struck out Kaline and Cash three times each while Northrup, Freehan, and I were victimized twice.

"I didn't know God was Black," Northrup said after the game.

When Gibson was peering in at you from the mound, he looked as if he wanted to do bodily harm to you. On that day, Gibson would have beaten any opponent he faced. You can't describe the intensity he had. He was breathing fire.

After Cash struck out in the second inning, he walked back to the dugout like a defeated warrior.

"This is going to be a short day," he said.

That was probably the best pitching performance I saw in my lifetime. It was Gibson's day in the sun. The funny thing was that Gibson didn't even seem to enjoy it.

Cardinals catcher Tim McCarver tried to get him to look at the scoreboard.

"Give me the damn ball," he said.

Gibson fanned me for his 17th strikeout. I knew his out pitch was a slider that would break outside against a right-handed hitter. What I didn't know is that he also had an inside slider that he liked to throw against right-handers. It locked me up. I took a called strike. McCarver told me years later that I grunted when I was called out. I can tell you that there was nothing I could do with that pitch.

Bob Gibson told me years later that he developed the inside slider to use against the National League's top hitters, such as Willie Mays and Hank Aaron.

Gibson was king in 1968. His 1.12 ERA that season was the best baseball had known since 1914, when Red Sox hurler Dutch Leonard established the record of 0.96.

We were beaten soundly, but even though the Cards chased McLain after five innings, I don't think we were overly concerned by the one loss. Lou Brock hit a home run and swiped a base, which was a sign of things to come.

But we expected Game 2 to be different and it was. Mickey Lolich was the hero, going the distance and striking out nine. Lolich also hit the first and only home run of his 16-year career. He'd borrowed one of Al Kaline's bats, and Al joked afterward that he wouldn't let Lolich use his bats again "because he's taking all the hits out of 'em."

Cash and I also smacked home runs in Game 2, and maybe that was important simply because much had been written before the World Series about how our power wouldn't be as effective in spacious Busch Stadium. The Cardinals only hit 31 home runs at home all season. Busch reminded us of the Coliseum in Oakland, except the ball carried better at Busch. In one of our first batting practices, Bill Freehan hit the glass windows of the Stadium Club in deep left-center field, and the local reporters seemed impressed. We never doubted our own power, but the fact that one of our pitchers cleared the fence there—and that we hit three home runs total—should have sent a message to the Cardinals.

My home run came in the second inning, and it carried 10 rows beyond the 335 marker. The late right-hander Nelson Briles served me up a slider down and away, and knew I hit it well. It was our first home run of the Series, and it felt as if the Tigers were off and running. But it was actually Lou Brock who was off and running.

Brock's speed and his bat had become significant factors in the Series. As the Series moved back to Detroit for Game 3, he had three hits and stole three bases, and we lost 7–3. We dug ourselves an even deeper hole in Game 4. Baseball is a team game, and a player only gets up four or five times in a regulation game. But Brock and Gibson seemed to be carrying the Cardinals all by themselves. Gibson struck out 10 more batters, and Brock smacked another home run and stole his seventh base of the Series. We lost, 10–1, and many people—maybe even some of our own fans—thought all the fun of the summer of 1968 was coming to an end.

But we didn't feel that way. After the game, Northrup said, "We're giving Gibson too much respect. We're giving the Cardinals too much respect. We have to go out there and play the way we know how to play."

We talked about how we had to minimize the damage Brock was doing on the basepaths. Somebody had to step up and harness him. But nobody suspected it would be me.

# Chapter 11

# We Knew Lou Wouldn't Slide

EVERYONE IN THE BASEBALL world seemed shocked that Lou Brock didn't slide in Game 5 of the World Series. But everyone on the Detroit Tigers would've been surprised if he had slid.

When the ball left my hand in the fifth inning, I believe the throw was going to nail Brock at the plate because our scouting reports indicated that he'd developed some bad habits.

Brock was probably too dominant for his own good in 1968. He stole 62 bases in 74 attempts during the regular season, and he'd swiped an unprecedented 294 bases over a five-season span. During that era, Brock and all of his teammates—and maybe even the entire National League—began to believe that he owned the basepaths. He always raced from first to third on a base hit. And he always scored on a single from second base. Our scouting reports indicated that no one was challenging him. Teams were just conceding runs to his world-class speed.

Given that kind of treatment, it was easy to understand why Brock began to take his dominance for granted. According to scouting reports, he usually drifted around third base, and Cardinals third-base coach Joe Schultz usually didn't offer him much guidance because Brock didn't need it. Lou always had the green light on the basepaths. Likewise, the on-deck batter usually didn't move to the plate to signal Brock when to slide on close plays because Lou never *had* close plays.

Before the Series started, the Tigers outfielders vowed we would challenge Brock if the situation presented itself.

Unquestionably, the throw I made to nip Brock at the plate was the most important moment in my professional career. The general consensus seems to be that the throw was the turning point of the 1968 World Series. But plenty of people deserve credit for making that play possible.

Going into Game 5 at Tiger Stadium, we were already trailing the Cardinals 3–1 in the best-of-seven series. And in that contest, we were already down 3–0 after the Cardinals' first at-bats. In the fourth inning, we chipped away at their lead with a pair of runs. Mickey Stanley tripled to start the inning, and Norm Cash drove him home with a sacrifice fly. Then I launched a triple out near the 440-foot marker in center field, and Jim Northrup chased me home with a single to right, cutting the Cardinals' lead to 3–2.

As I said before, we were confident in our ability to come from behind. But we also knew that we couldn't afford to surrender any more runs. When Lou Brock doubled with one out in the fifth, we all understood that the World Series might hinge on our ability to prevent Brock from scoring.

Cardinals second baseman Julian Javier stepped to the plate. Since he batted right-handed, I was fully expecting him to hit the ball in my direction. Many years of training would all come together at this exact moment. It started with my father, who taught me to listen to my coaches and respect my opponents. My old teammate Rocky Colavito played a role in that throw because he had helped me with my outfield play when I first joined the Tigers. So, too, did Charlie Dressen, who was the law to me in my first couple of seasons in the major leagues. And although Gates Brown had primarily talked about hitting, he also made me realize that I had to start mentally preparing for a game the minute I got out of bed in the morning.

Playing in the outfield alongside Kaline and Northrup also helped me with my positioning. In my early years, I would chase balls into the corner a lot. But by watching those guys, I learned to play the caroms the right way. Playing a ball off the walls is just like billiards; you simply have to understand your angles. There were others, too, but the biggest influence on that throw was probably Mickey Stanley, because he'd spent hours with me, talking to me about patrolling the outfield. He'd helped me tremendously with my throwing motion.

Remember, I had been a catcher in high school, and I had a quick release—a short-arm motion designed to throw a ball from home to second. Stanley had worked with me about positioning my body to get more on my throws. He was an incredible outfielder. In fact, he didn't have a single error in the outfield in 1968. When I watched him make plays in center field, I often felt as if I should take off my glove and applaud. Nobody in the league could climb a wall like Stanley. When he went up a wall, it was like steps had suddenly appeared to get him above the fence line.

In terms of the throwing motion, Stanley always told me, "It's like being on a bus and reaching up to let the bus driver know you need to stop—reach up, extend the arm, and pull down."

Likewise, I had studied how our pitchers worked against hitters. That's why I knew Javier would probably hit the ball in my direction, because Lolich was going to work him down and in. Based on all my knowledge, I moved out of my normal position. And when Javier lined that single, I was right there to cut the ball off and fire it in—in one fluid motion.

My objective on that throw was to hit our third baseman, Don Wert, right on the nose. He was my cutoff man in that situation. People tend to forget that catcher Bill Freehan also made that play happen. I've always said that Freehan was as important to our team as Johnny Bench was to the Cincinnati Reds in their heyday.

After I uncorked the throw, it was Freehan's call to either let it come through to home plate, or to instruct Wert to cut it off and fire to second to prevent Javier from taking an extra base. This was the kind of fundamental baseball that made the Detroit Tigers successful in 1968.

Freehan read the play perfectly. He realized the throw was on line with good velocity, and he could see that Brock had broken stride around third base. Brock thought he was home-free. But Freehan let the throw come through and blocked the plate beautifully. And just as our scouting report indicated, Brock didn't slide. Frankly, I think Brock was shocked that I even tried to throw him out at the plate.

He was definitely shocked that he was out.

The next batter, center fielder Curt Flood, hit a routine fly ball to me in left, and we were out of the inning. As we came to the infield, I hugged and thanked Stanley.

"Squirrelly," I said. "You were right there with me on that throw. All that time you helped me with my defense paid off."

Although I had plenty of important hits in my career, I never felt prouder than I did at that moment because I had worked harder at my defense than anything. Hitting came easier to me, but I had to work at defense. And at that moment, I felt as if I didn't take a back seat to any left fielder in the American League.

People also forget that in Game 2, manager Mayo Smith removed me from the lineup in the seventh inning of an 8–1 victory. Ray Oyler went to shortstop, while Stanley went to center and Northrup went to left. Sportswriters portrayed that situation as me being lifted for defensive purposes, and I was insulted and angry.

Much later, Smith would tell me that he was simply giving me some rest, thinking that he didn't want to risk me re-injuring my Achilles, which had given me trouble on and off during 1968. But my removal from Game 2 might have motivated me even more in Game 5. I had thrown out six guys that season trying to get an extra base off me, and there were only two or three other left fielders in the A.L.—Carl Yastrzemski among them—who threw out more.

After the fifth inning, we still needed runs to win the game and force a Game 6 back in St. Louis. We got them in the seventh, with Mickey Lolich starting our rally. With one out, he singled to right, ending the day for Cardinals starter Nelson Briles. St. Louis manager Red Schoendienst then brought in left-hander Joe Hoerner to pitch to Dick McAuliffe. Mac responded with a big hit, pulling one of Hoerner's offerings between first, where first baseman Orlando Cepeda was holding Lolich on the bag, and second baseman Javier.

Mac understood how pitchers worked. He noticed that Hoerner liked to pitch inside, so he decided that the hole on the right side of the infield looked rather inviting.

Stanley then walked to load the bases, and Al Kaline drilled a two-run single to give us a lead we wouldn't lose. Norm Cash also singled off Hoerner to drive in Stanley and give us a two-run cushion.

The funny thing is that Mayo would've been second-guessed for not lifting Lolich for a pinch-hitter if Lolich hadn't delivered. But Lolich had hit a home run in Game 2 of the Series. In fact, he had two hits and two RBIs in that game, and he was pumped up. More importantly, we wanted Lolich to stay on the mound because we all knew that if you were going to get to Lolich, you had to get to him early. He got tougher as a game wore on. And in Game 5, Lolich was getting sharper with each passing inning.

After the game, Brock complained that he'd gotten his foot in safely under Freehan's tag. But according to the *Detroit Free Press*, Cardinals play-by-play broadcaster Harry Caray said replays showed that Brock was indeed out. And still photos provided more evidence.

But even with the victory, the Tigers were still down three games to two in the Series—with a long way to go. But Game 5 had to be demoralizing to the Cardinals, and it was a huge morale boost in our clubhouse. The tide had started to turn. Even before my throw nailed Brock, Freehan had thrown him out trying to steal in the third inning. Brock led the inning off with a single, but Freehan called for a pitchout and cut him down. Before then, Brock had stolen seven bases against us and was batting over .500 in the Series.

There wasn't anyone like Brock in the American League, so we had to learn how to deal with him. Before the Series, we talked about Brock more than any other Cardinal, including Gibson. The year before, Brock batted .414 with seven stolen bases, two doubles, a triple, and a home run to lead the Cardinals over the Red Sox in the World Series. But after Game 5 in 1968, he didn't seem so invincible anymore.

Although it's easy for me to say now, I believed going into the World Series that it would be either Mickey Lolich or Earl Wilson who would be our pitching hero—not Dennis Dale McLain.

I felt that McLain had probably pitched too many innings during the regular season and I suspected he was getting tired.

While winning his 31 games, McLain pitched 336 innings. That was 116 more than Lolich and 112 more than Wilson. If everything else were equal, I would've taken McLain against anyone.

Although Lolich would win the MVP of the 1968 World Series, we still needed Denny to win one game for us. That was Game 6.

Stakes were higher in the World Series. The spotlight was brighter. The pressure was more intense. But Denny was still Denny.

Before the Series started, reporters asked McLain if he was going to be nervous in Game 1. "No, I'll probably be more nervous when I play Vegas," said McLain, referring to his two-week organ-playing gig after the season.

The night before the Bob Gibson–Denny McLain showdown in Game 1, Denny played the organ at the Sheraton Jefferson's Gashouse Parlour. The players and their wives were all there the first night. As I've said before, when you found one of us in 1968, you found most of us. Jim Northrup served as emcee, and we all had a good time.

At one point, Denny joked, "I may not be a better pitcher than Bob Gibson, but I'm sure I'm a better organist."

We weren't the kind of team where everyone was tucked in bed by nine o'clock. Everyone started to head to their rooms after 11:00, and supposedly Denny played encores until just after midnight.

When Al Kaline was asked about it, he told the *Detroit Free Press*, "That's just the way Denny relaxes."

Denny was also ticked off that he'd been removed from Game 1 after only five innings. The *Free Press* reported that Denny and Mayo had to have a morning meeting early in the Series to clear the air.

But we all knew that none of that mattered because when the game started, Denny was always a bulldog on the mound. Heading into Game 6, back in St. Louis, a local writer asked Mayo if losing to Gibson in Game 1 destroyed any of McLain's confidence.

All of the Detroit writers laughed, and Mayo said, "Obviously you don't know Denny McLain."

Weary or not from a long season, McLain was dominant in Game 6. With a 13–1 thumping of the Cards, we tied the Series at three games apiece. Denny scattered nine hits, fanned seven, and didn't walk one batter. Meanwhile, we pounded starter Ray Washburn and the next two Cardinals pitchers, Larry Jaster and Ron Willis. Kaline was 3-for-4 with a home run and four RBIs. Believe it or not, Northrup had another grand slam. I had a couple of hits, including a double and two RBIs.

This forced a deciding Game 7—still in St. Louis, against the legendary Bob Gibson. But clearly we were a more confident team. Gibson had dominated us with 17 strikeouts and a shutout in Game 1, and then gave up just one run in Game 4. He'd actually won three games against the Red Sox in the 1967 World Series, and he now owned a new major league record of seven consecutive World Series wins. But somehow, we believed we could beat him in a deciding game. When Mayo asked Lolich to pitch on two days' rest, Lolich thought that Mayo was talking about a relief role. But when Mayo told him he'd be starting, Lolich said he'd be ready.

And he was.

I thought Mayo made the right call to pitch Lolich in Game 7 because Mickey had an amazingly strong arm. He always seemed to be as strong at the end of the season as he was at the beginning. Even in a game, he always seemed to start strong, go into a relaxed mode, and then finish a game like a bulldog. I don't recall ever seeing him tire out. And even though he was a lefty, he seemed to be able to get right-handers out with regularity. He fanned about 20 percent of the right-handers he faced that season and 30 percent of the left-handers. His ball moved sharply; I certainly didn't like taking batting practice against him.

I believe McLain made Lolich a better pitcher, too. He woke Mickey up to the truth of how talented he really was. McLain wasn't shy about saying what he thought about how his teammates played. He would tell Lolich, "If I had your arm, I'd just go out there and blow 'em away." He was always needling Lolich.

Lolich was masterful in Game 7. It was a scoreless duel between Gibson and him until the seventh inning, when Cash and I delivered back-to-back two-out singles. Then Northrup hit a long fly to center field. People say that Curt Flood misplayed the ball, but when Jimmy made contact, I knew the ball was going over Flood's head. Flood did lose his footing for a moment, but it didn't matter because he wasn't going to flag that ball down. It was well beyond his reach.

Cash and I scored, and Jimmy legged out a triple. Then Bill Freehan doubled him home for a 3–0 lead. That's all the support Mickey needed. We added another run in the ninth when I got us going with a single. Mayo put in Dick Tracewski to run for me, and he eventually scored to make it 4–0.

With two out in the bottom of the ninth, Lolich surrendered a home run to Mike Shannon. But then he got Tim McCarver to pop up to Freehan to wrap up the Series.

We had beaten Gibson in the clinching game. He had struck out 35 Tigers in 27 innings and posted a 1.67 ERA in that series. But when everything was at stake, found a way to beat him. It made the title sweeter that we beat Gibson to earn it.

"We're champions of the world!" Earl Wilson kept saying over and over in the clubhouse. "We are champions of the world!"

It's difficult to describe the feelings you have after winning a championship. We were like a family and we celebrated like a family. We were all thrilled for Kaline, who had played for the Tigers since 1953, and had finally won it all. Despite the criticism Mayo took for reconfiguring our regular lineup for Al, he hit .379 in the Series, with 11 hits in 29 at-bats, including two doubles and two home runs. He also had eight RBIs. Only Northrup matched Al's RBIs.

Meanwhile, Stanley performed extremely well at shortstop—so well that people were saying he should be moved there permanently. He committed a couple of errors, but there wasn't a moment when anyone on the team believed the move was risky. I was very proud that I batted .304 in the Series, with a double, triple, and home run, plus five walks. Through the years, I'd learned to take what the pitcher gave me. And Gator had taught me to respect those hitting behind me. Those walks seemed like base hits to me in the World Series.

And with an ERA of 1.67 and three victories against the Cardinals, Mickey Lolich deserved the MVP—and he got it.

The clubhouse was raucous as we celebrated the championship. Tigers owner John Fetzer, a buttoned-down executive, was in the room taking swigs out of Stanley's bottle of champagne, like he was one of the players. McLain had stolen the microphone from NBC analyst Joe Garagiola and was trying to interview *him*. Broadcaster George Kell, an ex-Tiger himself, was celebrating so much you would've thought he was still with the team. Sportswriters say they don't care which team wins, but we were with those guys every day and we could see on their faces that they cared. The late *Detroit Free Press* and *Detroit News* columnist Joe Falls certainly cared. He was Mickey Stanley's neighbor and he congratulated everyone after the game. He told it "like it was" in his column every day, but he was a caring man. He interviewed me 30 to 40 minutes after the game, and my feet *still* weren't back on the ground.

"I looked over at the top of the left-field wall in the seventh inning, and I saw Rudolph the Red-Nosed Reindeer," I said to Falls. "Christmas came early! Man, oh, man. I've never been this happy in my life. Never. Never. Never."

That night, Tigers fans flocked to Detroit Metro Airport to greet us when we got home from St. Louis. But the authorities were so concerned about the security risk that we were re-routed to Willow Run Airport near Ypsilanti. Over the next few weeks, the city overflowed with love for the Tigers. Instead of killing each other like they'd done the previous summer in the riots, people were hugging each other. Black and White, blue-collar workers and white-collar workers—they all came together in one city-wide celebration. The newspapers reported that downtown Detroit had the feel of Mardi Gras when we won the championship.

In the Tiger Club at Comerica Park today there's a quote of mine on the wall. It says, "I believe the '68 Tigers were put here by God to heal this city."

Though I said that 54 years ago, I still believe that passionately today. My spirituality just tells me that there was a connection. God knew the city of Detroit needed something to restore some harmony to our neighborhoods, and the 1968 Tigers did the work for Him.

Years later, 1968 Tigers relief pitcher Jon Warden was eating in a Cincinnati restaurant wearing a Detroit Tigers cap. He was approached by an elderly man who asked Jon if he was from Detroit. Jon's wife coaxed him into telling the guy that he had actually pitched for the 1968 championship team.

The guy's eyes lit up and he shook Jon's hand. "Thanks for saving our city," he told Jon. "Thanks for saving our city."

# Chapter 12

# Time to Take a Stand

I ADMIRED THE KENNEDYS for their civil rights views, and I campaigned with presidential candidate Hubert Humphrey in 1968. I protested at the infamous Polk Theatre in Lakeland, Florida, because it refused to admit Black people. That actually amused me because when I first joined the Tigers, a young White man who worked around the clubhouse (coincidentally named "Gator") once took me to the Polk after we'd gone fishing. No one said a word when I bought a ticket.

When Dr. Martin Luther King was assassinated on April 4, 1968, it certainly made every Black person in America realize that we hadn't changed enough. And the shooting death of Robert Kennedy was another terrible reminder later that spring. In Detroit, we had gone through the riots in 1967 and the following year, the Tigers had helped heal the city by winning the World Series.

But by 1969, it started to bother me that I was the only starting Black position player on the team. Every other team in the American League had at least two minority starters—even the Red Sox, who were the last team to integrate. Reggie Smith was in the Boston outfield, and George Scott was at first base. The Baltimore Orioles had four Black players out of their starting eight. And the National League was even more integrated, with the Atlanta Braves using six or seven minority players in some games.

Gates Brown had only 14 at-bats in the first month of the '69 season. And starting pitcher Earl Wilson was the only other Black player on the team.

My mother and father had taught me not to think in racial terms, to view people for what they stood for rather than for the color of their skin. But it began to gnaw at me that Detroit, a city with a large Black population, had only three Black players on the team. There were certainly

119

Black players in the organization—particularly Les Cain, Wayne Redmond, and Ike Brown—who were capable of playing in the big leagues.

Redmond was a talented player with some pop in his bat. He'd hit
26 home runs for Montgomery in the Class AA Southern League in
1968, and showed plenty of promise. I never thought he received a true
opportunity to make the big leagues. Redmond was a minister, and back
then I remember it was suggested that his religion held him back. But
would they have said that if he were White?

Just the mere fact that we have to wonder whether race held him back
says to me that even by 1969 we hadn't come far enough yet.

To be honest, I never felt a hint of racism with my Tigers teammates.
We were a family, and I believed that most of those guys would've done
anything for me, and I would have done anything for them. Gates Brown,
Earl Wilson, and I were in the middle of every social event, and none of
us ever felt out of place for a minute in our clubhouse or when we were
with the guys. General manager Jim Campbell was like a second father to
me, and I certainly didn't view him as a racist. But certainly there was a
sentiment in baseball, specifically among the Black players, that in some
organizations a Black player had to be much better than a White player
to make the team. Ties always went to the White player.

Back when I joined The Tigers, there was an outfielder in our system
named Jesse Queen. He was the best hitter I'd ever seen. He was a few
years older than I was, and I thought he was a better ballplayer than I
was. I never understood why he didn't make it to the big leagues.

"You just pay attention to what you're doing," my dad told me, "and
never mind him. There must be a reason why he hasn't made it."

Was it the color of his skin? I didn't know. Just like I didn't know
why the Tigers still didn't have many Black players. Near the one-year
anniversary of Dr. King's death in April of 1969, those discrimination
issues began to dance in my mind. Just six months before this, African
Americans Tommie Smith and John Carlos won the gold and bronze
medals, respectively, in the 200-meter run at the Mexico City Olympics.
At the awards ceremony, they bowed their heads and gave the Black
Power salute during the national anthem, raising their fists in the air to

protest racism in America. Black athletes all over were feeling that more needed to be done. I know I began to feel that way.

By mid-May 1969, I was in a 2-for-24 slump and fans were booing me. All my thoughts, issues, frustrations, and convictions boiled over on May 15, 1969, when I walked out on the Tigers in the middle of a game against the Chicago White Sox at Tiger Stadium. Apparently, in the sixth inning, after left-handed sinkerball specialist Tommy John struck me out for the second time, I dropped my bat in the middle of the infield and walked slowly to my position in left field.

When the White Sox had been retired, I went through the dugout straight to the clubhouse, showered, and left the ballpark. Reportedly, Norm Cash and Gates Brown tried to convince me to stay, but I wasn't listening to whatever they had to say.

The reason I say "apparently" is because I really don't remember doing any of that. In fact, a day after it happened, I still didn't remember doing it. It was front-page news in Detroit when I also didn't show up for the team flight to Minneapolis the next day. Manager Mayo Smith suspended me $340 per day, based on my salary of $60,000.

Although Detroit had talented sportswriters, no one was able to dig up the true story of my departure because I didn't tell anyone. Everyone focused on my slump, or whether the boos had simply overwhelmed me. Reporters talked to Cash about how he had handled the boos over the years. Some suggested that I was "oversensitive."

Channel 4 reporter Al Ackerman had reported that I was unhappy with Tigers management and that I wanted to be traded. When I heard that, tears welled up in my eyes, because I never wanted to be traded—never even thought about being traded. This was my city, and I came up with most of the guys on that team. They were like family to me, and I didn't want to leave them.

Maybe the boos stunned me a bit because we had just won the World Series seven months before. And clearly I was disappointed in my performance because I wanted to help the team more than I was. I hit .285 in 1968, and when I left the team in May of '69, my average was .213.

My buddy Gates Brown was quoted as saying, "I don't think any of us really knew what was going on inside Willie. He seems like a mild, easygoing person, but he keeps things bottled up."

An article in the *Detroit Free Press* did suggest there were racial issues bubbling beneath the surface. Managing editor Frank Angelo wrote:

*"There is one aspect to this attempt to understand the Horton incident which none of his friends wanted to discuss, but which cannot be overlooked. Willie is a Negro. He's fully aware of the civil rights fight.*

*"He is the only Negro who is a Tiger regular outside the pitching staff and being as sensitive as he is, it is also certain that he feels there is even greater pressure on him to succeed.*

*"The fact that living arrangements at Lakeland were not the best as far as he and other Negroes on the team were concerned undoubtedly triggered other thoughts about his role as an athlete and a Negro.*

*"Put those personal concerns together with a horrendous batting slump, a desperate desire to win, and general overall sensitiveness, and you have the makings for this phase of the Willie Horton story."*

The mere fact that the story still referred to Blacks as "Negroes" should illustrate that the civil rights fight was still ongoing in 1969.

Although Angelo's story had the element of truth, he didn't have the whole story. What Angelo didn't know was that when I had walked away from the team, I had asked for a meeting with owner John Fetzer and GM Jim Campbell to discuss why there weren't more Black players on the Tigers' roster.

The two of them listened and acknowledged my point. No promises were made. "You can't change things overnight, Willie," Campbell said. "It takes time."

I was away from the team for four days. When I returned, I told reporters that there were no racial issues. The *Free Press* quoted me as saying, "I don't want any trouble to come out of this.... I believe every man is a man and we can live together. It doesn't have anything to do with racial issues."

It was necessary to say that because I'd received some nasty telegrams. This was nothing new to me. Since I arrived in the major leagues, I heard racial slurs raining down from the outfield stands. I had received hate mail and even death threats. One man was actually arrested for making threats against my family. I never wanted it publicized because I was afraid it would just fuel even more trouble. You didn't want to admit to the hate-mongers that they could get to you, because that would only encourage them.

That's why I had to say that there weren't any racial issues connected to my departure in 1969. Some of the mail was so hateful that my first wife, Patricia, fainted because of all of the stress. My son, Darryl, found her lying on the floor one day when he got up to go to school.

When I returned to the lineup in Detroit for the first time, 25,990 fans cheered loudly when I was introduced. I received more applause when I singled in my first at-bat. Mickey Lolich fanned 16 batters to break Paul Foytack's 13-year-old strikeout record, and we beat California 6–3. Soon the focus was back on the pennant race and not on me.

After talking to Campbell, I felt as if a weight had been removed from my shoulders.

A month later, without any fanfare, a 27-year-old Black infielder named Ike Brown was promoted to the Tigers, and he ended up playing parts of six major league seasons. Before his promotion, Ike had never been given an opportunity to play in the majors, even though he played seven years in the Tigers' minor league organization.

He could play several different positions, and he was one of the strongest men I'd ever known. You wanted him on your side in a team fight.

"But when we get into a fight," I told Ike, "keep your glasses on because you can't see shit without them."

Ike could talk some trash. He would let the other team know that we came to the field whether it was in a fight or a ball game. He kept everyone on their toes.

I can't say for sure whether my discussion with Fetzer and Mr. Campbell played a role in the decision to promote Ike. But I certainly know that I made Mr. Campbell think about the situation. It didn't change overnight, but I could feel a difference.

In August 1970, infielder Kevin Collins joined the team, and he started rooming with the Gator. I think that was the first instance of a Black Tiger and a White Tiger rooming together on the road. In 1972,

I started to room with Frank Howard. By then I don't think anyone gave it a second thought. "Big Daddy" and I were great friends, and he used to help me organize our barbecues in spring training.

As close as we were on that 1968 Tigers team, maybe I should have roomed with Mickey Stanley or Wayne Comer or Jon Warden or one of the other White players. I'm sure it would've been accepted, but it never occurred to me that I needed to do that. By 1969, I had started to think it was important that we push away the last traces of racism in the sport.

In my basement at home today is a montage of newspaper stories and pictures about Hank Aaron and his chase of Babe Ruth's record of 714 home runs. When Aaron was in the midst of that chase in 1973 and 1974, I carried those clippings on every road trip. Everyone in baseball knew what Aaron was going through. The threats he received were undoubtedly scary for his family. But I was proud of Hank, and it made me feel strong to carry those stories.

The Black men who played in the major leagues in the 1950s and early 1960s were pioneers in the truest sense of the word. They blazed trails, cut through barricades, and cleared away debris to make a clear path for Black players who followed them. Maybe they weren't all great ballplayers, but they were all exceptional men, rich in fortitude and strong of spirit. They had pride in the face of prejudice. And they had the mental toughness and survival skills necessary to play at a time when owners demanded that both uniforms and players be all White. In that era, Black players endured taunts, threats, and isolation, just to be part of a group that acted as if it didn't want them. They did it because they loved the game—and because they knew that a Black man should have the same right to live his dream as a White man has. These were indeed exceptional men.

By my last full season in Detroit in 1976, there were three Black players getting regular playing time—Ron LeFlore, my good friend Alex Johnson, and me—plus three other minority players in the starting lineup—Panamanian Ben Oglivie, Mexican Aurelio Rodríguez, and Puerto Rican Pedro García.

To this day, I'm glad I made a stand in 1969. It was payment for the debt I owed to Robinson, Doby, Bruton, Wood, and all of the other

Black players who put up with the abuse to allow me to wear a major league uniform.

The strength that I received from those Black players wasn't mine to keep. It was a gift I had to share with others. And after I met with Fetzer and Campbell in May 1969, I felt as if I'd done my part.

# Chapter 13

# Beanballs and Billy

For years, left-handed pitcher Rich Hinton assumed I was angry with him for drilling me in the eye socket with a fastball. But despite the beaning, I believed that Hinton actually saved my life.

Hinton was a rookie making his first major league start for the Chicago White Sox on Friday, August 27, 1971, when a heater sailed on him in the bottom of the third inning. He clearly knew he'd uncorked a wild one because he sounded an alarm the instant he released the pitch.

"It got away from me!" he screamed.

It was a night game, but as I stepped into the batter's box to face Hinton, a bit of twilight still peeked into the ballpark. I never saw the ball clearly, but I recall hearing Hinton's warning yelp, and I reacted by dipping and turning my head to the left. Had I not reacted to Hinton's warning, the 85 to 88 mph pitch could've struck me right on the temple. When you don't pick up the ball right away, you're in serious trouble. Usually I would've turned away to the right and fallen back at the same time. That movement also might've put the ball on a direct path to my temple. For some reason, I turned left and it struck me in the right eye.

Eight years later, when I joined the Seattle Mariners, Hinton and I actually became teammates. When we were introduced, he seemed to be concerned about how I was going to react to him. I told him that my attempts to contact him after the incident were simply to thank him for warning me. In my stance, I crowded the plate, and pitchers habitually put me on the ground. I knew who was throwing at me and who wasn't. I was confident that Hinton's pitch got away from him.

Dr. Clarence Livingood, our team physician, theorized in the local newspapers that the pitch might've also just nicked the visor of my helmet, which had slowed the ball's velocity enough to prevent permanent eye damage. My eye was grotesquely swollen, and my face looked as if I had resumed my boxing career and gone 10 rounds with Muhammad Ali. Although there were no broken bones, there was nerve damage that required surgery. Livingood wouldn't even offer an opinion about how long I'd be out of action, and manager Billy Martin only told the press that it would be longer than 10 days.

It was close to a month before I returned to the lineup, and even then I had some fear. I had reasons to be scared about my career. Seven weeks before, Tony Conigliaro, then playing for the California Angels, had called an early morning press conference to announce his retirement because of deteriorating eyesight—the result of a 1967 beaning.

In 1982, Conigliaro, 37, suffered a massive heart attack. And at age 45, he died of pneumonia in 1990. But at age 19 in 1964, he hit 24 home runs as a rookie outfielder for the Boston Red Sox. The following year, he jacked out 32 round-trippers to capture the A.L. home run crown at age 20. At 22, he became the youngest player ever to hit 100 career home runs. But on August 18, 1967, Tony C. was struck in the face by a fastball from California Angels pitcher Jack Hamilton at Fenway Park. There's a famous *Sports Illustrated* cover with Conigliaro's disfigured face on the cover. His cheekbone was fractured and his eyesight was damaged so badly he missed the entire 1968 season. He was able to come back and play for a couple of seasons, but his injury had long-term consequences. His improvement turned out to be only temporary.

The season before Hinton beaned me, on May 31, 1970, Baltimore Orioles center fielder Paul Blair was carried off the field in Anaheim after suffering a broken nose and several facial fractures when he was hit by a pitch from Angels reliever Ken Tatum.

Blair was an improving player who had batted .285 with 26 home runs in 1969. But after his beaning, Blair just wasn't the same hitter. That was clear to everyone in baseball. As I started my recovery, I couldn't help but think of Blair and Conigliaro. It was worrisome. That's why I'm thankful, even today, that Billy Martin was my manager that season. But at the time, I was angry with his approach to my injury.

Injuries are just part of baseball. Right before Hinton's pitch found my face, I had just returned to the lineup after missing a week with an injured wrist. And in 1970, my season ended in late July because of torn ankle ligaments. Those injuries were easily resolved. When the injury healed, I played again. But this injury involved psychological bruising as well as nerve damage. Shortly after the beaning I worried that I might not see pitches clearly ever again.

Martin, to his credit, pushed me to return to the lineup quickly. Twenty-nine days after the beaning, I went 3-for-3 in my return against the Yankees on September 25 at Tiger Stadium. I ended up playing the last four games of the season. Truthfully, I was furious with Martin at the time because I felt that he was forcing me into the lineup before I was ready. I resented his actions.

At the time of the beaning, I was flirting with .300 for the season. But when I ended the season with an 0-for-11 slump to drop my average under .290, I wondered if Billy knew what he was doing.

Not until Martin insisted that I play winter ball in Florida did it occur to me that my skipper was actually trying to speed up my recovery. Veterans just didn't go to winter ball. But Martin realized that if I didn't regain my comfort level in the batter's box, I was going to think about the beaning all winter. No one talked about sports psychology in those days, but Martin was clearly trying to get my mind ready for the 1972 season. Everyone knows the old adage that if you're thrown from a horse you have to climb back on it as soon as possible. But that idea really didn't mean much to me until Martin insisted that I face as much live pitching as possible before the 1972 season.

What I know today is that 0-for-11 slump at the end of the 1971 season—and my winter ball at-bats—might've been some of the most important at-bats of my career. Even if I'd had an 0-for-50 slump to end the season, I'd feel the same way today.

Martin understood that he had to be tough on me to help me feel normal again. Not only did Martin insist that I play winter ball, he came to Florida with me. His favorite coach and good friend, Art Fowler, was also down there working to reconstruct my swing. The two of them forced me to take batting practice with a barrel around my chest because they wanted me to stand straighter in my stance to give me a better look at the pitch. At first, they wanted me to wear a helmet with an earflap, but I couldn't get comfortable with that. By standing straighter, they convinced me that I would never again lose sight of a pitch.

When I look back on my major league career, I think that Billy Martin was the smartest manager I knew. No manager was willing to sacrifice more to make his players better. I don't mean to suggest that I agreed with every move he made. Billy was a tyrannical manager, and he didn't send candy and flowers to his players. He was direct and confrontational. Some managers leave veteran players alone, feeling that they've proved themselves capable of being professionals. But that wasn't Billy's approach. He didn't care who you were, he would be in your face if he didn't think you were pushing yourself to achieve the standards he established for his players.

Back on August 6, 1969, Billy was managing the Minnesota Twins. And during a trip to Detroit to play us he got into an argument with his pitcher Dave Boswell behind the Lindell A.C. on Michigan Avenue. Billy punched his lights out, and two months later, he was fired. The following October, the Tigers hired him to replace Mayo Smith. Billy visited every Detroit player to discuss his expectations. Honestly, I was impressed that he came to my house and sat in my living room, rather than just sending me a letter.

Martin laid it on the line for me. He said he believed I could be a better ballplayer than I had shown in the two previous seasons. "If you play at times the way I saw you play when I managed in Minnesota, you're going to get a lot of splinters sitting on the bench," he told me.

I was already a three-time All-Star by then, and I had been a .300 hitter in 1970. I can't say I was ready to hug Martin when he laid those words on me. But over the years, I realized that Martin was always motivated by winning. He wanted his players to succeed, and if he had to offend some people along the way or hurt his own reputation to accomplish that, he was willing to pay the price.

That night, he assessed my strengths and weaknesses for me. It was such a serious conversation that I started to laugh when Martin abruptly said, "Okay, grab your coat. We're going to Gates Brown's house."

At the Gator's house, we held some serious baseball discussions about where our team was at, and then we shot pool most of the night. That was Billy Martin. When he was serious, he was like an army general addressing his troops. But when the work was done, he wanted to be one of the guys and have a good time.

If Jim Northrup were alive today, he would probably still say that he disliked Martin because Martin pushed him probably harder than anyone on the team. But I would argue that Martin made Northrup a better player because he played him against some tougher left-handers. Not wanting to be embarrassed, Northrup learned to handle those pitchers.

"You can score a run without getting a hit," Martin liked to say.

And that's the way he managed. He didn't believe that you needed three-run homers to win games. He liked the leadoff walk, a swipe of second, a ground ball to the right side of the infield, and a sacrifice fly. And in subsequent years, it came to be known as "Billy Ball." He was very tough with his pitching staff, too. He liked his pitchers to protect his hitters, and he rode all of his pitchers mercilessly about surrendering too many walks. "Walks set up big innings," Martin would say.

Billy liked to manage his team, and he never wanted anyone—even a veteran—to be comfortable with his place in the lineup. He wanted his players to believe they had to re-earn their starting positions every day,

Martin didn't hesitate to shake up his lineup. He proved that on August 13, 1972, when he put together the strangest possible lineup to shake us out of a slump. Norm Cash batted leadoff, and shortstop Eddie Brinkman, a .224 career hitter, batted cleanup. Batting third, I hit a home run and a triple. Cash had a couple of hits, too. We won, 3–2, over the Cleveland Indians.

In his three seasons as the Tigers manager, Martin was able to get under everyone's skin at one time or another. Billy and I had our issues, particularly in our first spring training in Lakeland, when we had a disagreement over what I considered an unreasonable pinch-hitting appearance he wanted me to make.

Specifically, I remember Martin telling me that if I wasn't in a game by the sixth inning, I wasn't going to play that day and I was free to finish my running ritual. My training habits were well established. Gates would drive my car to the park with my bicycle in the back. I would don army clothes and run from the Holiday Inn to the ballpark on the path around the lake. When the exhibition games moved past the sixth inning, I would do my sprints, put on a sweat suit, and ride my bike back around the lake to the hotel.

In my mind my schedule was cleared with Martin. But one day, we were playing the Los Angeles Dodgers, and after I returned to my room, coach Frank Skaff knocked on my door. "Did we win?" I asked, not thinking this was anything but a social call.

"No," said Skaff, "the game is still going on, and Billy wants you to pinch-hit,"

"Pinch-hit?" I said. "By the time you drive me back over there, the game will be over. What are you going to do? Hold the game up till we get there?"

"No, I'm not driving you," Skaff said. "Billy wants you to ride your bike back around the lake and then pinch-hit."

"Ride my bike?!" I said. "People will be home by the time I get there. I'm not going."

Billy was clearly just trying to provoke me. Forty-five minutes later, the phone rang and team president Jim Campbell was on the phone, saying he wanted to see me in his office the next morning.

Early the next day, I was in the clubhouse ready for the meeting, and Billy acted as if nothing happened. He was talking about how we had lost a tough game. He didn't say a word about my refusal to ride five miles for a pinch-hitting assignment.

When we entered his executive office, Mr. Campbell started the meeting by saying that it's important to always have good communication between the manager and the players. Clearly, Mr. Campbell could see that Martin and I somehow had our wires crossed on what was expected of me. But before Mr. Campbell could finish his statement, Martin leaped up out of his chair and threw a pipe at Mr. Campbell.

Apparently, it was a pipe that Mr. Campbell had given Martin as a gift. Billy screamed, "You can keep your pipe! No one will *ever* tell me how to run my team!"

Obviously, I didn't have anything to say, and Mr. Campbell just told me to go back to work. Martin left the team for a couple of days, and Tony Taylor was put in charge. I saw Billy in front of the hotel and tried to talk things over. He just grumbled at me and walked off. The next day, there was a knock on my door. When I opened it, Martin walked in and started talking.

"First, let me tell you that I was wrong to ask you to pinch-hit the way I did," Martin said. "But you were wrong for challenging me. When it comes to this team, you have to remember that I'm the captain of this ship, and what I say goes. I'm the one who gets fired if we don't win. I have the responsibility."

When he was done, he shook my hand, and I told him that I appreciated his effort to make peace. After that, I had a better understanding of Martin. I vowed that if I ever got the chance to manage, I'd embrace some of Martin's philosophy. You always knew where you stood with Martin.

Martin could be extremely funny, and his humor played well with the media. He was making $35,000 when he was fired by the Twins, and the Tigers gave him a raise. After the Tigers fired Martin, the Rangers gave him a hefty raise to lure him to Texas. The New York Yankees gave him even more money when they hired him. In fact, when I was coaching for Martin in New York, he'd essentially joke that if he got fired a couple more times, he was going to be the richest man in baseball.

My biggest issue with Martin came in the 1972 playoffs, when he started me in only three of the five games against the Oakland A's. I had battled injuries throughout the season, but Martin knew that I would have played through those injuries if given the chance.

We lost that best-of-five series in the last game. In Game 5, Martin left me on the bench and started Duke Sims in left field, even though Sims hadn't played left field for us and had limited major league experience there. We'd claimed Sims off waivers in August, and he played 25 games as Bill Freehan's backup catcher, plus four games relieving Kaline in right.

Gates Brown believed the Series might've turned in the ninth inning of Game 1, when Martin pulled me out of the game. The score was tied, 2–2, and we had runners on first and third with nobody out. I was due up against right-handed Rollie Fingers, but Martin decided to play the percentages and use Gator as a pinch-hitter because he hit left-handed. But Gator popped up and then Jim Northrup hit into a double play to end the inning. We ended up losing in the 11th.

No one can say what would've happened if I'd been allowed to bat for myself in that situation, but I like to think that I could've driven in that runner from third. Four years before, in the 1968 World Series, I'd proved my ability to produce in big games. If the Tigers had taken Game 1 in 1972, maybe we would've won that series.

As angered as I was by what happened in 1972, it might surprise you to know what I've said for years—that if Martin would've been our manager in the late 1960s, we might've won three or four World Series instead of just one. We weren't a broken team—or over the hill when Martin took over in 1971. But we were banged up from injuries, and I think Martin got what he could out of us, especially in '72.

In 1969, there were probably a series of factors that hurt our chances to repeat as champions. Dick McAuliffe was injured in July and was lost for the season. Our chemistry also wasn't the same. Eddie Mathews had retired, and he was missed around the clubhouse. It also was an expansion year, and the Tigers lost Jon Warden, Ray Oyler, Wayne Comer, and young pitchers Mike Marshall and Dick Drago, who could've helped us. The Tigers brass thought the expansion draft went better than expected because the team didn't lose Gates Brown or Tom Matchick, but our chemistry was certainly altered. John Wyatt also was released before the 1969 season.

Interestingly, we actually scored more runs in 1969 than we did in 1968, but we also gave up 109 more runs. Our pitching probably wasn't as sharp, and we definitely didn't play as well defensively as we did in '68. We also didn't have the same knack for coming from behind to win games. In my opinion, we weren't hungry enough. We were still celebrating our championship. We really didn't get going until August, when we were 21–9, but then we suffered through a sub-.500 September. We ended up with 90 wins that season and finished 19 games behind the Baltimore Orioles.

One of the few regrets I have about my career is that we didn't seize our opportunities for championships the way we should have. People can talk about the Oakland A's dynasty, but I thought our team was as strong, if not stronger, than the Oakland A's.

Mayo Smith might've been the right manager for us in 1968 because we were a self-starting team., We were driven to success. We didn't need a manager harping on us. But I think we would've won again in 1969 if Martin had been our manager. He wouldn't have allowed us to keep celebrating our 1968 championship. He wouldn't have let us get complacent. We needed our tails kicked in 1969, and that just wasn't Mayo's style.

Some of my teammates felt that Martin took the fun out of the game because he was such a dictator in the dugout. But I remember having plenty of good times under Martin, especially after the team acquired Frank Howard in 1972. He's the man I called "Big Daddy."

As the Tigers chased the A.L. East title in late August, management bought Frank from the Texas Rangers. He was 6'7", 255 pounds, and he certainly was as powerful as anyone who ever played the game. He had been the National League Rookie of the Year for the Los Angeles Dodgers in 1960, and his career was filled with incredible feats of power. He was one of the few men to hit a ball over Tiger Stadium's left-field roof. In 1968, while we were winning a pennant in Detroit, big Frank went on a tremendous home run binge for the Washington Senators. In one span of 20 at-bats, he hit 10 home runs. He finished with 44 that season.

From almost the minute he arrived in Detroit, Frank and I became friends. Soon, we decided to become roommates. The first day I woke up with Frank on the road, I heard him on the phone ordering room service.

"I'll need eight scrambled eggs with cheese, six pieces of toast, four milks, half an apple pie, and a couple of steaks," Frank said.

In my sleepy haze, I thought, "Man, I got myself a good roommate. He's ordering breakfast for me." Just then, he turned to me and asked, "And what do you want, Willie?"

But when I think of Frank, I think of him coming down to my Club 23. He loved playing Gladys Knight & the Pips' "Midnight Train to Georgia" on the jukebox. He'd be dancing around the club, snapping his fingers to the music, and when he snapped his fingers, it was like someone firing a .45-caliber pistol. "We're all on the last train to Georgia!" he'd say with a laugh.

When my training camp barbecue for players and fans grew too big for me to take care of it all by myself, it was Big Daddy who stepped in to help. He helped pay for some of the supplies, and he worked the grill with me in Lakeland. Frank was the strongest man I'd ever met, and he had one of the biggest hearts of anybody I'd met in baseball. He truly is a beautiful man.

Eddie Brinkman was our shortstop on that 1972 team, and he and I were tight. Remember, I had played against him as a teenager in Altoona. We had a lot of history, and we had a lot of fun together as major leaguers. People sometimes forget how well Eddie played for us during that period. In 1972, he set a league record of 72 consecutive games without an error, and that wasn't broken until Cal Ripken played 95 consecutive games without an error in 1990. "Uncle Ed," as we called him, had only seven errors that season in 156 games. And he won the Gold Glove.

He was a lifetime .224 hitter, but I thought he was actually a better hitter than even he knew. In my mind, he was a decent hitter when the game was on the line, or when there were runners in scoring position. He also had a terrific sense of humor. He hit .342 in April with a handful of extra-base hits. One day, he came into the dugout after scoring a run and tried to look exhausted. "I'm just tired from carrying you guys," he said with a grin on his face.

The Tigers could've saved some money if they'd just gotten one room for the three of us, because Eddie was always down in our room, laying on the floor. We would talk baseball till all hours of the night.

Eddie Brinkman will be most remembered for the night we captured the A.L. East. During a live television interview, he said we were all "a great [bleeping] bunch of guys."

But Eddie didn't actually say "bleeping." He uttered a word that you cannot say on television. We always kid Eddie, because if anyone else made that comment, he would've been heavily criticized. But Eddie was such a lovable guy he actually picked up some promotional appearances out of it. From what I heard, he was quite a hit on the ladies shows.

It's funny how some players can get away with non-conforming behavior because it's part of their personality and charm, while others can't. I still laugh when I remember how Gates Brown would sometimes show up at formal team gatherings with an open shirt and a big gold chain, while the rest of us were all dressed in suits. If I did that, someone from the team would have been on me. But nobody would say anything to the Gator because that was just part of his personality. He was a leader on our team, and he was a colorful character. The Tigers needed Gator to be Gator.

The Tigers finished third in 1973. Billy Martin was fired in late August because of his continuing differences with the front office. He was a non-conformist, but he wasn't a lovable character. Management had been clear to him that if they could find a reason to fire him, they would. But Martin accepted that. In fact, he told me later that if his reputation had to suffer to make his teams better, he was willing to accept that.

What I know is that he did what he thought was right to make me a better player. In fact, I believe that Martin extended my career by six or seven years. I played until 1980—much longer than others in my age group. I think I lasted as long as I did because I heeded some of the advice that Martin gave me about my conditioning and my approach to the game.

When Ralph Houk took over as manager in 1974, I thought the change might not be in my best interest. I was right. As it turned out, Ralph Houk was the reason I didn't play my entire career in a Detroit Tigers uniform.

# Chapter 14

# Goodbye, Motown

WHEN THE DETROIT TIGERS traded me to the Texas Rangers on April 12, 1977, I told the media that "it was probably the best thing for me," even though in my heart, I knew it was a lie.

The Old English "D" was a part of my life. It wasn't tattooed on my body. It was tattooed on my heart—and in my mind. When Mr. Campbell traded me, it was a shock to my system. It was like my father was disowning me.

Even though Mr. Campbell completed the deal to bring right-handed pitcher Steve Foucault and $25,000 cash to the team, I knew that the trade wasn't his idea. It was obvious to me that Ralph Houk was behind it.

What bothered me the most about leaving the Tigers was that Houk told the media he had spoken to me about embracing a new role on the team but that I "wouldn't accept the role." He told the media that he wanted me to become more of a role player, and that I had resisted. But there was no such discussion. I had no idea what Houk was thinking because he didn't communicate with me whatsoever.

I certainly understood my situation on Opening Day of 1977. Remember, I was going to be 35 at the end of the season and one by one my 1968 teammates had begun to leave, either through retirement or in trades. Al Kaline had retired after the 1974 season. Norm Cash was released on August 7, 1974, and Jim Northrup was unceremoniously sold to the Montreal Expos the same day. By the start of the 1977 season, John Hiller, Mickey Stanley, and I were the only holdovers from that World Series squad. I knew I wasn't going to play 162 games in 1977. I was hoping I might play 100 games and get close to 400 at-bats.

Houk was trying to rebuild the team, and we had a surplus of out-fielders. Ben Oglivie was on that squad, along with Ron LeFlore and

Rusty Staub. Houk also wanted to give young Steve Kemp a chance to play out there. He saw Kemp as a key building block for the future, and I could see that, too. The Tigers also had some quality infield prospects emerging, including Alan Trammell and Lou Whitaker.

But just two seasons before, I had been named the American League's Outstanding Designated Hitter after hitting .275, with 25 home runs and 92 RBIs. I thought that I'd play 100 to 105 games at DH and in the outfield in 1977, and that I'd serve as a mentor to Kemp. To be honest, I looked forward to that because I remembered how much Rocky Colavito had helped me early in my career. As a player, I felt it was important to give back to the game. And I felt it was important that I pass along the knowledge I had learned. A baseball team is like a family, and you should do what you can to guide and tutor the younger members of the family.

It's funny that on the day Houk was quoted as saying that I wouldn't accept my new role, Kemp was quoted as saying that I'd done all I could to help him become comfortable in the organization.

It was a tough situation for Kemp because he felt like he was trying to take my job. But I told him not to worry about that. He was 22; I was 34. I told him not to let the boos bother him. I told him what Colavito had told me: Fans get used to a ballplayer and appreciate him like they appreciate a comfortable pair of shoes. At first they don't think the new shoes will be as comfortable as the old ones. But sooner or later, they grow accustomed to the new shoes, and they make for a comfortable walk."

I told him that when fans boo him, it just means they care about what goes on with the team. And those who boo will cheer even louder once they get comfortable with you.

"I really like Willie," Kemp told the *Detroit Free Press* the day I was dealt. "I respect him as a person and as a player. He was a good fellow. He tried to help me. He gave me advice and he tried to give me some extra confidence. I felt he was behind me all the time."

Do Kemp's remarks give the impression that I was a man who didn't understand his role?

Any suggestion that I didn't want to stay in Detroit is simply untrue. Detroit was my city. It was my home. I had grown up in the Jeffries Projects, and I had learned to play ball on the inner-city fields. I stood on the hood of my car and spoke to a mob during the 1967 riots. I owned and operated Club 23 on Livernois, just a few miles from Tiger Stadium. Why would I want to leave the Tigers?

My relationship with Mr. Campbell might've allowed me to block that trade. But knowing Mr. Campbell the way I did, I knew that when Houk asked him to trade me, Campbell felt obligated to do so because he strongly believed that a GM must support his manager. Mr. Campbell always put the team first—even above his personal feelings. He was a man of principle.

When it came to my career, Mr. Campbell often acted as if he were my father—or at least my guardian. Maybe if I would've gone to him at the start of the 1977 season and told him how badly I wanted to stay in Detroit, he might've tried to persuade Houk that it was best to keep me around. But because I saw Mr. Campbell as a father figure, I think I wanted to prove something to him. In the back of my mind, I think I believed that if I went to Texas and had a great season, then Mr. Campbell would bring me back home.

I probably also wanted to prove to Houk that I was still a productive major leaguer. I remember thinking that I was going to Texas to do for the Rangers what I wanted to do for the Tigers in 1977. I wanted to contribute on the field as a player and as a mentor to the younger players.

To be honest, I was a bit insulted by the trade. I had played in four All-Star games, while Foucault, 27, had been a .500 pitcher in just four major league seasons. He'd signed as a third baseman, switched to catcher, and only tried pitching after suffering a serious knee injury.

Was that the best deal the Tigers could work out? When I got to Texas, I was determined to have a strong season.

I shed tears on my last day with the team, but I kept my composure the best I could for my final interview as a Tiger. The media reported that I showed no anger or bitterness. And they accurately portrayed me as more hurt than mad.

On the day the trade was announced, we were on the road in Toronto. After I was told of Campbell's decision, I returned to the field and finished batting practice. I wanted to say goodbye to my teammates, particularly Mickey Stanley, who was a very close friend.

This was what I told the media that day: "As long as I live, I will be part of the Tigers, part of Detroit. I've been a member of this organization since I was 17 years old. I'm never going to outgrow that. The Tigers and the city of Detroit are two of the most important things in my life.

"I'd be lying if I said I'm not going to miss the organization. It's been a part of me for too long. The ballpark [and] the people who work there will be a part of me until the day I die. I'll remember them wherever I go."

The late Joe Falls, then a *Detroit Free Press* columnist who would become a good friend through the years, wrote that the trade seemed pretty callous on the part of the Tigers.

"Let's come right out and say it," Falls wrote. "Willie was always more than just a ballplayer to the city of Detroit. He was the first Black star the Tigers ever had—the only one who gave the Black community a sense of pride. He was one of their own—a kid off the streets who came up the hard way and made it. Who wouldn't be proud of someone like that?"

Joe wrote that I appreciated everyone in the game, including the grounds crew. It was true that I considered most of the groundskeepers my friends. I would occasionally take them to dinner and invite them down to my club for a drink. Falls said that he admired that I left with class and didn't criticize the team. There was no temper tantrum. In the Detroit newspapers the next day I even thanked Houk for playing me in the outfield in spring training so the Rangers would know that I could still play in the outfield.

"I liked [Willie] because he had all the basic instincts of honesty, integrity, and decency," Falls wrote. "These traits were ingrained in him, and I always liked to think his parents had something to do with that. In his own way, Willie Horton was a regal man."

His words meant a lot to me. While I was proud of how I played the game, I've always known that it was more important to be judged as a man than as a player.

That's why it bothered me so much that Houk said I wouldn't accept a lesser role. I used to call him "Major Smile" because people warned me that there wasn't always truth behind his smile. But I never really believed Houk was like that until the moment I was traded.

Before I left the Tigers clubhouse in Toronto that afternoon, I shook hands with everyone, reserving my firmest grip for Steve Kemp. "Remember what I told you," I said. "Just relax."

In the sports world, trades often are boiled down to one line in the transactions column in the newspaper. But they are truly traumatic events to the players involved. Your family, your business relationships, and essentially your life is thrown into chaos.

Club 23 had become a fixture in the community. After I opened it, I wanted someone to help manage the business, so I turned to a former classmate at Northwestern High School. Her name was Gloria Reid. In high school, I had run around with her brother Sam, and she didn't like me initially because she thought I was keeping Sam out too late and getting him into trouble. But I had always been impressed with the way Gloria carried herself. She had gotten herself a good job at Ford, and I remember when I asked her to work for me, she said, "I don't know anything about running a club."

But she took the job, and she worked with my friends Donald Wayne Neeley and Bob Reynolds to turn Club 23 into a successful operation. I was very proud of my club. Many of the players from other teams would visit when they were in Detroit, and it became a regular hangout for airline pilots. People from Wayne State University would come over. We served good food. One of our specialties was the "Boomer Burger," named to honor one of my many nicknames. My sister Virginia worked at the club and made many of these Boomer Burgers. When Magic Johnson was in high school playing summer basketball at St. Cecilia, he would come into Club 23 for a Boomer Burger. And on the night of the 1971 All-Star Game in Detroit, there was a long, long line to get into my place.

People knew me because I was a ballplayer, but Club 23 also reminded people that I was a Detroiter. We worked with other businesses in the area to help teenagers find jobs because unemployment was high in those years. We also bought tickets to take local kids down to Tiger Stadium.

One day in 1978, Mayor Coleman Young came into Club 23 looking for me. He said he needed my help to calm down a mob that had formed in protest of the shooting of a Black youth by a White bar owner on Livernois. The bar owner had come across some kids breaking into a car. As it turned out, the youngster who was killed had actually stolen my wife's car—twice.

But when a mob of 700 people formed on Livernois around that bar, Mayor Young was concerned that another riot would break out. When he asked me to come out and address the crowd, I did it because this was my home. There was some looting in the area and some property damage. And one man was badly beaten. But Mayor Young's approach seemed to work, because the few hours of violence didn't evolve into a full-scale riot.

We made money on Club 23, and I probably would've made more if I'd listened to Gloria. I always put money back into the business when I should've been putting more money in the bank. Gloria started out as the manager, but over time, she became a companion—and then my wife. And that was the best decision I've ever made.

When I was traded, I knew that Club 23 wasn't going to be able to survive. Gloria was crucial to the business—but she was coming with me to Texas. There are so many details to deal with when you're traded. For instance, my sister Ruth and her husband—I called him Mr. Robey—used to attend every Tigers game. I'd leave them tickets at the box office, and they'd just walk on over from the Jeffries Projects. Suddenly, I was worried about how they were going to attend the games. But my teammate Ben Oglivie immediately said he'd take care of them.

Oglivie and I only played together for three full seasons, but we became the best of friends. The Tigers had a habit of having new players room with me, and when "Benji" came over from the Boston Red Sox for Dick McAuliffe, we hit it off right away. We had very different approaches to physical fitness, which was quite interesting at first. Remember, this was 1974. And when I woke up one morning to see Benji on the floor with his legs crossed doing meditation and yoga, it scared me.

"He was exercising by lifting himself on two fingers!" I remember telling Bill Behm.

Actually, it was Benji who got me thinking about the role proper nutrition plays in an athlete's conditioning. Benji was 6'2" and weighed 160 pounds. My diet wasn't as strict as his, but I began to think about eating less fried food and more vegetables. By the end of my career, I was probably in better shape than I was at the beginning. In fact, during my final two seasons in the major leagues, my playing weight was 210 pounds.

It was hard saying goodbye to Ben Oglivie. But considering his approach, I certainly wasn't surprised that he played until he was 37 years old—of that he had some great seasons late in his career, hitting 41 home runs one season for the Brewers.

You'd think it would've been hardest to say goodbye to my teammates. But it was also hard saying goodbye to the support personnel—like the members of the ground crew, and certainly Bill Behm.

Bill had been taking care of me since I signed my first professional contract, and we had some funny moments together over the years—like the first time I chewed tobacco in the outfield. I ended up vomiting in left field. Behm had a birth defect that caused him to limp, but no one hustled out on the field to tend to his players with more urgency than Bill. When he saw me get sick, he raced out there like an Olympic sprinter. He might've given my old Northwestern classmate Henry Carr a run for his money that day.

"Willie, what's the matter?" Behm asked.

"I swallowed my chewing tobacco and threw up," I said.

"You have to be careful that you don't accidentally swallow it," Behm said.

"You mean I'm not supposed to swallow it?" I asked, incredulously. "Nobody told me that."

Behm laughed so hard that the game was held up a couple of minutes longer than it should've been.

Another funny moment came in 1968 when I re-injured my Achilles tendon chasing a fly ball. When I went down in a heap and didn't get up, Mayo Smith and Behm both sprinted out of the dugout toward the outfield.

Along the way, Mayo pulled his hamstring and went down like he'd been shot. Behm had to stop and treat Mayo, and he eventually ended up helping carry Mayo off the field. Meanwhile I was left lying in the outfield. My teammates all had a good laugh about that one.

When you're saying goodbye to your friend, you remember all the laughs you had with them. And saying goodbye to the people at Tiger

Stadium was like saying goodbye to my family. Remember, I had worked at the stadium when I was a kid and essentially had been around the corner of Michigan and Trumbull for two decades.

As sad as I was, I took some comfort in the knowledge that I was going to a team that wanted me. Some members of the media wondered where I was going to play for the West Division–contending Rangers because they had recently acquired Claudell Washington from the Oakland A's, presumably to play left field. They had two right-handed designated hitters in John Ellis and Tom Grieve.

But I knew they didn't trade for me so I could sit on the bench. Having gone through a trying experience with the non-communicative Ralph Houk, I went to manager Frank Lucchesi when I got to Texas and told him I was ready for whatever role he had for me, and that I wanted to help the young players as much as I could.

This was a young, hungry ballclub, and I was excited about playing for a team that believed it could win. Somehow that season, the Rangers found 519 at-bats for me, including more than 400 as the cleanup hitter. I batted .348 in May, hitting safely in 17 of 24 games that month. In one game against Kansas City, I walloped three home runs and had five RBIs in a 7–3 win at Royals Stadium.

After some games, I'd call Mr. Campbell and tell him to "check the box score" the next day in the paper. I called Mr. Campbell often that season, and not because I wanted to razz him. In my heart, I knew he was following my performances as if I was still playing for him. I knew that he cared what happened to me. I think he was as proud as I was that I helped the Rangers win 94 games that season. That was 20 more wins than the Tigers had under Houk. I finished the season hitting .289 for Texas, including .313 on the road.

In retrospect, it was one of the best seasons of my career. I really enjoyed playing with the Rangers. And I think we might've won the Western Division if management hadn't fired Lucchesi on June 22. In spring training, Texas infielder Lenny Randle attacked Lucchesi after being benched. Lucchesi suffered a fractured cheekbone, and ended up suing Randle as well. I can't help but think that this had something to do with the firing because we 'd just won 10 of 13 games when Lucchesi was canned.

Eddie Stanky, 60, replaced Lucchesi. Stanky promptly quit a day later, either because he was homesick or because he didn't like the "modern player." Both were given as his reasons for leaving. Connie Ryan filled in as interim manager, and then six days later we got Billy Hunter, the former St. Louis Browns and New York Yankees infielder. He decided to conduct spring-training-style practices right then during the hot Texas summer. We finished eight games behind the Royals in the West, and to be honest, we were a tired team by the end of the season.

I really didn't think much about Houk until the moment in 1979 that I became the 43rd major leaguer to hit 300 career home runs. The two-run shot came off Tigers ace right-hander Jack Morris. The blow was a big deal in Seattle because they hadn't had much history yet. Just before my next at-bat, they stopped the game and brought out a fourth-grader who had caught the ball—and he gave it to me.

I remember when I was rounding the bases after hitting number 300. I thought about my major league career. And after the game, I told the media that I dedicated that home run to Mr. Campbell and to Ralph Houk.

Years later, I ran into Houk at an Upper Deck Legends game, and I politely told him there was something I wanted to get off my chest. I told him there were no hard feelings, but I was curious to know why he had told the media that I wouldn't accept my role, when in fact, he had never even said a word to me about what he expected from me.

In the newspaper, Houk said he had explained to me that I was going to be a part-time player.

In fact, I don't believe he said 50 words to me the entire time we were together in Detroit.

Gates Brown told me that Ralph gave him the same story about me not wanting to be a part-time player. I had to tell Gator that conversation never happened.

I was in my thirties and I was willing to give back to the organization. As I said, like Rocky Colavito, Kaline, and Gator did for me, I wanted to mentor Kemp. I liked being his role model.

When I ended up playing in Texas and Seattle, I did everything I could to help the younger players.

After I confronted Houk, he stuttered, stammered, and eventually said that he'd been misquoted. It was hard for me to believe. I didn't think he was being straight with me—just as he hadn't been straight with me in 1977.

I have one theory about why Houk didn't like me or appreciate my abilities: Once, when we were playing the Yankees when Houk was managing, we had a melee. I picked Ralph out of the crowd and pushed into the dugout. I have no idea whether that had anything to do with our issues in Detroit, but it was odd that Houk never talked to me in Detroit.

After my last full season with Houk in 1976, I began to think about how I'd approach managing if I was ever given the opportunity. I was sure I'd communicate better with my players than Houk ever did. I figured I'd manage like a combination of Charlie Dressen, Casey Stengel, and Billy Martin.

If given the chance, I would demand as much from players as Martin did. I would push them to be the best players they could be. But I wanted to be more of a teacher. I wanted to motivate, inspire, and encourage younger players as Dressen had done for me. And I wanted to have good rapport with my players the way Stengel did all those years. I never played for him, but it was clear that Casey Stengel got along with his players. I believed I could be a good manager if given the chance. What I didn't know was that I would be managing in just two years.

# Chapter 15

# My Other World Series

WHEN A RINGING TELEPHONE wakes you up at three o'clock in the morning, it's usually not good news. But the pre-dawn call I got on November 4, 1978, was a mixed blessing. My friend Cookie Rojas had been forced to resign as manager of the Valencia Magallanes in the Venezuelan League, and team owners wanted to talk to me immediately.

The fact that I was playing in the Venezuelan winter league at age 36 just goes to show what a strange journey the 1978 season had been for me. Cookie's mandate with the Magallanes had been to assemble a roster capable of winning the Caribbean World Series. But that was no easy task because everybody plays quality baseball in that part of the world. They just love their baseball down there, and Valencia's park was always packed when we played. The winter-league rosters are always full of promising major leaguers. The pitching is good, and the hitters are better. There are no easy games in the Venezuelan League.

At the start of the winter season, it looked as if Rojas had picked the right players to do the job. Major leaguers Jerry White, Tim Blackwell, Mitchell Page, and Rodney Scott were on our team, along with a solid-hitting minor leaguer named Dave Coleman. Mike Norris was also on the pitching staff. We looked impressive early on, launching our season with a lengthy winning streak. I was hitting over .300 and I enjoyed mentoring the younger players.

But then the Magallanes suffered one of those inexplicable losing streaks. One loss became two, two became three, and when a slump hits four or five, everyone starts to tighten up. Given the expectation that management had placed on Rojas, it seemed that there'd be a shake-up. We figured the lineup would be juggled, and maybe we'd sign a new player or two.

But when the team's directors rousted me from a sound sleep in the middle of the night, I didn't know what to expect. They summoned me to the office immediately, and before the sun came up, they'd offered me the manager's job. This came as quite a surprise. Pablo Penton, one of the owners of the team, would tell me later that the board of directors had debated whether to "go back to the States" to hire an experienced manager or to hire me. They decided on me because they believed I had good rapport with the players. Apparently, Rojas had also recommended me as he was headed out the door, and they respected him, even though our talented team was now at .500 for the season after 20 games.

Initially, I had reservations about taking the job because I felt indebted to Cookie. He'd given me the opportunity to play in Venezuela at a time when I really needed it—for a variety of reasons.

It wasn't an easy decision to replace him because I honestly felt that he was saving my life in Venezuela. I still tell him that today. Cookie brought me down there and took care of me when I was going through the strangest time of my career. And as it turned out, my Venezuelan managerial experience was one of the highlights of my career.

The 1978 major league season had been rough on me. First the Rangers shocked me with a trade to the Cleveland Indians during spring training. Then the Indians released me over the Fourth of July weekend. I was out of work 10 days when the Oakland A's signed me. I thought I'd found a new home. When I got there, the A's were a few games over .500, and analyzing the division race, it seemed that a team would win the A.L. West with fewer than 90 wins.

I distinctly remember telling A's owner Charlie Finley that if we could deal for another big bat—like Toronto's Rico Carty, who was rumored to be available—I felt we could contend. I got off to a good start in Oakland, batting over .300. We also had Mitchell Page (who would later join me in Venezuela), and a 24-year-old kid with a lot of promise named Tony Armas. With some good breaks, I felt like we could really make some noise. I was sure of it.

Then a few weeks later—just as I suggested—the A's actually did trade for Carty. But who did they send to last-place Toronto in return? A minor league pitcher named Phil Huffman—and me. After hitting

.314 with Oakland, I went to Toronto and hit only about .200 there. But that wasn't the worst of my troubles.

Before a Blue Jays game against the Tigers in Toronto, my three sons were involved in a frightening altercation outside Exhibition Stadium. An overflowing crowd was jamming into the game, and there was congestion near the players' parking lot. To this day, I'm not sure exactly how the event unfolded, but my wife, Gloria, remembers that some bystanders made unseemly remarks to my sons and words were exchanged. A fight ensued. Gloria had my daughters with her, and she was trying to protect them. She was screaming. Someone tried to lead her inside to safety, but she wouldn't leave us.

"Those are my boys and my husband," she said, and handed off the girls to a woman, who took them inside.

As I was making my way over to help my boys, a member of the Royal Canadian Mounted Police—on horseback—saw me running toward the melee and thought I was planning to join the fight. Presumably, he didn't know I played for the Blue Jays, but either way, he struck me upside the head with a billy club. Then his horse reared up and came down on my son Deryl Lamar's foot, breaking it.

Not knowing who'd hit me, I turned around and slugged the horse. For the next month, people all around baseball were talking about how Willie Horton knocked out a horse. I don't know if I knocked him out, but the horse went down. Blood was running down my head. Two of my sons, Darryl William and Al, were standing back-to-back, fighting against the crowd. I had bats in the trunk of my car and the danger level was high enough that I thought about getting them.

"Don't let Willie get those bats!" Gloria said. It was certainly one of the scariest moments I've ever experienced—maybe scarier than the night I addressed the mob during the 1967 riots.

Finally, a Blue Jays executive arrived, informed the police that I was a ballplayer, and we were escorted into the building. But the ordeal wasn't over. As the doctor began to examine my injuries, we realized the police had handcuffed my sons and were trying to cart them off to jail. It took some time to untangle the mess.

Apparently, I kept telling Gloria I was fine, but I really wasn't. At the hospital, doctors told me that I'd suffered a concussion, but it was far more severe than anyone realized. Over the next few weeks, my vision was hazy and people were telling me that my mind wasn't right. Sometimes I was disoriented—and depressed. Other times I would be angry. I would be in the outfield, but I couldn't maintain my focus. When the season was over, I was trying to drive from Toronto to Detroit and I ended up in Cleveland in front of the ballpark. That's when I knew my brain wasn't functioning properly. Today, I'd probably be diagnosed with post-concussion syndrome. No one called it that then, and the treatments that were prescribed didn't seem to work.

What seemed to bring me back to reality was my decision to play winter ball.

When that brutal 1978 season was over, I didn't know what my baseball future would be.

When Pablo Penton and his manager, Cookie Rojas, suggested that I travel to Venezuela to play a 60-game winter ball season for the Valencia Magallanes, it seemed like a good idea. Penton was also a scout for the Oakland A's and knew my reputation. They were willing to pay me $5,000 per month, plus bonuses and living accommodations in a nice condominium. Retirement was a possibility for me at that point, but I thought that if I played well enough down there, some major league team would sign me before spring training.

Usually players with more than three years of major league experience aren't allowed to play in winter ball unless they're natives to that country. But Penton, a part-owner and vice president of the team, petitioned Major League Baseball commissioner Bowie Kuhn to let me play, on the basis that I was trying to recover from my concussion. Kuhn gave his blessing, and soon, Gloria and I were on our way to Venezuela, along with our daughters, Pam and Gail.

My friend Louis Burrell had to stay with me all the time because I would want to go running in the middle of the night. Cookie helped me re-train my mind. In fact, he trained me like a racehorse. He just worked with me all the time. And even after he was fired as our manager, he told me that he wanted me to have the job.

To be honest, I don't think the Magallanes realized that I had some very strong ideas about managing, even though I'd never managed before. The board of directors was surprised at some of my moves and shocked by my opinions on personnel moves, too, especially when I told them I didn't want to add a major league All-Star shortstop to the team as we headed to the Caribbean World Series.

Management also looked at me a little funny when I went in and asked them to give my native Venezuelan players more money because I felt they were underpaid.

"You're like a labor union leader," Pablo said to me.

"You have to give these boys what they deserve, and you have to keep them happy," I said. "You can't just take care of the star players. You have to spend time with each of them."

According to league rules, you had to play three native players at all times, and I always felt it was important to make sure the native players realized how much I valued their contributions. I also wanted to make sure the role players felt needed.

Pablo's a dear friend of mine today, and we still laugh about the time I decided to insert a pinch-hitter—a guy named Raphael Escalona—for myself, with the winning run at second in an important game. Escalona was a backup catcher and hadn't yet distinguished himself as a player when I made the move.

In my mind, it was the right moment to motivate Escalona. I figured if we were to win the Caribbean World Series, he might need to be a key player. And I also felt that some of the native players needed a morale boost. I also wanted to see what Escalona was made of.

After making that move, I had to pass the owners' box seats as I walked back to the dugout.

"Are you crazy, Willie?" Pablo asked. "What are you doing?"

"I know what I'm doing," I told him.

Fortunately for me, Escalona smashed a triple and we won the game. And as the season progressed, he became a more confident player and an important player for our team.

What's interesting about my player/manager job is that once I accepted it, my mind began to become sharp again, and I started to emerge from the fog of my concussion. It was almost as if the added responsibility forced my mind to heal itself and deal with the extra workload.

The Magallanes went on a roll after I took over and we made up ground quickly. We won the regular season and playoff crown. And after we won our league title there was plenty of excitement about our possibility of winning the Caribbean World Series, which was held that year in Puerto Rico. In that part of the world, the Caribbean World Series is as important as our World Series. Even today, Caribbean World Series games are broadcast on Spanish-speaking stations in Miami and other parts of the United States with a large Hispanic population.

The Caribbean World Series dates back to 1949, and Venezuela was one of the original competitors. Many top major leaguers have played in the tournament. Through the years, the Caribbean World Series has included major leaguers Don Zimmer (1955), Earl Battey (1958), Tommy Davis (1960), Manny Mota (1971), Carlos May (1972), Bobby Valentine (1973), and even my old Tigers teammate Norm Cash. Cash played for the Venezuela team that finished second in 1959, and he's best remembered for hitting two home runs and driving in eight during the tournament.

Rules also allow teams to pick up three native players for the tournament, and the Magallanes management wanted me to add Cincinnati Reds shortstop Davey Concepción. By then, Concepción had already been a regular National League All-Star. He'd won four Gold Gloves and had hit .300 that season. Many people thought that he was the best shortstop in the game during the 1970s.

But I told the owners I didn't want Concepción because we had a young native shortstop in Alexis Ramírez, who had blossomed into one of our top players. I couldn't look him in the eye and tell him I was benching him because we could sign Concepción. It wouldn't have been fair to Ramírez.

Owners were upset by my decision. We had an intense argument over the Concepción issue. Likewise, I disagreed with management about how we should've handled the situation when a couple of our star players, Mitchell Page and Rodney Scott, wanted to go home for Christmas. To me, it didn't seem fair that some players could go home and others could not. My position was that if Page and Scott left, I didn't want them coming back.

"We're all on this ship together," I told Mitchell and Rodney, "and nobody jumps ship when we're still sailing."

Pablo begged me to take them back, and eventually I relented, but I made no promises about how I would play them. I didn't start either one of them in the first two games of the playoffs—not bringing them in until the fifth or sixth inning. I think the other players respected me for that decision. Mitchell and Rodney were young men then, and they still had some growing up to do. Later, they would tell me they appreciated my approach with them. Imported players wanted more relaxed rules in winter ball, but I had a stringent set of rules for our team, and no one was exempt from them.

Essentially, I made good on my promise to myself that my managerial type would be a blend of Billy Martin, Charlie Dressen, and Casey Stengel. I thought I was tough when I had to be, much like Billy. But I came to the park early every day to work with the young players. I talked to them and tried to give them confidence. I told them stories like Dressen did. And I tried to keep the clubhouse loose like Casey did.

We didn't have Tim Blackwell to catch for us in the Caribbean World Series, because he only signed a contract until December. Apparently, Rojas had been anticipating signing another catcher late in the season, but that catcher backed out. Blackwell agreed to extend his stay until after the playoffs, but he wouldn't go to the Caribbean World Series. We ended up using major leaguer Bo Díaz at catcher.

The Caribbean World Series includes the top teams from the Dominican Republic, Puerto Rico, Venezuela, and Mexico. You play each team twice, and the team with the best record is declared the champion.

In the opener, New York Mets pitcher Nino Espinosa beat us, 1–0, on a two-hitter, and the board of directors was nervous. "Don't worry," I said. "We're going to win this thing." And we did.

We didn't lose another game. Page wrapped it up for us when he hit a three-run homer in the ninth inning to beat Mexico's Enrique Romo, 9–6, to win the final game. Romo pitched for the Pittsburgh Pirates. We had to win that game, too, because if we lost, we would've been tied with the Dominican Republic. If there had been a tie, we would've had a playoff game—and we were out of pitchers.

Much to my delight, Alexis Ramírez hit over .300 for me and played flawless shortstop. He was the runner-up in voting for the top short-stop in the tournament. That was important for me, because I'm not sure they would've let me back into Venezuela if we would've lost that series. Everyone had questioned my decision not to take Concepción. But White batted .522 in the series, and Page drove in 11 runs. He was simply amazing.

Obviously, winning the 1968 World Series was a more important moment in my baseball career, but when we won that Caribbean World Series Championship game in Puerto Rico, we celebrated as if we were champions of the world. We weren't any less excited than we were in 1968. It was a proud moment, particularly for me, because when I came down to Venezuela, it was possible my career was over. I proved down there that my bat still had pop, and maybe more importantly, I proved that I could contribute beyond my playing ability.

My time in Venezuela helped me considerably because I hit .313 and finished among the top 10 hitters in the league. The Seattle Mariners liked what they saw from me and gave me a tryout contract in late January. The only negative of my Venezuela experience was that my daughters Pam and Gail contracted an eye disease, and we were worried for a couple of days that they might lose some of their eyesight. You can imagine how hard it is to concentrate on baseball with that on your mind.

Pablo Penton told me a couple of times that he thought I could manage in the big leagues because I seemed to be getting the most out of my players. Mostly, though, I was thinking about getting my chance to play again with the Mariners, but I also thought that I might be able to manage, too. When my career was over, I thought teams might come to me about managing. My dad always taught me that if you work hard at your profession, you will be discovered. He believed you created your own opportunities with your work ethic. Unfortunately, he never taught me that sometimes you have to knock to get inside the door. I didn't send out résumés. My feeling was that the baseball world knew who I was, and my record in Venezuela was certainly no secret to anyone in baseball. I ended up with coaching jobs with Oakland, the New York Yankees, and the Chicago White Sox. But no one ever asked me to interview for a managing job.

It's well established that major league teams haven't been enthusiastic about hiring Black managers. The first Black manager was Frank Robinson, named in 1975. That was 28 years after Jackie Robinson broke the color barrier for players. It's not like Robinson's hiring opened the floodgates for Black managers.

In 1972, Jackie Robinson criticized baseball for the lack of Black managers. He died shortly after making that statement. He would not be pleased with the progress.

Of the 44 managers of color who have been hired since then (including interim managers), 25 have been Latino, 16 have been Black, and two have been Asian. The Los Angeles Dodgers' manager Dave Roberts is considered both Black and Asian.

Even if I had rapped on some doors, would I have been given fair consideration for a manager's job? It's hard to say. In 1999, the MLB introduced the "Selig Rule," named after then-commissioner Bud Selig. The rule states that all teams must consider hiring women and/or a person of color for every front-office position.

Since then, we have not seen the influx of minority managers that I had expected. We only have two Black managers today in Dusty Baker and Dave Roberts. It seems to me that teams are interviewing minorities to fulfill its obligation to the Selig Rule, but they aren't hiring them.

# Chapter 16

# Mull Digger Becomes
# the Ancient Mariner

WHEN I SIGNED with the Seattle Mariners for the 1979 season, I owned a glove and two batting helmets that were five times older than my new team.

The Mariners craved a media-friendly, high-profile player to heighten the team's identity and I was looking for a team willing to offer a fresh start to a 36-year-old power hitter. We were a perfect match.

Remember, this was only the third season of the Mariners' existence—more than a decade before Ken Griffey Jr., Randy Johnson, and others would arrive in the Northwest. In 1978, the Mariners had lost 104 games and they were drawing fewer than 6,500 fans per game to the Kingdome. Even at the start of the season, only about 11,000 or 12,000 were going to the ballpark. The Mariners didn't have an Al Kaline or a Mickey Mantle or a Hank Aaron in their history, and the public seemed to view my signing as a significant move.

Originally, I'd signed a tryout contract with the Mariners. But when I began to consistently launch the ball with authority during spring training, the Mariners' management got anxious to convert my tryout deal to a regular contract.

When I was playing in Venezuela the previous few months, Pablo Penton kept telling me that my swing looked sweet and powerful. He had armed me with confidence.

"These are major pitchers down here in Venezuela," Pablo would tell me, "and you're hitting .300 against them. You're going back to the majors and hitting .280 or .285 and 25 home runs."

At the end of the 1978 season, it seemed as if I was on retirement's doorstep. But I got the little boy back in me while I was playing and winning in Venezuela. The Mariners signed an aging veteran, but they got a player who felt invigorated. It's not an exaggeration to say that I was in the best shape of my major league career at age 36. In the photos featuring me in a Mariners uniform, I look almost thin. I showed up at training camp weighing 210 pounds, a full 15 pounds lighter than when I was playing for the Detroit Tigers. With Billy Martin's preaching about conditioning, Ben Oglivie's nutritional advice, and my own desire to continue to be an impact player, I was suddenly overflowing with confidence.

The funny thing with the Mariners is that management was worried about me. I was pounding the ball so well, they were afraid I was going to leave at the end of spring training and sign with a contender. The more hits I got, the more the Mariners fretted.

"I just want to concentrate on getting my game together," I told team executives Danny O'Brien and Lou Gorman. "We'll talk about a contract at the end of spring training. I'm not going anywhere."

Mr. O'Brien should've known what kind of man I was because he had been the general manager in Texas when the Tigers traded me there in 1977. Seattle had given me a chance to be an everyday ballplayer again, and I felt indebted to them. Loyalty should be mutual. People who know me well know that I'm loyal to a fault. One of the reasons why I signed with Seattle was that I respected Danny O'Brien.

O'Brien presumably expected the worst when I finally came into his office to negotiate with him. He seemed stunned when I made my contract demand.

"I want a rookie contract," I told him.

"A rookie contract?" he repeated. "What do you mean?"

"I mean, give me what rookies get, and then let's work in some incentive bonuses," I said. "If I hit those bonuses, it'll mean the contract has worked out for both of us."

My agent at the time, Charlie Dye, was against my decision to ask for an incentive-laden contract, but I felt very strongly about it.

O'Brien could not have agreed quicker and that deal ultimately paid me more in one season than I'd earned in many seasons with Detroit. I reached all of my bonus incentives by the All-Star break, and it turned out to be the most lucrative contract I ever signed.

That season I would joke with other players about my rookie contract. When the Tigers came to town in June, the *Detroit Free Press* reported me as telling Ron LeFlore, "I'm losing money playing. I bet I'm the only one in the majors for 15 years and making $36,000."

The 1968 season was probably the best of my career. My 36 home runs, .285 batting average, and 85 RBIs contributed to a world championship. But 1979 might've been my second best individual season. For the first time in my career, I played all 162 games, and my 29 home runs were my highest total since '68. My 106 RBIs and 180 hits—Seattle franchise records—were also personal highs.

Certainly, some people believe my home run total was aided by the homer-friendly Kingdome in 1979. But I actually hit more home runs on the road than I did in Seattle that year. I did take advantage of the Kingdome's deep alleys for more extra-base hits. Twelve of my 19 doubles and all five of my triples came in the Kingdome. Over the years, I learned to take advantage of a park's design. If it had power alleys, I tried to smack the ball into the gaps.

In my first game in Seattle, I had three hits, including a home run, to help beat California, 5–4. From that point on, the Kingdome fans treated me like royalty. It was like being home in Detroit.

At times, I remember thinking that people in Seattle were almost too nice to me. It was like I could do no wrong there. Even members of the media seemed to treat me that way. No one in Seattle wanted to hold me accountable.

I remember flagging down the late *Seattle Times* columnist Emmett Watson once, after he had written some really flattering things about me in the paper. "Thank you very much, Emmett," I said to him. "But when I don't play well, you have to kick me in the butt. That's the way it's supposed to work."

He laughed, but I was serious. When Joe Falls would criticize me in his column in Detroit, it motivated me. I considered Joe a friend, but I understood his job description. I knew it was his job to analyze my performance. And if I didn't measure up, it bothered me. I feel the same way about retired *Detroit News* columnist Jerry Green. Old-school journalists like Green and Falls didn't write columns simply to stir up controversy. It was their job to hold teams and players accountable, and they were quite serious about their business—as serious as I was about mine.

That's why I worried in Seattle when everyone treated me with almost too much respect. I didn't want a free pass. And I didn't want to get complacent. Fortunately, I didn't.

The Mariners won 67 games that season, and that was actually a respectable number, given that our pitching staff had an average age of about 24 or 25. The team boasted some talented ballplayers. Ruppert Jones was 24 and coming into his own, and Bruce Bochte was a fine hitter. If he hadn't had injury problems, he might've developed into one of the major leagues' finest hitters. When I initially signed with Seattle, Bruce actually offered to give up No. 23 so I could have my old number. I appreciated the gesture, but I decided to wear No. 53 instead. I picked that number because Dodgers Hall of Famer Don Drysdale had worn it. I'd always had a lot of respect for him, and he was a credit to the game.

The Mariners had a wealth of interesting characters, including Tom Paciorek, who is one of baseball's all-time funniest people. We also had Mario Mendoza, who was to Seattle what Ray Oyler was to the Detroit Tigers in the '60s. Mendoza gobbled up ground balls with amazing accuracy, but he just couldn't hit the breaking ball. Today, a .200 batting average is referred to as "the Mendoza line." Some say Paciorek invented the phrase, but he insists it was Bochte. Either way, it was developed during that 1979 season with Seattle.

Mendoza was always fooling around with me—razzing me and playing little pranks, and I was always shooing him away. I called him "the Crazy Mexican." Paciorek has often told the story of sitting next to me while I was sleeping on a spring training bus ride. Apparently, I was dreaming, and when I woke up suddenly, I said, "Get away from me, you crazy Mexican!" Mendoza and my old teammates had a good time with that one.

In Detroit, I was "Willie the Wonder," and in Seattle I was the "Ancient Mariner." But my teammates called me "Mull Digger." I often used that term because my father did. And so did his father. But I have no idea where it came from. I just assumed it was a mining term down South, but a search for a definition yielded no results.

My father and a former Detroit Tiger from Mississippi named Bubba Phillips used that term to describe a hard-working player—someone dependable who came to work and did his job every day. To me, that was a mull digger. And in Seattle, some of the guys even had a jacket made with my nickname "Mull Digger" sewn on the back.

That 1979 season provided me with many wonderful memories, including my 300th career home run. My heart has told me that God has a plan for all of us, and I believe that it was more than coincidence that my 300th came against the Detroit Tigers.

On June 4, 1979, I parked my 299th into the outfield stands of the Kingdome. Milt Wilcox was on the mound for Detroit, and he threw me a breaking pitch that was outside and so close to the dirt that a sand wedge might've been more useful than a bat. When I connected, I was leaning over the plate with one arm extended. It was more like a golf swing than a baseball swing. The ball flew to the outfield on a long arc, and fell into the left-field stand like a wedge shot landing on the green.

"I don't know how I hit it," I told the *Detroit Free Press* that night. "I guess I was just meant to hit that pitch." But looking back, maybe it was prejudice that helped me learn to hit a pitch like that. Early in my career, when someone in Detroit's front office was tipping teams on how to pitch to me, I didn't see too many fat pitches. I learned I had to take what I could get. Late in my career, I hit as many balls as strikes because I would move the plate in my mind by adjusting my body positioning. If you're leaning way over the play, a ball a foot outside can be in your power zone.

I was expecting Wilcox to throw me a pitch down and away, and so I moved closer to the plate as he finished his windup.

Early in my career, I didn't like to be cheated on my swings. I felt the same way late in my career, too. I tell young players that if you're relaxed and confident at the plate, and your eyes are in control of your strength, then you're in a perfectly balanced position. You're using your inner strength. You aren't searching for your swing. You have your swing. When you're in that position, you don't hold back. All of my energy went into each swing.

The only exception I made was when I knew my swing wasn't quite right. People who followed my career closely would probably argue that I never choked up on a bat in my life. But that's not accurate. If I was slumping or out of sync, and if we had a runner in scoring position, I would let the bat handle slide down between my fingers a couple of inches. Not even the catcher would notice. I made sure I made contact in those situations. If I wasn't swinging the bat well, I would actually strike out less than if I were on a hitting tear.

In that same game against Detroit, in my next at-bat, Wilcox hit me in the hand with a fastball. I charged the mound, benches emptied, and it took several minutes for the umpires to restore order.

"He wasn't trying to hit me," I admitted to the press afterward. "But when you're mad, you don't think about that. Besides, I was hurting anyway."

At that point, I showed the media my badly scabbed hand, which had been injured a few days before when I was spiked against the Texas Rangers. Whenever you see someone charge the mound, there's usually an underlying cause.

Back in the mid-1970s, when I was playing for the Tigers, I charged the mound one time after the Angels' Frank Tanana hit me. To be honest, I wasn't mad at Frank. I was mad at his manager, Dick Williams. As I got to the mound, I kept telling Frank that he shouldn't listen to Williams when he orders him to hit a batter. Then I turned to Williams and told him if it happened again, I was coming after him. I was pretty animated at the time.

People tell me how intimidating I was in those situations, but most of my close friends find that amusing, especially those friends I met after my playing career. Today, people see me as a playful, friendly guy. That was probably true back then, too.

The night after the Wilcox fiasco, it looked as if I'd hit my 300th homer, but my long drive off Tigers reliever John Hiller hit a speaker

132 feet above the Kingdome playing surface in left field. It was one of the most bizarre singles in baseball history. That didn't bother me in the least, though. I remember how Al Kaline had lost a couple of home run because games were rained out before the fifth inning. One was in 1958 and the other in 1963. He finished his career with 399 home runs. If it weren't for some bad weather, Al would've had 401 official career home runs.

At least I ended up on base. Six years later, A's designated hitter Dave Kingman smashed a ball off Seattle pitcher Dave Geisel that struck a wire hanging from the Kingdome roof. Instead of being a home run, it fell safely into left fielder Phil Bradley's glove for an out.

Somehow, I knew I would hit my 300th the next day against Jack Morris. Before I left for the game, I told Gloria to make sure she had the family in their seats by the end of the start of the first inning. It was Wednesday, June 6, 1979.

The Tigers jumped out to a 3–0 lead against us in the top of the first on a Rusty Staub home run. In the bottom of the inning, I came up to bat against Morris with Ruppert Jones on second base. I dug in and ripped a shot over the left-field wall for number 300. It made me proud that I hit it off a quality pitcher like Jack Morris. He had established himself as the Tigers' ace that season. He had that nasty forkball, and even when he was young, you still had to work Morris to get a good pitch to hit.

Rounding the bases, I was crying tears of joy and laughter mixed together. I really didn't know whether I was happy or sad. Mostly, I was confused. Playing against the Tigers was the most difficult part of my career. I didn't even like to go on the field with them before the game. I preferred to stay in the trainer's room. If I went out and socialized with the Tigers, I didn't think I would be able to compete against them. The Tigers had raised me. My emotions overwhelmed me that night. The Tigers' players congratulated me, but I couldn't help but think I should've been in their dugout.

The Mariners organization and their fans were first-rate. Three nights after my 300th, it was "Willile Horton Night" at the Kingdome, and the team presented me with artwork commemorating the home run. The piece had 300 silver dollars framed in the shape of the number 300.

In that era of baseball, we didn't think much about milestones. But late in a player's career, he begins to ponder them more, and his legacy becomes important to him. Heading into the 1980 season, I was looking forward to my 2,000[th] hit. Obviously, making that list wasn't going to change the way I saw my career, but the 2,000-hit club did include plenty of outstanding ballplayers, and at the time, it still included a relatively short list of African American players. I needed just 81 more hits. Based on my 1979 output, I expected to be there by midsummer.

As it turned out, I never got there at all. In spring training of 1980, I ripped open my hand sliding into a base. I didn't think much of it until the wound refused to heal. Doctors diagnosed it as a rare disease that interfered with the healing process. The hand bothered me all season, even forcing me to the disabled list a couple of times.

The situation was so bad that at the time, I would pull off my glove and my bandage would be soaked in blood.

When I came off the disabled list in September, I still had a reasonable shot at reaching 2,000 hits in a career. I needed 20 more. Seattle manager Maury Wills, who'd replaced Darrell Johnson that season, didn't use me immediately.

Bruce Bochte was playing some DH at the time, and he came to me and said he thought I should be playing DH to get the hits I needed.

"Pops, we are all pulling for you and if you are the DH, I'm sure you will pick up the hits," Bochte said.

But Wills didn't see it that way. And he told Bochte if he didn't DH, I still wasn't going to play.

When I talked to Wills about getting enough to get my at-bats, he mumbled something about picking up some now and more the following year. But I was 37 years old and didn't know if I would have a next season.

"Imagine if someone had said that to Roberto Clemente," I said to Wills. "Next year is never promised."

Clemente ended up with exactly 3,000 hits after the 1972 season and then was killed in a plane crash in the off-season.

Wills wasn't in his right mind that season. We knew he was into drugs, and a few of us tried to help him. But he wasn't ready for help. He did start me for several games in a row in September, but then he benched me for two games down the stretch and only used me as a pinch-hitter in another game. Right before that, I had nine hits in eight days. I certainly wonder if I would've played those three games, plus a couple of others earlier in the season, whether I would've made it. I ended my career just seven hits shy of my milestone, tallying 1,993.

Now 89, Wills has been clean and sober for many years now, and I'm happy for him because in 1980, his problems were obvious to his players. I sometimes wonder if Maury didn't play me those games because he knew that I knew what was going on in his life. I wanted to help him, but he didn't want my help at that time. I hit .286 that September. It wasn't like I was hurting the team chasing my 2,000 hits.

Did he want me off the team? That was certainly my impression. But I was still surprised when I got a call from the Mariners in December of 1980 to tell me I was part of an 11-man trade with the Texas Rangers. It was an odd situation because I was actually on the Mariners media public relations tour—talking about the upcoming season—when the deal was made. They waited until after that was over to tell me I'd been traded.

Seattle traded Rick Honeycutt, Mario Mendoza, Larry Cox, Leon Roberts, and me to Texas for Richie Zisk, Rick Auerbach, Ken Clay, Jerry Don Gleaton, Brian Allard, and minor leaguer Steve Finch. At the time, only four trades in major league history had involved more players.

At the time, it seemed like a good move for me. I thought the Rangers had a chance to win their division. Looking at their lineup, I saw myself batting cleanup. Battling through my injury with Seattle in 1980, I batted only .221 with eight home runs. But my hand finally healed in the off-season, and I looked forward to working with the kids in the Rangers' system. In spring training of 1981, I was hitting the ball well. So I was a bit surprised when the Rangers started playing me less often as we got closer to the regular season.

At that time, my good friend Dennis "Hoggie" Gordon was staying with me at the Rangers' spring training home in Pompano Beach, Florida. I had gotten to know Hoggie well when he was running the kitchen in Lakeland at Tiger Town. He had played some Negro League baseball back in his day, and I more or less adopted him as a grandfather for my kids. He even moved to Seattle to live with us for a while. Hoggie knew his baseball, and people liked having him around. The Mariners had even allowed him to sit on the bench with the team, although Hoggie was such a straight-shooter that manager Darrell Johnson didn't always appreciate what he had to say.

One time on the bench, Johnson asked Hoggie what the problem was with the team. "Well," Hoggie said, "you're the problem." He sure didn't pull any punches.

Hoggie watched me bang the ball around the ballpark in spring training for the Rangers in 1981, and he couldn't figure out why I wasn't playing more often.

"Something's wrong here," Hoggie told me. "You have to find out what's happening."

I told him not to worry. I could still see myself batting fourth, with Al Oliver in front of me. It was going to be a great season.

"I'm tellin' you, something is wrong," Hoggie insisted.

I figured that the Rangers wouldn't have traded for me if they didn't have plans for me. I thought they were just trying to get a good look at the kids on the roster. I was content to put on my army clothes and do my workout every day. I wanted to be ready for Opening Day.

But day after day, my name was missing from the lineup card. Hoggie finally convinced me to go talk to manager Don Zimmer. I called Zimmer "Uncle Popeye" because he really did look like the cartoon character.

When I went to Zimmer to discuss the situation, he raised his hands in the air and said, "I have nothing to do with this. You have to talk to Hopalong." That was everyone's nickname for general manager Eddie Robinson.

Robinson was honest with me. And as he ushered me out the door, at least he had some kind words for me. "You did everything we asked of you, Willie," he said. "But we just want to go in another direction."

I couldn't help but wonder… couldn't they have gone "in another direction" earlier in spring training? The real issue I had with the Rangers was that they released me on April 1, when it was too late to catch on with another team. Teams had already finalized their rosters. Of course, I also couldn't help but wonder if Maury Wills was indirectly responsible for my predicament. Maybe the Rangers hadn't wanted me at all, but were simply doing me a favor by taking me in a trade. Had Seattle simply released me, there would have been a backlash. By trading me, they had at least eased the public relations pain.

And there was another issue: At that time in baseball, there seemed to be a push to sweep out older players like me. Even though I didn't find work with another team in 1981, that might've said more about labor issues than about my playing ability. A strike loomed on the horizon, and it came later that season in June. Nine years later, in 1990, Major League Baseball was found guilty of collusion for some of its actions in the 1980s. Maybe I was just at the launch point of that line of thinking.

One of the most difficult issues that a professional athlete faces is deciding when to hang the spikes out in the garage.

After the Rangers cut me, I wasn't initially thinking about retirement. I returned to my home in Seattle, believing that someone would call. Injuries happen in baseball and I'd hit consistently enough in spring training to convince anyone that I could still play. If someone got hurt somewhere in the majors, I felt like I'd be called on to take his place. But the call never came.

Then one day I was mowing my lawn in Seattle when I heard a baseball broadcast on the radio and I heard the announcer mention Luis Tiant and Rusty Torres. I figured it must've been an exhibition game. But after a minute, I realized Tiant and Torres were playing with the Portland Beavers of the Pacific Coast League.

A Philadelphia native named David Hersh had bought the team at age 21 and made a name for himself with a variety of promotions, including the signing of former major leaguers. The important fact for me was that they were affiliated with the Pittsburgh Pirates. Maybe this was my ticket back to the major leagues. I called Hersh and asked him for a tryout. I was 38 years old.

"Can you still hit?" he asked.

I laughed. "I can still hit," I said.

In my tryout I ripped a few balls beyond the confines of the Portland ballpark and busted out some windows across the street. The Beavers had to reimburse the building owners. They signed me on the spot.

In my first season in Portland, I batted .302 with 25 doubles, 17 home runs, and 75 RBI. The following season I delivered 22 home runs and 82 RBI with a .275 batting average.

But the call never came.

Willie Stargell called me from Pittsburgh because he believed the organization was going to call me up. But they promoted a young prospect. Truthfully, how could I blame them?

They paid us very well. Management ran Portland like a major league team because we had former major leaguers. I remember we played in Hawaii and sold out the stadium because we had so many players fans recognized.

After two seasons in Portland, I decided to look elsewhere for a last effort to stay in the game. I signed with Nuevo Laredo Tercolates in the Mexican League. I was thinking about 2,000 major league hits. But mostly, I wanted to continue to play.

But it didn't take me long in Mexico to realize it was time to put an end to this chapter in my life. I looked around at the young players on my team, and I realized that if I played there, I'd be taking playing time from a younger player who needed those at-bats to develop. And that's just not what Willie Horton's about.

My son Deryl Lamar was also in southern Mexico, playing with a semi-pro team. We didn't speak a word of Spanish. I played 49 games and hit .324. But I ended up becoming ill from a parasite, which caused me to lose weight and my strength. I told my son to pack up our van. It was time to move on.

From Mexico, we drove to Houston to visit my niece. Then we drove to Florida to pick up my daughter April. Next, we drove to Detroit. Then we drove to visit my son Al at Drake University in Des Moines, Iowa. He had been a high school standout at Redford and had earned a basketball scholarship to Drake. Then we drove back home to Seattle. It was a beautiful trip with Deryl. Over all those miles of driving, I was able to make peace with my retirement. I realized how much I needed my family, and I was ready to go home.

My parents, Clinton and Lillian.

My childhood home in Virginia.

Me and Larry Munsey on our Little League team.

DETROIT SCORER'S ASSOCIATION
NEWSPAPER BOX SCORE
Played at BRIGGS STADIUM

League METROPOLITAN    Class CHAMPIONSHIP    Date 6/9/59

| Team NORTHWESTERN | | AB | R | H | RBI |
|---|---|---|---|---|---|
| CHARLES BOYD | 2B | 4 | 2 | 1 | |
| BOB MARSHALL | SS | 2 | | | |
| WILLIE HORTON | C | 4 | 3 | 2 | |
| JOHN HOLMES | CF | 5 | 1 | 2 | |
| MATTHEW SHORTON | 3B | 4 | 1 | 2 | |
| ALEX JOHNSON | RF | 3 | 1 | 1 | |
| CLARK NEYLAND | 3B | 3 | 1 | 1 | |
| TYRONE PETERSON | LF | 3 | 2 | 2 | |
| BILL STREET (RH) | P | 0 | | | |
| JERRY NIXON (RH) | P | 3 | 2 | 1 | |

| Team CASS TECH | | AB | R | H | RBI |
|---|---|---|---|---|---|
| ROY KRUPA | 3B-LF | 5 | 2 | 2 | |
| JACK TRELOAR | 2B | 4 | 1 | 2 | |
| CARMEN FANZONE | SS | 3 | 2 | 1 | |
| RON POSOCH | 1B | 3 | 2 | 2 | |
| DOUG VILNIUS | CF | 3 | | | |
| FRANK PALAZZOLA | LF-RF | 4 | 1 | 2 | |
| TOM MULLINS | RF | 2 | | | |
| LARRY HARRISON | C | 3 | 1 | 1 | |
| GEORGE COJOCARI (RH) | P | 2 | | | |
| AL STUBBE (RH) | P | 0 | 2 | | |
| RON ORLOWSKI | | 1 | | | |
| RAY KRUPA | 3B | 1 | | | |

Total 31 13 12    Total 31 10 10

TEAM

| TEAM | 1 | 2 | 3 | 4 | 5 | 6 | 7 | 8 | 9 | 10 | 11 | 12 | Total |
|---|---|---|---|---|---|---|---|---|---|---|---|---|---|
| NORTHWESTERN | 1 | 0 | 3 | 0 | 6 | 1 | 2 | | | | | | 13-13-3 |
| CASS TECH | 0 | 6 | 0 | 0 | 0 | 2 | 2 | | | | | | 10-10-3 |

Errors PETERSON - JOHNSON - NEYLAND - TRELOAR 2 - FANZONE
LEFT ON BASE CASS 12 NW 5 1
2 Base Hits FANZONE - POSOCH 2 HORTON    RBI HARRISON - KRUPA - POSOCH 4 - PALAZZOLA 2 HORTON 3
3 Base Hits    NIXON - PETERSON - HOLMES - MARSHALL 2 SHORTON 3
Home Runs HORTON    SHORTON    TRELOAR
Hits Off STREET    PO-A CASS TECH    NW 21-9

Winning Pitcher NIXON    Losing Pitcher COJOCARI
TIME - 2:35

89

Spring training with the Tigers.

Over the years, I can't tell you how many people have told me they copied my batting stance when they were kids. *(Photo courtesy of the Detroit Tigers)*

Mickey Stanley, Gates Brown, Mickey Lolich, me, and Bill Freehan. *(Photo courtesy of the Detroit Tigers)*

Me and Denny McLain embrace after my double scored the winning run against the Oakland A's on September 14, 1968, to give McLain his 30th win of the season. *(AP Images)*

My home run in the second inning of Game 2 of the '68 World Series. *(AP Images)*

My throw nails Lou Brock at home, as he's tagged out by catcher Bill Freehan in the fifth inning of Game 5 of the '68 World Series. *(AP Images)*

Working on a bat. Always ready to hit. *(Imagn / Detroit Free Press)*

In the middle of things. Here I am getting ready for a Men's Social at my place, Club 23.

Gates Brown, Billy Martin,
and me relaxing after a big game.

The end of my playing career
in Detroit. *(AP Images)*

Me and Judge Damon Keith, who was such a large
part of my life.

At Comerica Park with
my lovely wife, Gloria.
Our partnership has been based
on love and deep religious beliefs.

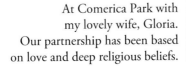
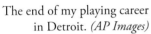

Hugging Mr. Ilitch at the ceremony retiring My No. 23 jersey in 2000.

It's an exceptional honor and I was touched to have my number retired.

I got emotional during my speech, as my wife, Gloria,
and legendary announcer Ernie Harwell looked on.

Speaking at the Northwestern High School field dedication, which was an amazing honor.

Hanging with legends: Al Kaline, me, and Mark Fidrych.

Al Kaline and I wave to the crowd before the start of Game 1 of the 2006 World Series in Detroit. *(AP Images / Morry Gash)*

Detroit mayor Mike Duggan, me, former senator Carl Levin, and Detroit police chief James Craig pose with shovels during a Detroit Police Athletic League (PAL) groundbreaking at the site of old Tiger Stadium on Wednesday April 13, 2016. The site would become the Corner Ballpark, where the field is named in my honor—The Willie Horton Field of Dreams. *(AP Images via Steve Perez / Detroit News)*

I'm still part of the Tigers family today. From left: Tigers GM Al Avila, owner Chris Ilitch, Miguel Cabrera, manager A.J. Hinch, and me commemorate Cabrera's 500th home run in September 2021, at Comerica Park. *(AP Images / Jose Juarez)*

My statue at Comerica Park; a symbol of the city's love for me and my love for Detroit. *(AP Images via Steven King / Icon Sportswire)*

# Chapter 17

# You Can Go Home Again

WHEN YANKEES MANAGER Billy Martin brought me to New York in 1985, my job title was coach. But really I was the morale officer. My job was to try to help maintain a happy working environment. Little did I know that my new peacekeeper duties included preventing Billy Martin and player Ed Whitson from beating each other senseless. Veteran player Don Baylor jokingly referred to me as the team's new "tranquility coach."

During a road trip to Baltimore, the phone rang in my hotel room late one night and I was informed that I needed to come downstairs because "Skip is in a fight."

That didn't seem like an emergency to me, because Billy fancied himself a seasoned barroom brawler. "Billy can handle himself," I said. "I'm going back to bed."

"You don't understand," the caller said. "He's fighting with Tex and it's been going on for a while."

"Tex" is Ed Whitson, who was a Yankees pitcher at the time. He was 6'3", around 200 pounds, and Billy was 5'10", 155 pounds.

"I'll be right down," I said.

When I arrived downstairs, I heard the story that the fight had started at the Cross Key Lounge, continued in the parking lot, moved into the hotel lobby, then the elevator, and finally they fought in the hallway between rooms on the third floor. Witnesses told me it had gone on for more than an hour.

I found Billy in his room, and the trainer already had him in the bathtub with his body encased in ice up to his neck. It was clear that he had taken a pretty good beating.

"You have to go take care of Whitson," Billy said.

"I'm not going to beat up anyone," I said. "What happened?"

Billy's explanation about the fight was that Whitson had sucker-punched him because he thought he heard Billy bad-mouthing him in a conversation. According to Billy, he had gone over to help Whitson, because he was told Whitson was having words with another patron.

Revenge and anger still owned Billy's emotions when I first showed up. He claimed Whitson had kicked him in the groin, a charge that was also reported as fact in *Sports Illustrated*'s version of the fight.

The funny part of the story was what made Billy the maddest was that he had let Whitson sucker-punch him. "I usually make sure I throw the first punch," said Martin, who had plenty of fighting experience.

By the time I arrived, I assumed the fight was over. But I was mistaken. Whitson was still angry and I made sure he stayed in his room. It was not my powers of persuasion that kept him there. It was the power in my arms.

I didn't fight Whitson. There was no need, and no desire on my part to do that. By then, my reputation was usually enough to calm down any situation. Most of the people in baseball knew about the time in 1975 that I charged the mound against Frank Tanana because I had grown tired of getting knocked to the dirt by inside pitches.

My view was that pitchers were entitled to pitch me in tight, but if I had to hit the dirt in order to prevent being hit in the head, then I had a problem with it.

Umpire Marty Springstead said after that game that he wanted to stop me before I got to the mound, because then he would not have had to eject me. But neither he, nor Angels catcher Ellie Rodríguez, could hold me back.

"He's the strongest man in the league," Springstead said at the time. "Nobody can hold him."

Tanana was from Detroit and grew up as one of my fans. "The last thing I wanted to do was get Willie Horton mad," he remarked.

That summed up my reputation. The boys on the 1968 team were always out to play baseball, but if the opposing players wanted to fight, we would accommodate them. I had to watch myself in those days. I received a letter from the commissioner one season. He told me no more fighting or I would be suspended. I told him I was a "man of peace."

Maybe it was good that some people didn't believe that. My reputation for strength dated back to my minor league days. Former major league pitcher Bill Monbouquette has occasionally told the tale of a Double-A pitcher who happened to throw too close to my head. I chased him into his clubhouse. When he shut the sliding door behind him, I just pulled the steel door off the tracks and went inside.

The famous line from Monbouquette is: "Willie is so strong, even his spit has muscle."

On that night, Martin and Whitson went crazy, and I just had to wrap up Whitson with a bear hug until he calmed down. In later years, Whitson called me the "strongest SOB" he ever wrestled.

I called Lou Piniella and we agreed to order a car to take Whitson back to New York. Billy was definitely the loser in his scrap with Whitson. When I went to see him the next morning, he was wrapped up like a mummy. He had me help him with his coat. "Can't let them know that I'm hurt," he said, even though everyone knew what happened.

Although Billy always climbed on the team bus last, he climbed on first this particular morning. And he made sure I walked next to him as we exited, just in case he needed to steady himself. Martin had a broken right arm and bruises all over his body. When we got him into the coach's room, he sat down and promptly fell over because he was wrapped so tight. He told the television crews not to take video of him in the dugout, and then he toughed it out during the game.

Martin admitted to the media that he lost the fight. "I can't fight feet," he said, before adding that he should probably go to karate school. Whitson had a rib injury and a fat lip.

That night, after watching Billy tough it out to manage, I realized how mentally strong he was. Nothing would have kept him off the bench. Billy would not give Whitson the satisfaction of knowing that he knocked Martin out of action.

Once, I heard Reggie Jackson talking about Billy in an interview. Reggie made some derogatory comments about him. Even though I have great respect for Reggie, that bothered me. I know Billy wasn't perfect, but he certainly wasn't a racist. If anyone would know Billy, it's me. I saw the kind side of Billy that others didn't. I saw Billy give money to people who had none. He wasn't perfect, but he was loyal to his people.

The question people ask me about this story is why I was with the Yankees, and not the Tigers, in 1985. And here's the story:

Not long after I retired, the phone rang in Seattle. A voice boomed, "Hey, Roids!" I knew immediately it was one of my 1968 Detroit Tigers teammates. Nobody even knew that nickname except those guys. Only a few seconds of razzing was necessary before I realized it was Jim Price.

"What the heck are you doing in Seattle?" he asked. "You belong in Detroit. Get your butt back here. Detroit is your city."

Mostly, Jimmie was giving me the business, but he was serious about believing I should be in Detroit. I explained that I still had kids in school in Seattle, and that it wasn't easy to pack up and move. But he persisted, telling me that I was more "marketable" in Detroit than I was in the Northwest.

"We're putting together a fantasy camp using the 1968 Tigers, and we want you to be involved," Jimmie said.

"Fantasy camp?" I said. "I don't want to go on any cruise."

Jimmie started laughing because he realized I didn't have any idea what he was talking about. When he said, "fantasy camp," all I could think of were the old TV shows *Fantasy Island* and *Love Boat.*

But once he explained the concept that he and his friend Jerry Lewis had put together, I liked the plan. The idea was to bring together fans and members of the 1968 Tigers for a week of playing baseball. It turned out to be a great idea, and Jim Price's phone call may have altered the course of my life.

I decided to participate. Great decision. I probably benefited more from those camps than the participants. By reconnecting with those Detroit fans, I think it made me realize that at some point I had to come home again. It makes me misty-eyed when I think about all of the devoted, wonderful fans I've met at these camps.

Unfortunately, I wasn't able to take a direct route back to Motown, but eventually I returned. Billy Martin hired me to coach in Oakland for a couple of seasons. But right after the Tigers won the World Series in 1984, I thought I had an opportunity to come back. I remember calling

Gates Brown, who was the Tigers' hitting coach at the time, and laying out my plan to approach the Tigers about becoming their minor league hitting instructor.

"We could really lay down a strong foundation here," I told Gates. "We can work with each hitter individually and take him where he needs to go."

Gates seemed excited about the possibility. But after I was given the job, he told me that he was probably going to resign. Gator was offended, maybe even insulted, that the Tigers had only offered him a $2,500 raise after the World Series.

"Don't tell anyone I'm resigning," Gates told me. "But send the Tigers a letter and tell them that if my job ever opens up, you want to be considered for it."

Following Gator's advice, I sent the letter. As soon as Gator's resignation became official, ex-Cincinnati Red Vada Pinson was hired, and the Tigers said they never received any letter. It was a bit off at the next spring training in 1985 because some players thought I was the major league hitting coach.

But the situation became stranger still when the New York Yankees called the Tigers to ask permission to talk to me about a coaching position. Martin had been hired to manage the Yankees again, and he wanted me on his staff.

With the season about to start, I had driven through the night to Nashville to coach some of our prospects. Tigers general manager Bill Lajoie woke me up with the news that the Yankees wanted me. Our conversation went something like this:

"That's really a decision I don't want to make," I said. "Maybe I can't make it."

"It seems to me that you can't pass up this opportunity," Lajoie said.

"But it took me so long to get back here, that I really don't want to leave," I said. "I waited too long to get back to Detroit."

"I'll help you make the decision—this is the best opportunity for your future," he said. "You should go."

And that's how I ended up wearing the Yankees' pinstripes. Bill Lajoie helped me reach that conclusion. And I thought he was trying to help me.

That would've been fine with me, except a few years later people started asking why I wasn't with the Tigers organization. Lajoie essentially told everyone that the Tigers had given me an opportunity before and I had run out on them. That scarred me deeply, because that's just not an accurate portrayal of our phone conversation.

As it turned out, the Yankees situation worked out nicely for me. When I met with owner George Steinbrenner, he asked what my salary had been in Detroit. I told him $25,000. He then asked how much more I had deferred. "None," I said.

He couldn't believe it. He raised my pay to $60,000 per season.

People have mixed opinions about Mr. Steinbrenner. However, I watched him in action. He was five or 10 years ahead of everyone else in terms of his approach to the game.

After a year in New York, Chicago White Sox general manager Ken Harrelson asked for permission to talk to me, and then he hired me to coach in Chicago. I was at least getting closer to Detroit. And there in the Windy City I met a rising young executive named Dave Dombrowski, who years later would become my boss in Detroit.

On December 23, 1989, Billy Martin called me and told me that he was going to end up back with the Yankees. "Don't take another job," he said. "You're going to end up working for me again."

Two days later, he was killed in a car accident.

By then, I'd made up my mind that I really didn't want to work anywhere but Detroit. The fantasy camps had really reminded me that my roots were in this community, with the many fans who'd supported me for so many years. They gave me strength when I played, and they were still giving me strength.

Before the great Yankees legend Joe DiMaggio died in 1999, I was blessed with the opportunity to meet him. He was well up in years, but he knew every ballplayer who came to compete in his Joe DiMaggio Classic exhibition game. And he knew more about my career than I knew about his. "You should've been able to play your whole career in Detroit," he said. "That's what's wrong with baseball today. We don't have loyalty."

I've never forgotten what Joe said to me.

Actually, I did return to work in the Detroit area, working first in a job-training program, and finally for the City of Detroit as the Police Athletic League (PAL) director.

Detroit mayor Coleman Young had recruited me for PAL through Charlie Primas, who was president of the city housing commission from 1985 to 1994. Primas was a well-known athlete himself, having played for the Harlem Globetrotters.

I was hired as PAL's deputy director, working under former Detroit Lions great Dick "Night Train" Lane.

PAL was struggling a bit when I arrived, but I made it clear to Mayor Young and Charlie that I had tremendous respect for Mr. Lane, and I planned to be extremely loyal to him. As long as Mr. Lane wanted to be there, he was going to be there. In my mind, Night Train Lane and WJR broadcasting legend J.P. McCarthy were PAL. The organization had been around since the 1967 Detroit riots. Once I showed Mr. Lane how much I respected him, he put me in charge of PAL operations.

He told me that he thought his football mentality had probably gotten in the way. He hadn't been able to get the staffing he needed from Detroit police chief William Hart.

Once I got involved, I made an effort to develop a better relationship with the police. I learned to do what was necessary to get the staffing I needed. I even went to the shooting range. In fact, by the time I resigned, I was a second deputy chief and executive director of PAL. I had Officer Butler working for me, and Officer Nail and Joe Howard were assigned to me. We put together a career-development program, and with the support of Ford Motor Company, we took our membership from 9,000 to 22,000.

Again, it was the Tigers fantasy camp that helped me. There I met a man named Carl Manoogian, whose brother was a top executive at Ford. Through him, I met others, including Gary Nielsen, and I began to work with Ford's marketing company. They showed me how to develop a budget to help meet my needs at PAL.

When we started, we were hanging on with a $1 million budget. By the end, we had almost a $2 million budget.

Our career development program was based on sports and recreation, but it was really about education. All of the outreach programs in the city, including after-school babysitting—we started those at Pal. People have patterned themselves after us, and I'm very proud of my work with PAL.

I was actually still living in Seattle, but I commuted to Detroit and lived with my in-laws until I could save up enough comp time to go home for a month. They were two wonderful people, and they treated me like a son. It was a difficult home life situation, but my father had taught me long ago that you had to do what's best for your family—and my girls needed to finish school in Seattle.

Thanks again to the fantasy camp, I was able to move back to Detroit permanently a few years later. Bobby Milano, owner of Ort Tool and Die in Erie, Michigan, came to the Tigers fantasy camp and offered me a job as a salesperson. I enjoyed working for Ort. I liked the company, and more importantly, I liked the people.

Yet, I didn't have any more thoughts about rejoining the Tigers, especially after an incident one day at Tiger Stadium. I showed up to attend a game, headed to the same gate I'd been going to since I was a kid working in the clubhouse in the 1950s, and was informed I needed to show identification to enter the park. I needed a pass, and I didn't have a pass.

Shortly after that happened, my friends from Windsor, Ontario—photographer George Brooks and Arsene and Bonnie Bondy—were at my house to help me put in a flower garden. We were planting impatiens. I had met Arsene and Bonnie at Eastern Market, and their family owns a farm in Essex County, Ontario. All of us became the best of friends, and maybe they figured that my spirits needed a boost because they wouldn't accept my contention that my days in baseball were over.

As we were spading up the earth, George planted a seed of hope in my mind. "There's still more good you can bring to the sport of baseball," he told me. "Too many people around here feel like we do about you."

Apparently, Tigers owner Mike Ilitch was among them. And he believed that I needed to be more involved with the Tigers family.

Behind the scenes, many people, including Detroit mayor Dennis Archer and deputy mayor Freman Hendrix, had been lobbying for the

Tigers to retire my No. 23. My good friend Dr. Turner had also been pushing in the background, along with City Council member Brenda Scott and council president Maryann Mahaffey. Mr. Ilitch apparently had also decided that it should be done. But not only would they retire my number, that honor would also come with a statue in the outfield, which would stand with those of Al Kaline, Ty Cobb, Charlie Gehringer, Hank Greenberg, and Hal Newhouser at Comerica Park. Each statue rests atop a granite pedestal and reaches a total height of 13 feet.

When Tigers president John McHale called to tell me the news, I was driving home from Tennessee on I-75 near Lexington, Kentucky. I had to pull over because I was shaking. Tears filled my eyes, and I remembered walking down those railroad tracks in Virginia and meeting Larry Munsey. That was almost 70 years ago. Can't help but wonder whether I'd be where I am today if I hadn't taken that walk.

Anyone who thinks he can get to the top without help is simply a fool. My father. Judge Keith. Ron Thompson. Sam Bishop. Charlie Dressen. I could list a thousand names, and still only be halfway done.

My jersey-retirement ceremony was held at Comerica Park on July 15, 2000, and I needed 400 tickets for all my friends and family. Just as George Brooks had predicted, my baseball career was far from over. Mr. Ilitch brought me into his office several months later and asked me to become a member of a special committee to help turn around the Tigers. Al Kaline was also on the committee, and he told me to see if I liked the job. If I did, I could work full time.

A year later, I returned to Mr. Ilitch's office, telling him I wanted to do more for the Tigers. I wanted a permanent place in the organization. It was difficult to say goodbye to Bob Milano and Ort, but baseball is my love, and the Tigers are my family.

I think Mr. Ilitch understood that the city is in my soul because he was a native Detroiter himself. He went to Cooley High School and was offered $5,000 to play for the Tigers in 1948, but he turned them down to join the military. He has never been given enough credit for his commitment to Detroit. He could've built Comerica Park in the suburbs. He didn't have to put as much money into the city as he has. But Detroit is also tattooed on his heart, just as it is on mine.

It's been my great fortune to be around former bullpen coach Lance Parrish, a quiet man who's never received enough credit for his playing career. He played 19 seasons in the major league and much of his career was spent as one of the A.L.'s best catchers. He was an eight-time All-Star and a three-time Gold Glove winner. To me, he's a Hall of Famer.

In my opinion, there are some former Tigers who should be in the Hall of Fame. Let's start with Lou Whitaker. Now that Alan Trammell is in, Lou must follow. My former teammate Mickey Lolich should be inducted. I've been in the game, or I have watched the game, for more than 45 years, and Mickey is clearly one of the most dominant left-handers I've ever seen.

Speaking of Hall of Famers, I can't say enough about the late Ernie Harwell. Although he didn't play the game, he was as important to me as any player in the clubhouse. During spring training, I would go to his house almost every Sunday for dinner. I would call his wife "Mother Lulu." He was a special man, and he always gave you something to think about when you left him.

People also forget that Ray Lane was doing radio when the Tigers won the pennant in 1968. My son Darryl William's first plane trip came when he was four years old, and Ray volunteered to bring him to Lakeland for me.

When my number was retired, it occurred to me that another Tiger wore No. 23 as proudly as I did—Kirk Gibson. I'm proud that my number was associated with him because he played the game with passion.

Since rejoining the organization, we have headed in the right direction and the Ilitch family has the team headed in the right direction today. Also, since my return, I've enjoyed being with the Tigers. Another friend who has influenced my life significantly is my agent, Mark Dehem. Given how my previous agent negatively affected my life, it's a real joy now to have an agent who's like a member of the family.

Many years ago, a fellow named Cliff Cooke had asked me why I didn't sign autographs at trading-card shows. "I don't believe in charging people for my autograph," I told him. But Cliff said I should be doing those shows because my fans wanted to see me, and he figured how to structure deals so fans wouldn't have to pay.

When Cliff died, I assumed my signing days were over. But Mark Dehem said, "Willie, let me take care of you."

And he's done just that. I have trouble saying no, and Mark has made sure I'm sheltered from having to deal with those situations. He's also taken the load off my wife, Gloria. And, frankly, he's been by my side during some tragedies in my life.

Happiness surrounds my life these days, but it's not only because of my return to baseball. I've always been a spiritual person; my parents raised me in a Baptist household and God had always influenced my life. I have to admit that I strayed from His word at times during my career, but I always knew His presence, even if I wasn't a regular at Sunday services.

My three sons, Darryl William, Deryl Lamar, and Al, jointly owned a record label and management company with MC Hammer for a while. It was called Bust It, and they lived a lifestyle that involved the rich and famous. But eventually, each of my sons decided that wasn't the kind of lifestyle they wanted to live.

Deryl Lamar became close friends with NFL star Deion Sanders along the way, and in fact, Deryl introduced Deion to his future wife. Deryl also fondly remembers the day he and Deion had an important phone conversation.

"Deion, there's something I want to tell you," Deryl Lamar said.

"No, first there's something I want to tell you," Deion replied. "I've accepted Jesus Christ as my Lord and savior."

Deryl was stunned. "That's what I was going to tell you!"

That's a true story.

At different times, under different circumstances, all of my sons and daughters have been saved.

And what I found out later is that Deryl Lamar, a deacon at New Light Baptist Church in Detroit, would pray with his mother that I would find my way to God.

God sent a messenger to help me find the right path. My family experienced a series of tragedies that left us in mourning. My niece, Mar-Kecia, a student at Western Michigan University, was murdered in 1998. A woman ran her over with a car because she didn't like that my niece had paid attention to a young man. Mar-Kecia had lived with us in Seattle for a time, and it was like losing a daughter. It was a senseless death—almost impossible to discuss without being overwhelmed by the horror of it.

Just three days after Mar-Kecia was killed, my brother Robert, who would call Gloria every day to say hello, strangely didn't call. We were concerned, so Deryl and I went to Robert's house. I held Robert and I cried, but we were too late. He had passed away.

On December 8, 2000, my nephew David Griffin died. Gloria's mother, Thelma, also died that year. She was very, very close to us. Then, on December 20, 2001, my brother Ray passed away in Tennessee, and five days later we were all on the highway on Christmas Day, heading to his funeral. In 2002, we lost our 19-year-old nephew, Kenyon. Each death brought us so much pain. But Deryl says the pain was taking me where I needed to be.

In 2003, another nephew named Raymond Tyner—we called him Mr. T—was suffering from cancer, and I had called to see how he was doing. In the midst of that conversation, I mentioned some minor aches and pains I was having.

Mr. T cut me off. "I respect you greatly, Willie, but there's no need for you to complain," he said. "The only thing you should be worried about is your soul."

I tried to talk to him about how he was feeling, and he told me not to worry about him. "You should be worrying about your soul."

His words hit me like a fastball in the ribs.

Mr. T was a spiritual man, and his cancer was in remission. That's why I was stunned a couple of days later when I got a call that he had died of a heart attack.

At his funeral in Dayton, Ohio, I told the congregation what Mr. T had told me two days before he died. He was at peace with God.

But God's message overwhelmed me 18 days later when our nephew Durand Ferris was gunned down at a gas station in a case of mistaken identity.

At his funeral at New Light Baptist Church, I could feel God in my heart, and I remember what Reverend Dr. Benjamin Stanley Baker said that day: "Anyone who believes in their heart and wants to confess with their mouth that the Lord Jesus Christ is the Savior should please come forward."

At that moment, I rose from the pew and marched to the front of the church.

Reverend Baker asked if I had any words to say. "It's time," I said. "The Lord has always put His hands on me and has been right there for me. I do believe in my heart, and I am confessing this with my mouth. He has always held my hand and now it's time for me to hold Him."

Deryl Lamar says that Gloria cried when I went to the front of the church. My daughter Pam was actually in charge of taking down the names of new members, and she hadn't looked up to see it was me who had come down the aisle. Reverend Baker said to her, "You have someone else to sign up."

When she turned and realized I was a new church member, you could feel the joy in her heart.

Deryl Lamar's son, Deryl Jr., also accepted Christ that day. And when Darryl William was told of my acceptance of the Lord, he broke down over the phone.

Despite the tragedies that my family endured over the years, I have peace in my life. I'm closer to my team, closer to my family, and closer to my God. My life seems complete.

# Chapter 18

# Family

MY PARENTS' FIRST HOME in Detroit had one bedroom, a sitting room, a kitchen, and a shared bathroom. But there always seemed to be plenty of room for friends and family.

These days, we hold family reunions once a year. But back then it seemed as if we had family reunions every weekend. All of Lillian Horton's children came to see her often, and no one ever considered paying for a hotel room. Family sometimes would visit from down South and some would bunk at my sister Faye's house, or over at my sister Virginia's. When I was young, my cousins were so involved in my life that they seemed like brothers and sisters. And my mother was always bringing home someone for supper. Even if you didn't have much, my mother believed that you did what you could for those who had less than you.

When I close my eyes, I can still see Poppa looking out the window, shaking his head and laughing. "Who's Sis bringing home for supper tonight?" he would say.

It was chicken or fish every Friday night, bologna and crackers on Saturday, and a special meal on Sunday.

Family was important to my mother and father, and that belief rubbed off on their youngest child. When I think about my baseball career and my life, the family atmosphere has always been a central theme.

The Detroit Tigers always seemed like a second family to me, and Jim Campbell was like a second father to me when my own dad passed away. When I think about my first few years in organized baseball, Black players like Billy Bruton, Sam Jones, Gates Brown, Jake Wood, and others made me feel like I'd joined another family. In the early 1960s, it still was a struggle for Blacks to make it to the major leagues. But you knew you weren't in it alone. Black players looked after one another. They helped each other make the climb up.

Down in Lakeland, Florida, Charles and Madeline Brooks made sure Black ballplayers had a place to live when no hotels would accept them. Madeline worked for the NAACP, and the Brookses didn't just talk the talk. They walked the walk.

And when I barbecued every spring for players and fans down in spring training, it was undoubtedly inspired by my need to feel surrounded by "family."

My former Tigers teammates remain close to me to this day. Some have passed on, including a few who died far too young. Bob Christian, Joe Sparma, Norm Cash, and Ray Oyler all died very young. Sadly, we've also lost Pat Dobson, Dick McAuliffe, Gates Brown, Earl Wilson, Jim Northrup, Eddie Mathews, Don McMahon, Al Kaline, Bill Freehan, John Wyatt, and Tom Matchick. I keep in touch with many others, including Jon Warden. Jon and I talk regularly, and when I had health problems one winter in Florida, he stepped up to help me. I'll never forget his kindness.

Jim Price still works in the Tigers radio broadcast booth, and still operates the team fantasy camps. I always suspected he'd make a name for himself.

I'm proud of my own family, and I thank my wife, Gloria, for how my children turned out. George Brooks called her "the matriarch" of our family. My daughter Pam says Gloria's "the rock" of the family. Gloria really is the backbone of our family.

Although both of us had children before we were married to each other, we decided that we weren't going to use the word "stepchild." All of my children are Hortons. And we raised them and loved them like they were Hortons. Gloria was the perfect person to raise this family. And I never worried when I was on the road because Gloria was always in control.

Gloria was my perfect match because she could both support me and guide me at the same time. Late in my career, when I had doubts about whether I should still be playing, she would tell me, "Willie, you can still play—and you love to play, so you keep on playing."

She's always been a strong woman, and she wasn't afraid to tell me when I was about to make a mistake. "Willie," she would say, "when you're wrong, you're wrong. And you are wrong here."

Remember, she had managed Club 23, and she had good business sense. I really needed to listen to her more than I did. Sometimes, people would ask me to get involved in financial deals, and she would say, "Willie, not all of these people are your friends."

Her patience with me was almost unbelievable. When people would come up and ask me for an autograph at an inopportune moment, she could've said, "Willie, this isn't the right time." She could've made an issue out of it. I saw other baseball wives do that. But Gloria understood that I wanted to treat the fans like kin. So she let me be me, and I'm thankful for that.

When I traveled with the team, she always kept me informed about what was happening with our children. They were always surprised that I would know the scores of their games when they called me. But Gloria always tried to keep me involved in the parenting process, even if I wasn't at home. My daughters joke that one of Gloria's talents was making me feel like I had some input even when the decision had already been made.

"Go ahead and do it, but don't tell your father," she would say to the kids. "Let me talk to him." We all laugh about that now because it's the kind of maneuvering that has to be done when you have a father who's traveling more than 100 days a year.

People probably believe that it was me who got my children involved in sports. But during my career, Gloria was more involved with the kids' athletics—and she was well qualified. She also went to Northwestern High School in Detroit, where she played basketball and field hockey. She also worked with a teacher named Miss Nelson to try to convince school board officials to launch a girls track program at Northwestern. It wasn't started in time for Gloria to join, and it's too bad because she probably would have been an outstanding track athlete.

Even today, she knows more about basketball than I do. When we were living in Seattle, she worked at the Sheraton Hotel, managing a restaurant. She convinced the hotel to sponsor a men's recreation basketball team, and she coached the team to the championship. The trophy is still on display in the hotel. She was extremely serious about the team, calling our sons occasionally for advice because they also knew the game. When the boys were young, Gloria was often in the driveway playing hoops with them.

The funny aspect about my relationship with my wife is that she wasn't sure she even liked me when we were teenagers. We both attended Northwestern High School, and we knew each other well, even though we didn't date. She wrote for the school newspaper. Her brother Sam Reid and I were good friends, and he used to get in trouble at home for coming home late. Gloria used to blame me for that.

Years later, when I invited her to go to a party with me, she said she wasn't even sure she wanted anything to do with me. My father's parenting style was firm and confrontational. My mother's style was soft and caring. Hopefully, my children see my style as a combination of the two. I wanted to be softer with my children than my dad was with me, but I felt I had to give them some tough-love lessons. You have to push your children to be the best they can be.

Deryl Lamar has thanked me for the tough-love approach I took with him after he was diagnosed with scoliosis. He had a curved spine, and doctors recommended risky surgery to insert a metal rod to straighten it. Deryl was a second baseman with pro potential, and doctors told us he would likely not be an athlete after the operation. They told us that it would be a year before he would even be able to walk again.

"Don't you worry about that," I told the doctors, already believing in my mind that we were going to get Deryl moving long before that.

Just a teenager at the time, Deryl wasn't even sure he wanted to endure that level of rehabilitation. But he also didn't want to ensure the pain of scoliosis.

"Son," I told him, "you have to take chances in life. You have to have the surgery. You have to believe that it's going to work out."

Doctors warned us that "it was a 50/50 proposition," and if there were any complications with the surgery, the damage could be severe. They were already concerned about his flexibility. They really did effectively rule out his hopes for pro baseball.

"Son, don't ever let another man tell you what you can or can't do," I told Deryl. "If you work hard, anything can happen."

My father had said those same words to me many years before.

After the surgery, he was in a full body cast. We would go into his room and lift him three times a day. After a few months, his spirits were down, but Gloria and I weren't having any of that. We told him it was time to get out of bed and rejoin life. We bought him a weight bench and an exercise bike, and I worked out with him.

In just five months, he was walking again. And after nine months, Deryl could dunk a basketball.

His rehabilitation went so well that he actually went to an Oakland A's tryout camp in Medford, Oregon, a year later. He ran well and looked terrific, but his bat speed wasn't where it needed to be. He survived the first cut, but didn't get through the second.

I thought I'd need to console Deryl, but he told me he would be fine.

"This wasn't about baseball," Deryl said. "This was about the commitment you had in me. It was about what we accomplished when people told us we couldn't do it."

When my boys went off to school, my only request was that they continue to communicate with one another and remain close. They all promised they would, and they've lived up to that promise. Darryl William had tremendous talent, and maybe he could've been a major league outfielder. I remember when he was in the minors in the New York Yankees chain, Bucky Dent would call and ask me to speak to Darryl about working harder. Darryl was invited to the Detroit Tigers' spring training camp once, and he also spent a season in the Chicago White Sox farm system.

He was a terrific all-around athlete at St. Benedictine High School in Detroit. He was 6'2", over 200 pounds, and had a 38-inch vertical jump, which came in handy on the basketball court. He averaged 27.5 points per game as a junior at St. Benedictine, which made him one of the top 10 scorers in the state. He averaged 24 or 25 points per game as a senior and finished with more than 1,500 points at St. Benedictine. He played one season at Navajo Junior College in Arizona, but was injured during his time there. He also ended up playing one season of football at Saginaw Valley State University.

Al is 6'4" and he had a strong basketball career at Redford High School. He held the school record of 38 points in a game before it finally fell a few years ago. When he played there, my daughter Gail was the team's mascot. Al later played at El Camino Junior College and then Drake, but his college career was undermined by two knee surgeries. He ended up in the military, before settling into the entertainment business.

My daughter April lives in Florida, and my other three daughters have settled in Michigan. Terri, who went to Oregon State, worked for the Detroit Board of Education. In college, she was an exchange student in Paris. We lost her too soon.

Pamela attended Clark Atlanta University. My wife says Gail is a lot like me—tough and stern in her approach. When she played soccer back in Seattle, they called her "Thunderfoot" because she could kick with authority. During one softball game, Gail walked into someone swinging a bat. Gail's face swelled up dramatically, but she wouldn't let Gloria take her out of the game. She was a tough athlete.

One funny story about Pam is that—believe it or not—she married a man named Darryl. So when you count our two grandsons, we now have five men named Darryl or Deryl in our immediate family. I joked that it's like boxer George Foreman naming all of his boys "George."

Gloria and I raised our grandson Dominique, and that again reminds me of my life growing up in the projects. My mother helped raise her grandkids like they were her own children. As I've said before, my nephews seemed more like siblings to me. And in the Horton family, everyone helps raise the children.

Dominique is studying to be a minister. He sends the family a weekly devotion every Monday.

The older members of the family talked about that when my nephew Michael passed away. Michael, of course, was one of the youngsters in the car in 1965 when my parents were killed in that car crash. Joe, the other youngster in the car, died years ago.

At Michael's funeral, I told the congregation: "Michael was a nephew, but he was raised like he was my brother, and I disciplined him like he was my son. And in the end, he was my friend."

At the funeral, I told Michael's mother, Faye, that she had been like a mother to me back in the days when I spent nights with her in the projects. I would eat at Mama and Papa's house, but I would sleep at her place in the projects. Really, all of my brothers and sisters were like parents to me. Even my late brothers-in-law, George and Ken, were also parental figures to me. George was married to Helen, and Ken was married to Frankie.

In the Horton family, my brothers and sisters always did what they could to help. My brother Joe went into the service to help the family, and I always believed that Billy's decision to go into the service helped me get through school because he was helping support the family.

Today, I draw my strength from my family, and it gives me great pleasure to talk to them all of the time. It's not hard to believe that all of my daughters have taught me—and maybe even humbled me—many times. One of the turning points in my life came when my daughter Pam, then 13, confronted me about all the days I'd spent away from home as a baseball player. At the time, I was playing for the Portland Beavers, the Triple-A affiliate of the Pittsburgh Pirates. Pam and I were driving to the store one day when she got very upset with me.

"You don't even know me!" she said.

"What are you talking about?" I said. "I know you very well."

I initially thought that this was just a teenage rebellion issue, but I knew I had to be careful here. However, that wasn't it at all. She was just trying to tell me that I needed to think more about spending time with my family. And I decided she was right. Maybe I had taken my family for granted.

Branch Rickey III headed up the Pirates organization then, and I got his permission to take Pam on the next road trip, which included stops in Arizona and New Mexico. Just to show how baseball is one big family, I should explain that Branch Rickey III is the grandson of Branch Rickey, who, in 1945, signed Jackie Robinson to his first pro contract with the Brooklyn Dodgers.

My trip with Pam was a memorable event, and it included one funny episode that's become a staple of Horton family storytelling.

Having just been paid, I stopped by a store in Arizona to make a quick purchase. I asked Pam to wait in the car. I removed the money I needed from my wallet and threw the wallet back into the car and told Pam to hold onto it.

Being young, Pam got impatient and eventually came into the store. "Where's my wallet?" I asked.

The mortified look on her face told me she had left it in the car.

The problem was that it was a very hot day, the windows were down, and someone walking by the car had larceny in their heart that day. When we got back to the car, the wallet was gone. Pam started crying, figuring her dad would erupt like a volcano.

"It's only money," I said. "Nothing bad happened here. We can always get more money."

Pam has often told that story, and maybe it'll be passed down through the generations. Maybe all of our descendants will embrace the philosophy that there should never be heartache over money.

While I might have some good parenting stories here, I would never suggest that my retirement from baseball went smoothly.

As I sorted through the emotional issues of leaving the game, there were some difficult times in my home. I'd been a professional ballplayer for almost two decades, and I really didn't know who I was outside the lines. When it became clear that the end was near, I started to think that I was letting my family down. Who knows, maybe deep down I believe I was letting my father down, too. I felt as if I could still play, so why couldn't I catch on with another team?

Even hitting 29 home runs for the Mariners in 1979 couldn't save me from the hardship of saying goodbye to a sport that was so intertwined with my life that it was hard to know who was beneath all those statistics.

I sometimes can't believe how well my life has gone after I stopped playing baseball.

Today, I'm told that I'm a national hero in Venezuela for winning the Caribbean World Series in 1979. There's even a bust of me at the stadium in Valencia.

That's surprising given that when I returned to the city to manage and play in 1980, it didn't go as well. We had different players, and more importantly, there was a different attitude in management.

When we struggled for a few games, I was called into the office. They told me either I was going or we were going to change some players. I said I wasn't going, and so I was fired.

Players were upset. Gloria was crying, and I was agitated. Then, Deryl Lamar overheard the team's traveling secretary bad-mouthing me to the media. Deryl's temper got the best of him, and he attacked the secretary. I had to pull him off. I knew there would be trouble after that—and there was.

We wanted to leave Venezuela the next day, but there were suggestions that Daryl would be arrested unless money was paid. I don't know who received the money or why, but no one was arresting my son for standing up for his father. I paid what needed to be paid, and didn't ask any questions.

If I would've listened to Gloria more, I probably would've had more money when I retired. But much of my financial difficulty was caused by a former agent who led me to believe that my finances were in order when they were not. Several other major leaguers were victimized by his actions, and all of us ended up with back taxes owed to the Internal Revenue Service.

When I appeared before the judge, I accepted responsibility because it was my fault for not overseeing my own finances. In the end, it was Gloria who was able to get us square with the IRS.

My troubles were weighing heavy on my mind when I retired, and I told my wife to take the girls and move back to Detroit while I sorted through the issues. Maybe I just needed to be alone. But I ended up spending most of my time with a friend named Jim Brown. He was an outdoorsman and a spiritual man, and he made me realize that life was really just beginning for me.

"You don't have to be rich and play baseball to enjoy life," he said. "Your job now is to raise your family."

He really just brought me back to my Southern roots and made me realize what was really important in my life. Jim was a man who had suffered catastrophic injuries as a teenager when he was hit by a train, but he persevered to become a man of exceptional character. He believed strongly in the Man Upstairs. And when my No. 23 was retired in Detroit, he and his wife drove all the way across the country to be there.

Although I would soon get involved in coaching, I had to find some immediate work, and I ended up working on a maintenance crew at the *Seattle Post-Intelligencer*. When some of the executives saw me sweeping the floors, they offered me a job in the office. But I stayed where I was.

Deryl Lamar was working with me, and one night when I was scrubbing toilets, he told me, "Dad, you shouldn't have to do this kind of work."

"Son," I said, "my dad taught me long ago that what's important in life if that you do whatever you need to do to support your family. If you have to wash dishes, you wash dishes. If you have to sweep floors, you sweep floors. And that's what I'm going to do."

By taking that job, I actually felt better about who I was. And only then was I ready to move on to coaching.

At 79, I still have much I want to do in the world of baseball. It's hard to describe how good it makes me feel when the young players ask me for advice and talk to me about their game.

I still want to do more with the children, which is why I still work with the Boys and Girls Club in Lakeland and Mulberry, Florida, and in the Tigers' organization in Lakeland. One of my other goals is to help resurrect baseball in the city of Detroit. Inner-city baseball seems to be dying all over the United States, and it's a shame because there are more Willie Hortons in the projects waiting for an opportunity.

To me, there's a three-fold problem that needs to be addressed. First, we need to place more emphasis on developing neighborhood leagues. People spend too much emphasis on travel baseball. That's fine, but it's the local leagues where the process starts. Second, we must offer more training for coaches. There are men and women out there willing to coach, but they need to be taught how to coach effectively. Finally, we have to restore the hunger of the African American players. Today, Latin American players have that hunger. They see baseball as their ticket to a better life and they work hard at becoming better players.

Better fields will help. We played on quality fields when I was a youngster. That's why I was very proud that Northwestern High School honored me, dedicating new softball and baseball fields in 2004. They were paid for by a $127,000 grant from the Baseball Tomorrow Fund.

I had trouble finding the right words at the ceremony, but this is what I said: "It's about people—my whole life is about people, my whole career was about the fans. The city, the park and the school—we and this family and our communities have to become a partnership for this to work."

There's a sense of contentment in my life these days. I call Deryl Lamar, and when I ask him, "What's the word today?" he knows I'm not making small talk. I want to know his take with the Scriptures.

People write new chapters in their lives every day, and I'm writing some beautiful chapters these days. I was in an automobile accident in 2003 and ended up with a hip replacement. But honestly, that just seems like a minor inconvenience. I like where my life is at, and I'm surprised every day about where it takes me.

In 2004, Gloria and I attended Major League Baseball's All-Star Game in Houston, and while we were there, Dave Winfield's wife spent an hour telling me how much I meant to her husband. He actually thought I was in the Hall of Fame. I can't tell you how touched I was by that.

Likewise, I was surprised when Deryl Lamar told me that famed boxing promoter Emanuel Steward once told him that my boxing ability was exceptional enough that I could've challenged for the heavyweight championship of the world, had I pursued it.

"Your dad was Mike Tyson before there was Mike Tyson," Steward told Deryl. "He was called 'One Punch Willie' because he would knock out grown men when he was 15 years old."

One of my hobbies is watching vintage black-and-white Western movies, particularly the old Roy Rogers classics. Apparently, the love of those films runs in my family.

Years ago, my late friend Arsene Bondy traveled down South with me. While we were at a hotel in Tennessee, I found one of those movies on TV and settled into watching it. We left the hotel in the middle of the movie to visit my brother Ray and his wife Pinkie. When we got to their house, Ray was watching the same movie.

Arsene started laughing, but he was really amused when Ray and I started to watch it together.

When Ray said "Hey Willie, look! He's behind the bush—he's going to get 'em," I thought Arsene was going to fall on the floor laughing.

My father didn't often hold conversations with me. He didn't care much about my opinion. But I remember having a couple of discussions with Poppa after I worked out at a park across the street from the family home on Edison. I would run laps around the park, and when I stopped for a breather, I'd sit on the bench next to Poppa. That's when he used to tell me stories about all of his children.

"They're all my kids, and I claim them all," he told me. But there are probably only four or five of them I would sign my name for."

I've always wondered whether I was one of those four or five.

Poppa never told me he was proud of me. That wasn't his way. But I always believed he was proud of me as a baseball player. I also want to believe he would have been proud of how Gloria and I raised our children. We raised seven children, and we've lost Terri. But we have 21 grandchildren, 23 great grandchildren. For the record, I've signed for all seven of my kids, and it made me feel good to be able to do that.

# Chapter 19

# Bird Left Our Nest

MARK "THE BIRD" FIDRYCH always knew where his pitches were going because he had given the baseball specific instructions on where he wanted it to go.

When the Cleveland Indians watched Fidrych talk to the ball during his first major league start, on May 15, 1976, they thought he was out of his mind. He would play with the dirt on the mound like he was about to start a garden. He high-fived teammates after routine plays. Then there were his conversations with the baseball. Fidrych talked, and the ball seemed to listen.

The Indians were all laughing about Fidrych's antics until they realized he was throwing a no-hitter going into the seventh inning, when Buddy Bell broke it up. He finished with a two-hitter in his 2–1 complete-game victory over the Indians.

It was one of the most remarkable performances I had ever seen, and Fidrych was one of the most beautiful human beings I ever met.

When I was told on April 13, 2009, that Mark Fidrych had died in a tragic accident while working on his 10-wheel truck, it felt like I had just lost another family member. He was only 54. It was such a shock that I had a hard time believing it was true. How can a man so full of life be dead?

Although I played only one full season with Fidrych, I was probably as close to him as I was to some of my 1968 teammates. He loved life and he loved to play baseball. He was always such a positive person.

The first time I met Fidrych, I thought he was the batboy. He had that moppy, unkempt curly hair. Somebody thought he looked like Big Bird from *Sesame Street*, and the nickname stuck. He seemed perfect because he was an animated character on the mound. He would address the ball before he pitched because he believed it needed guidance.

I immediately took "Bird" under my wing because he had such a wonderful spirit. We talked all of the time, and he made me laugh all of the time. He became an instant star, and it didn't faze him all. I remember well-dressed Tony Kubek, wearing a splendid bowtie, interviewing Fidrych on national television, and Fidrych had on jeans, a t-shirt and moccasins with no socks. He didn't even have a telephone installed in his apartment. He would go to a pay phone if he needed to call someone. That was "Bird."

But the boy could pitch. He kept the ball low and he picked away at the corners of the plate. His fastball had late movement. Sometimes, it would tail away from a hitter and sometimes it would sail in on a hitter. He posted a 19–6 record with an amazing 24 complete games to win the American League Rookie of the Year Award in 1976.

What impressed me the most about Fidrych was his ability to fill up stadiums around the country. Fans came to see him by the thousands. For years, I've said that Fidrych gave Major League Baseball a charge when it needed it. He brought fans back to the ballpark. In one stretch, more than 424,000 people showed up to watch him over 10 starts. I think you can say he saved baseball in that time period. He made the sport popular again by taking the game back to the people.

This is a kid who cared as much about the fans as he did about his own success. In 1976, he received about 20 birthday cakes and hundreds of cards, when he celebrated his 22nd birthday. And after he won a big game, his No. 1 topic for reporters was to make sure that they wrote in their stories that he wanted to thank all of the fans who send him cards and cakes.

Fidrych was one of a kind. We sang "Take Me Out to the Ball Game" at his funeral. It was the right thing to do. "Bird" would have enjoyed that.

Probably our best moment together came on August 11, 1976, when I hit a pinch-hit, walk-off home run in the ninth inning to give Fidrych a 4–3 win against the Texas Rangers.

For most of that game, I had been in the trainer's room getting treatment for a nagging injury. And I remember that "Bird" kept coming back between innings to tell me that I should stay ready because he may need me. That was a difficult season for me. I hadn't been playing much. But Fidrych didn't allow you to be down around him. He was always upbeat.

"How are you doing, Willie?" he would say. "You have to get yourself ready."

After Fidrych retired the side in the ninth, I put on my uniform and came into the dugout. As soon as I arrived, manager Ralph Houk told me to bat for Jerry Manuel. I had gone 19 games without a home run, but as soon as I hit the pitch I knew it was gone. Looking back, it was as if Fidrych knew that it was going to be my night. Even though he was 21 and I was 33, he was being the leader. He was trying to inspire me.

What I remember most about that night was the crowd response. They wouldn't leave the stadium until Fidrych and I came out to take a bow.

I was asked to give one of the eulogies at Fidrych's funeral and that's one of the stories I told. I also said Fidrych was the best teammate I ever had. I said that because long after we played together he was still by my side when I needed him.

Not long after my first book was published, we found out that my daughter Terri needed a double lung transplant because of exposure to asbestos through her employment.

It was a devastating, scary time for my family. At one point, doctors said there wasn't anything more they could do. But we got hope from doctors in Pittsburgh who said they believed the double-lung transplant could work. Tigers manager Jim Leyland and Detroit hitting coach Lloyd McClendon still had many connections from their days in Pittsburgh, and they made calls on our behalf.

When I received the call notifying me that a donor had been found for Terri I was so overwhelmed that I forgot to pick up my wife, Gloria, before I headed to Pittsburgh.

Doctors had tried to prepare us for how bad Terri would look after the operation, but it was stunning to see her in that condition. She was not recognizable. But I remember a kindly nurse telling me that Terri was going to perk up as soon as her sisters arrived at the hospital. She said she had seen it many times: When a patient's siblings arrive, they start to recover. And she was right. Terri has had some setbacks, but she is doing well today.

Although Terri had insurance, the cost of this surgery was expensive to the point that we had to hold a fundraiser to pay the costs that insurance didn't cover. Some of the former Tigers came in to help. Among those was Fidrych. We offered to pay him for his time, but he wouldn't accept any form of payment. He wouldn't even let us pay for his travel. And this is a man who didn't play long enough in the major leagues to stash any money away. He was just an honest, hard-working, blue-collar man after he left baseball. He was an everyday guy.

As I was delivering Fidrych's eulogy, I struggled to hold back tears. In summary, I said there should be a place in the Hall of Fame for players who are beautiful human beings. Fidrych had the credentials to be a first-ballot honoree in that category.

In addition to Fidrych, the Tiger family has lost Jimmy Northrup and Ernie Harwell since my first book was published. As previously mentioned, Jimmy was a fine player. We wouldn't have won the 1968 World Series without Northrup's contribution. And Ernie was probably one of Michigan's true treasures. He was a star in his own right, but Ernie never acted like a star.

Since the first edition of my book was published, I've had some knocks. I've lost friends and family members. But there isn't a day when I don't get up and feel that I've been blessed. I've always felt as if God has looked after me. My family is still strong, and I still have many of the same friends I had when I was a young man growing up in the Jeffries Projects.

I've had blessings great and small in my life. One of the more interesting stories involved my 1968 World Series ring that I lost shoveling snow at my bar in Detroit in the 1970s.

It seemed as if I would never see it again. But close to three decades after I lost it, I heard from a man whose brother had inherited the ring from his grandfather who owned a pawn shop in Miami. Not knowing whether to meet him or not, I turned the matter over to my agent, Mark

Dehem. The man said his brother lived in Hawaii and he had convinced him to part with the ring.

We asked him what he wanted for the ring, and he said he didn't want anything for it. He just wanted to return it to me. He didn't even want a reward.

Even after we agreed to meet him, we weren't sure we believed every word the man said. Mark's brother, Dave, is a police officer, and he agreed to join us.

We had the meeting and the man did indeed have the ring, and he handed it over. True to his word, he wanted nothing. He just said he wanted the ring to be with its rightful owner.

The funny conclusion to this story is that less than a week later I was at my grandson Dominique's youth baseball game when I suddenly realized the ring was gone. It must have slipped off my finger again.

We halted the game, and someone brought out a metal detector and we searched the entire infield, to no avail. The ring had disappeared.

I don't know whether I was more sad about losing the ring, or afraid of what Gloria was going to say about me losing the ring again.

"Don't tell your grandmother," I told Dominique.

Later that night, Dominique removed his cleats out of his bag and my ring tumbled out of the shoe. He had no idea how it got there. We don't even have a theory. As the saying goes, the Lord works in mysterious ways.

My blessed life continued several years later. I had a physical at the start of spring training and I was diagnosed with prostate cancer.

I remember shortly after hearing I had cancer, I had a talk with Tigers owner Mike Ilitch, who is a spiritual man. He told me simply to follow my doctor's advice and keep my faith and I would be fine.

Not long after that meeting, tests could find no evidence that I had cancer. But it returned, and I was forced to have prostate surgery. I joked with the surgeon that I was praying his hands were steady. He laughed.

The surgery was a success. It feels as if my faith helped me through this. I have such a strong faith that God is looking over me, that I never even think about having had cancer.

# Chapter 20

# Greenberg and Me

WHEN HANK GREENBERG played for the Detroit Tigers in the 1930s and '40s, opposing fans poured hate speech on him from every section of the ballpark.

You don't have to be Black to know the ugliness of bigotry.

Not many people knew that Greenberg and Jackie Robinson were close friends. Their bond developed over a mutual understanding of what it was like to try to play baseball in hostile stadiums where people would routinely taunt them or call them the ugliest of names.

Throughout Greenberg's career, he was verbally abused and discriminated against because he was Jewish.

Greenberg's and Robinson's paths literally collided during the 1947 season. Robinson had made history by becoming the first Black player in major league history. The Tigers had sold Greenberg to the Pittsburgh Pirates, mostly because the Tigers didn't want to pay his hefty salary. They also didn't want to face him. That's why they moved him to the National League.

On this day, Greenberg and Robinson both happened to be playing first base. Early in the game, Robinson laid down a perfect bunt. But it was a bang-bang play at first. He ended up colliding with Greenberg. They both went down in a heap.

In the next inning, Greenberg walked. According to the *New York Times*, when he arrived at first base he asked whether Robinson was okay after the collision.

Assured that Robinson suffered no harm, Greenberg began talking to Robinson. It probably wasn't common for White players to talk cordially to Robinson.

"Don't pay any attention to these guys who are trying to make it hard for you," Greenberg said. "Stick in there. You're doing fine. Keep your chin up."

What Greenberg didn't know was Robinson had been thinking about quitting. His family had recently been threatened.

The *New York Times* reported the Greenberg-Robinson conversation in the following day's newspaper. Robinson told the *Times*: "Class tells. It sticks all over Mr. Greenberg."

This was big news because Greenberg was a two-time MVP.

That meeting at first base launched a lifelong friendship. Even after Greenberg retired the next season, he remained supportive of Jackie. I learned more about Jackie's career from Hank than from anyone else.

When I was playing with the Tigers, Hank would be around from time to time. We hit it off. He took me under his wing and taught me about how the baseball world worked. Gates Brown was the first one to tell me that I was a "franchise player." At the time, I didn't know what he was talking about.

I thought it was something bad. I kept telling him, "My dad said I'm a ballplayer. I'm not a franchise player."

Hank also schooled me about being a franchise player and the responsibility that goes with that tag. Greenberg helped me understand that you can do other things to help people, but on game day you have to focus on playing baseball.

You have to push everything else aside. That's what Greenberg did. He didn't tell me exactly what he went through on the field, but we've all heard and read the stories.

Anti-Semitism was rampant in those days. Comments from fans were frequently derogatory words about his Jewish heritage. He was heckled mercilessly. Former teammate Birdie Tebbetts was quoted as saying that no ballplayer except Robinson faced such frequent verbal abuse as Greenberg.

I experienced some issues, but nothing compared to what Greenberg and Robinson went through.

When it comes to racism, every Black person has his or her own story. I remember how appalled I was that stadium officials wouldn't let my grandparents sit together when they came to watch me play minor league baseball in Knoxville in 1963.

Because my grandmother was White, she could sit in any seat among the general group of spectators. But my grandfather was Black and he was told he had to sit in the Blacks-only section.

Midway through the season, the all-Black section was gone. But it certainly had a lasting impression.

We also don't talk often enough about what Hank Aaron had to endure when he was chasing the career home run record.

My guess is that he probably had a stack of death threat letters that were a foot high.

Only one time did another player throw a racial epithet in my direction. The Tigers were playing the White Sox. They had a tall shortstop named Ron Hansen. He was 6'3". He is remembered for pulling off an unassisted triple play. He caught a line drive, stepped on second to retire a runner who couldn't get back. Then he looked up and saw Russ Snyder coming from first. He tagged him for the third out.

I don't remember what year I had my encounter with Hansen. All I remember is I was sliding into second with a bad leg. Everyone knew I had a bad leg. I thought Hansen purposely stepped on me. He was trying to hurt me. I jumped up and Hansen reacted poorly.

He called me the N-word.

Immediately, I went after him and he started running toward the center-field bleachers. Other players intervened and order was restored.

We didn't end up enemies. Back then, we got over what happened in the heat of competition. Today, players stay mad. That's one difference between my generation and today's players.

One time, Greenberg reached his boiling point and marched over to the White Sox dugout and threatened to fight everyone on the Chicago team.

I learned from Greenberg. I received many hate letters during my time in Detroit. I showed them to Tigers' management, but I never brought it up with the media. I thought publicizing them would just invite more hate letters.

Greenberg learned that quickly in his career. He didn't let those who hated him get in the way of his success. In 1938, he clubbed 58 home runs. That was only two shy of Babe Ruth's record at the time.

He produced some incredible seasons. For instance, in 1937, Greenberg banged out 49 doubles, 14 triples, and 40 home runs. He drove in 184 runs while batting .337.

Greenberg helped me with sorting out how to deal with all that and how to have clout on and off the field.

I was fortunate in my career to have met many high-achieving people who offered me guidance on how to get the most out of my career. Let's start with Judge Damon Keith. He was like a father to me, particularly after my real dad was killed in the car accident.

When the Tigers signed me, I was just a teenager. Judge Keith kept me headed in the right direction. He gave me advice for a lot of years. We just lost him three years ago. He was 96. I can't fully explain how important he was to my life. It wasn't just me. As a civil rights attorney and judge, he helped more people than anyone realizes.

He was tough on me when I moved into his house. One night I came home at 11:15. I thought he told me to be home by 11:30. I came in through the garage and he came out and hit me in the chest.

"Eleven o'clock means eleven o'clock," he said.

Never was late again.

Judge Keith always tried to make sure that I was around the right people. He introduced me to Dr. Martin Luther King, entertainer Sammy Davis Jr., and actor Harry Belafonte. He would invite me down to his office to meet influential Black people.

I met a number of great leaders, including Andrew Young. He started as a pastor and ended up mayor of Atlanta and the U.S. Ambassador to the United Nations. He was a statesman, activist, and diplomat. I was fortunate enough to be able to do some work with him.

Judge Keith was a mentor to many and respected by all within the civil rights community. I met countless number of Black activists in his judicial chambers when I was a young man.

After the Detroit riots in 1967, I became more active in the civil rights movement. I worked with Coleman Young before he became Detroit's mayor.

When I was playing in Detroit, I was tied to the political world, the entertainment and the sports world. I knew many of the top sports stars: Dave Bing, Alex Karras, Lem Barney, Charlie Sanders, Mel Farr. Sanders and I were particularly tight.

Charlie and I went to Bill's Barber Shop on 7 Mile and Sorrento. The place was always busy and people didn't always pay much attention to who was in the shop with them.

One day, I was in the chair getting a haircut when a man came in and started talking about Detroit sports. He didn't know Charlie and I were there. At some point, he started cutting me up. I don't recall exactly what he didn't like about my game. Maybe I wasn't hitting enough for average to suit him or maybe I hadn't hit enough homers. When he was done with me, he threw some criticism on the Detroit Lions, including Charlie.

"Those sons of a bitches," he said at one point.

My barber was getting madder and madder, but I told him to let it go.

When my barber finished my cut, I rose from the chair, walked over to the guy, shook his hand, and said: "How do you do? I'm Willie Horton."

The look on his face was enough for me.

Bill, the owner, said to him, "You've got to find another barber. Because you can't come in here no more."

I got to know tennis star Arthur Ashe really well. We had a connection to the Harlem Globetrotters and I played with them for about 12 or 15 games as part of their tour in the Midwest. They wanted me to continue on their tour, but it was too much for me. They were playing a game in a different town every night.

It was fun hanging out with those guys. I have great respect for their athletic ability and their creativity. Meadowlark Lemon and Curly Neal were exceptional athletes and comedic geniuses. Those two guys and some of the others would plan their comedic plays on the bus and then execute them in the game without rehearsing them once.

It was amazing to witness.

Major league pitcher Ferguson Jenkins was also on the tour, and the guys came up with some crazy routine that finished with me batting the basketball into the basket.

I had played some high school basketball. So I had some comfort being on the court. We definitely had some laughs. But I had had enough after 15 games. That's a hard life.

From the time I was a young man, I was around successful Black people. The Four Tops and the Temptations grew up in Detroit neighborhoods. I had a class with Melvin Franklin of the Temptations. My brother-in-law had him in a few classes. The Four Tops were a little bit older and they mentored us.

In school, Melvin couldn't stop talking.

"Shut up, Melvin," our teacher would say.

"Yes, ma'am," he'd say in his low, heavy voice.

We knew The Drifters as well. By my recollection, about 85 percent of the Motown greats lived in Detroit when they were young. Most of them lived around me.

When I first moved into my first home on Steele right off 7 Mile, practically everyone in the area was in the entertainment business. Marvin Gaye lived behind me, Aretha Franklin was around the corner on Outer Drive, Smokey Robinson stayed right off Sorrento. We enjoyed hanging around with Aretha because she liked to cook. She had talent in the kitchen. She could cook and bake.

Aretha and I have been friends a long time. Several years back, she received the MLB Beacon of Change Award in Chicago. She asked me to be the presenter.

Organizers flew me to talk about her accomplishments. But she became ill at the last minute and I ended up presenting the award and accepting on her behalf. Bo Jackson was there. I gave both speeches. It was one of the hardest things I have ever had to do.

She received a medal for that honor, and I'm still holding it for her. Now and then, she runs into my wife, Gloria, at Kroger or at the mall.

"Tell your husband, I still want my award," Aretha says.

Kawasaki gave all of the Detroit Tigers players motorcycles. I guess they thought if people saw Tigers riding them they would buy them for themselves. Gates Brown and Mickey Lolich enjoyed their bikes and became motorcycle enthusiasts.

Motorcycles weren't for me. I gave mine to Marvin Gaye. He learned how to ride in the alley behind our houses.

Before starting on this book, I talked to Abdul "Duke" Fahir about the Willie Horton Party they threw for me in Anaheim. That's the one that started at the Copacabana and ended up at Glen Campbell's house. The Temptations and Four Tops both sang at the party.

Those guys all called me "the Babe Ruth of Detroit." I had to play with a hangover the next day. It was the best party I ever attended.

Even when I was playing, I understood I had been blessed with a great opportunity. My parents and Judge Keith made sure I was grounded.

# Chapter 21

# The Capuchin Boycott

EVEN THOUGH I was playing during the heyday of the Civil Rights movement, it wasn't easy for Black players to take a stand against injustice.

Players had to worry about the consequences for their actions. Black players wanted to do all that they could, but they also wanted to stay in the game. They didn't want to be labeled as troublemakers.

Just because Black players were allowed to stay in the same hotels and eat at the same restaurants didn't mean the battle was over.

Black players still weren't always treated fairly, especially when it came to who made the roster. Other subtle forms of racism also existed, like whose face was out front when the organization was marketing the team.

Jim Campbell was good to me for sure. But when it came time to discuss decisions about the team, the Tigers talked to their White star, Al Kaline, not their Black star, Willie Horton. That has nothing to do with Al Kaline. I loved the man and he always treated me with great respect.

The American League seemed to be behind the National League when it came to racial issues. As I previously mentioned, I believed Blacks were underrepresented on the Tigers' roster.

Players from the National League like Tommy Davis, Hank Aaron, and Ernie Banks used to tease me all of the time about playing in the "Republican League."

"Keep your head up," Davis would tell me.

They considered the National League the "Democratic League" because there seemed to be more players of color, particularly stars, in that league. The N.L. was stronger—not perfect—but stronger on integration.

The American League was the Republican League because we didn't seem to have as many players of color.

In 2021, we observed the 50<sup>th</sup> anniversary of the Pittsburgh Pirates playing a lineup exclusively made up of players of color. Every player was Black or Latino. That was 24 years after Jackie Robinson broke the color barrier.

Although the Pirates had used a lineup that was mostly Black or Latino for most of the season, it wasn't until September 1 when it used the all-minority lineup. White players Rich Hebner, the starting third baseman, and Gene Alley, the shortstop, were injured and opened up spots for Dave Cash and Jackie Hernández.

Here was the Pirates' lineup card that day:

Rennie Stennett, 2B

Gene Clines, CF

Roberto Clemente, RF

Willie Stargell, LF

Manny Sanguillén, C

Dave Cash, 3B

Al Oliver, 1B

Jackie Hernández, SS

Doc Ellis, P

Curt Flood refused to report to the Philadelphia Phillies after being traded in 1969 and challenged baseball's reserve clause all the way to the U.S. Supreme Court. He lost his case on a 5–3 decision. His actions ruined his career, although he did inspire others to continue the fight that eventually led to the creation of a free agent system.

I'm sure Flood knew that as a Black player he was taking a huge risk for his actions. Racial tension at that time was high.

As a Black player, your concern is that a GM might hold activism against you.

But that didn't stop Earl Wilson, Gates Brown, Jake Wood, and me from deciding to boycott the Capuchin Dinner. The dinner, attended annually by the Detroit Tigers, was to benefit the youth in the Detroit area. The charity helped both Black and White kids. But there were never any Black kids at the fundraising event.

All of us agreed not to attend. That was in 1967. We planned to meet at GM Jim Campbell's office to let him know what we were doing.

So I was sitting outside of Jim Campbell's, watching the clock, and waiting for my friends to show up.

"Why don't you come into my office, Willie," Mr. Campbell said. "They aren't going to show up."

"How do you know?" I asked.

"Because I know how these things go," Campbell said. "They wanted you to come up and talk to me about it."

Mr. Campbell could be tough in negotiations, but I always found he was a fair man. He was generous with me. He listened to what I had to say. He warned me that changes weren't going to occur overnight. But he would see what he could do.

He also told me that when I talked to the other guys they would say they never agreed to join me in the meeting.

A week later, the Tigers were in Baltimore. Brown explained why he and the other Black players hadn't come to Mr. Campbell's office. "We went out for dinner and they gave me a speech."

"You're a franchise player," Gator said. "Willie, the Tigers can get rid of us, but they can't get rid of you. Fans wouldn't be happy if they tried to get rid of you."

I didn't initially accept Gator's "franchise player" label. Not fully understanding what it meant, I thought it sounded negative.

"Poppa always told me I was just a ballplayer," I said. "I don't want to be a franchise player."

"Whether you want to be a franchise player or not, you are one," Gator said.

And after he explained how I could use my stature to help others, I began to understand why the other Black players wanted me to be the spokesperson. I had more protection than they had so maybe I could get more accomplished.

The late broadcasting legend Ernie Harwell also talked to me about the responsibilities that come with being a franchise player.

In 1970, me, Gator, and Elliott Maddux boycotted the Capuchin Dinner. We were fined $100.

The following year, the Capuchin group sent tickets to Judge Damon Keith to distribute to the Black community.

I think one of the reasons why Judge Keith introduced me to so many successful Black people is he wanted me to use my stature to help others. The Police Athletic League programs allowed me to compete for free in my younger years, and I've worked with that program through the years to help other kids receive the same benefit.

We've introduced a similar program in Polk County, Florida, to make sure that children get a chance to compete. I still try to give back whenever I can. I've been involved with the military for many years and I'm still active in charity work.

When I was playing, I tried to do my part by mentoring young players when they came up. I did that whether they were Black or White. I remember Rocky Colavito did that for me and I tried to pay it forward.

Through the years, I had a bunch of young players stay with me, including Tim Hosley, Marvin Lane, Wayne Redmond, Art James, and even Jerry Manuel who went on to become a manager with the Chicago White Sox and New York Mets.

I even bought a gas station to give the young guys a job in the summer. Back when I started in the game, the pay wasn't as lucrative as it is today. You had to find an off-season job to support your family.

One winter, I worked for Chrysler. I also worked for a while for Learjet. After the Tigers won the World Series in 1968, Johnny Podres, Gates Brown, and I took a job with the Wonder Bread Bakery. We were sales executives, and it was our job to land new clients.

We'd go to work every day, but we weren't working. Johnny would talk us into going to the race track every day. One week, we received a check for two dollars. We got fired pretty quickly.

Today's players don't want to play winter ball, but players in my era would go because the pay was decent. I had great experiences in winter ball. That's how I got to know Roberto Clemente and Orlando Cepeda and others. Those guys provided me with a lot of knowledge about the game. I took their knowledge and passed it along. That is what you are supposed to do in the game of baseball.

# Chapter 22

# Empty Seats

IN THE 12 years I played with Al Kaline, I'm not sure he ever said more than 100 words to me. If you asked him a question, he would answer. But he wasn't a guy who asked what you did on your off day.

We had big personalities in our locker room. But Al wasn't one of them. Norm Cash and Gates Brown were outgoing. They would get up in your business and cut up with you. That wasn't the way Al interacted with teammates. He was quiet. He kept to himself.

As I said before, he was 18 when he hit his first major league home run. At 19, he was playing regularly for the Tigers. At 20, he won the American League batting championship. Al batted .340 that season. He accomplished all of that before he was old enough to hang out in bars with his teammates.

When he became a starter at 19, the Tigers had 10 guys over 30, including catcher Al Lakeman, who was 35. A teenager didn't have much in common with veterans.

I think Al decided it was best to keep to himself. And he stayed that way even when he was older. But don't confuse being quiet with being unkind. Al would do anything in the world to help you if you went to him and asked.

With Al, you needed to initiate the conversation. I learned that early in my career. Al couldn't have been more helpful to me.

I had immense respect for Al as a person and a player. All the years I played with him, don't believe I ever saw him make a bad throw. He taught me how to go out there and work. I remember I used to go out there in the corner and the ball would beat me up. The outfield can be a hard position, but Al made it look easy.

Players used to call Al "The Lion" because he could walk across a cement floor in his cleats and not make a sound. He was so light on his feet.

People didn't know that Al played a number of years with a bad foot. I can't remember exactly what the diagnosis was, but it resulted in Al having to wear a soft cast off and on.

I had the opportunity to be around Roberto Clemente, Willie Mays, and Kaline, and I put them all in the highest category when it comes to the classy way they conducted themselves on and off the field.

Al and I didn't talk much when we played together, but we made up for it when the late Tigers owner Mike Ilitch hired us to be advisers to the Detroit Tigers' organization.

We were friends when we played together, but it grew when we were older. Al told me that he thought he and I had similarities when we played.

Neither one of us said much in the clubhouse. We weren't the kind of players who yelled and screamed. We just went out and did our jobs. We were also alike because we loved our jobs. We loved Detroit and we loved playing for the Tigers.

"We didn't have to talk about it," Al said. "We just looked at each other and understood that's how we felt."

Our relationship was always propped up by mutual respect. We both knew the other.

Another thing Al told me was that he had no memory of the day in Milwaukee when I forced his jaws apart to pull out his tongue after he had an outfield collision with Jim Northrup. That happens sometimes with trauma cases.

When I came up with the Tigers, he gave me two pieces of advice that I carried with me through my career. First, don't take an unsuccessful at-bat into the field with you. If you strike out with the bases loaded, you have to let it go when you take the field. It will be worse if you flub a drive to the outfield because you are angry over a poor at-bat. Instead, go out and win the game with good defense. On days you fail at the plate, win with your glove.

Second, Al taught me never to show fear with any pitcher. Al and I had the same mindset about hitting. If a pitcher knocked us down, we wanted to drive the next pitch through the box or out of the ballpark.

After I rejoined the Tigers, Al and I spent a lot of time together, offering our opinions about what the Tigers could do to develop a winning organization.

Mr. Ilitch was always receptive because he wanted to win badly. He was such a Detroit sports fan. Before he bought the Red Wings and Tigers, he was involved in a variety of sports endeavors. Remember the Detroit Caesars softball team in the late 1970s? Mr. Ilitch paid former Tigers players Jim Northrup, Norm Cash, Mickey Stanley, and Jim Price to play for the Caesars team from time to time.

People forget that Mr. Ilitch was with Marvin Gaye as one of the many owners of the Detroit Wheels of the short-lived World Football League.

But Mr. Ilitch was primarily a baseball guy. He knew everything about the game. I loved sitting in the luxury box talking baseball with Mr. Ilitch and Al Kaline.

The 2021 season was hard on me for a number of reasons. Because of COVID protocols, I wasn't allowed to go to the ballpark until late in the season. I wasn't allowed to mingle with players, even though I was fully vaccinated. It was a medical decision to keep the locker room as closed as possible. The only people allowed in there were the people who had to be there.

But that was tough for me. I had been in major league dressing rooms continuously since the early 1960s. I feel like I still have more to give to the game. I want to talk to players about the history of the game.

Al and I used to talk about how today's players don't know the game's history. Some of the current Tigers don't know what a great center fielder Mickey Stanley was, or that Bill Freehan and Mickey Lolich should be in the Hall of Fame. Freehan was an 11-time All-Star and Lolich was one of the game's best for many, many years.

They don't know that Charlie "Paw Paw" Maxwell was a gifted pinch-hitter, as was Gates Brown.

Al and I used to talk about how Gator was one of the best pure hitters we ever saw. Gator could come into a game cold, stand in against the toughest pitchers, and drill the first good pitch he saw into the gap. Al and I would laugh about all of this talk about "launch angles" and "bat speed." To me, today's players are taking "softball swings."

One issue that Al and I certainly agreed on is that we need to get communities back involved, particularly Black communities. We need more Black players in the game. That means we have to get local businesses more involved.

My parents couldn't afford for me to play, but they didn't have to because the local grocery store or barbershop or car dealer would sponsor the team. Often, the sponsor was also your coach.

Bigger stores like Cunningham's and A & P were also active and we need a big company to step up. In hockey, the Ilitch family has helped local hockey through Little Caesars.

When Mr. Ilitch died in 2017, I told people he was more than a boss to me. I meant that sincerely. I learned so much from him.

Once, Mr. Ilitch told me the difference between a successful businessman and a homeless person is just the luck of the draw.

"God loves everyone, but you and I have been fortunate in our lives. But the homeless man hasn't," he told me.

Mr. I worked for everything he had, but he still believed he was blessed. I admired the humility he had in him. I have always felt the same way.

This past season I was particularly sentimental. Maybe that happens when you can't contribute the way you want to contribute.

I have too much time to think these days. I thought about how when I hit my 300th career home run was one of the most memorable days of my career. I was playing for the Mariners and they gave me 300 silver dollars.

I was happy that day. But I also cried that day because I wished I could have done that for the Tigers. Even though I have a fondness for all of my teams, I was always a Tiger in my heart.

Al Kaline died on April 6, 2020, and I have missed him every day since. But I am not thinking about retiring.

I feel like I have work still to do. I have talked to former major leaguer and current broadcaster Harold Reynolds about the need to find a way to commemorate the early Black players on major league teams.

My feeling is there should be a place in every stadium that recognizes the first few Black players on each team. In Detroit, we have recognized Jake Wood. But Jake, Ozzie Virgil, and others deserve permanent recognition. I would also like to see the Hall of Fame take a second look at players of color who might have been passed over for recognition.

Doing a second look seems like the least we can do for players such as Tommy Davis, Richie Allen, Rico Carty, and others.

These are the kind of issues I would discuss with Mr. Ilitch and Al in the luxury box. I cannot do that anymore. I am now the lone old-school voice. It makes me sad. But I don't feel alone when I'm up there.

I took my nephew to a Tigers game at the end of the 2021 season and he was looking to sit down and I stopped him.

"You're in Mr. Ilitch's seat," I said.

I still feel like he is with us.